Of Ice and Men

OF ICE AND MEN

Steve Yzerman
Chris Chelios
Glen Sather
Dominik Hasek
The Craft of Hockey

Bruce Dowbiggin

MACFARLANE WALTER & ROSS
TORONTO

Macfarlane Walter & Ross
37A Hazelton Avenue
Toronto, Canada M5R 2E3

Distributed in Canada by General Distribution Services Ltd.

Distributed in the U.S. by General Distribution Services Inc.
85 River Rock Drive, Suite 202, Buffalo, New York 14207
Toll-free tel. 1-800-805-1083; Toll-free fax 1-800-481-6207
e-mail gdsinc@genpub.com

CANADIAN CATALOGUING IN PUBLICATION DATA
Dowbiggn, Bruce
        Of ice and men: Steve Yzerman, Chris Chelios, Glen Sather, Dominik Hasek:
        the craft of hockey

Includes index.
ISBN 1-55199-028-8

1. Yzerman, Steve.   2. Chelios, Chris.   3. Sather, Glen.   4. Hasek, Dominik.
5. Hockey players — Biography.   6. Hockey coaches — Biography.   I. Title.

GV848.5.A1D68 1998   796.962'092'2   C98-932221-1

PHOTOCREDITS
page xviii: © Rocky Widner
page 82: Courtesy Chicago Blackhawks
page 154: © Toronto Sun
page 230: Courtesy Buffalo Sabres

Macfarlane Walter & Ross gratefully acknowledges financial support for its publishing program from the Canada Council for the Arts, the Ontario Arts Council, and the Government of Canada through the Book Publishing Industry Development Program.

Printed and bound in Canada

For Terry, who loved Henri Richard,
and Bill, who booed Doug Harvey.

Contents

Steve Yzerman / **Natural Leader**   1

Chris Chelios / **Defense Expert**   83

Glen Sather / **Master Builder**   155

Dominik Hasek / **Iron Butterfly**   231

Index   301

Acknowledgments

ASSEMBLING A BOOK OF THIS SORT is like organizing a photo exhibition on a particular theme. The result is the product of many lenses capturing the same subject. No two lenses see the hockey world in quite the same light, and I've tried to synthesize and arrange various approaches to the subject without jamming them all into a single frame.

I wish to thank Dominik Hasek and his agent, Rich Winter; Steve Yzerman and his agent, Larry Kelly; Chris Chelios and his agent, Tom Reich; and Glen Sather and his agent, Glen Sather. Their time, their insights, and their patience made this project possible. Allowing me to visit their working lives, and patiently explaining just what they do for a living, was not always easy for them, but they were unfailingly gracious and cooperative. Thanks as well to their wives and families who welcomed a stranger in their midst.

Special thanks to the many other hockey people cited in these pages who took the time to consider the topics and respond to my inquiries.

Whether at the NHL draft, rinkside in Nagano, or in the press rooms of North American arenas, they added tremendously to my knowledge, rebutted my opinions, and provided many insights into the game. Michael Gillis's friendship and advice were invaluable. Thanks, too, to Ron Yzerman for his photographs and memories. And to Chris Broadhurst for massaging my research.

The NHL officials and the public relations folks in Edmonton, Chicago, Detroit, and Buffalo were always cordial and supplied me with all manner of arcane data. Richard Martyn was an indefatigable researcher and producer who put me in touch with many of the voices in this book. My friend Steve Paikin also contributed to the interviews and arguments at the core of the book on our radio program "Double Play." "There's nothing like a well-produced radio show, and this is nothing like a well-produced radio show... "

Let me recognize my many colleagues and friends in the media whose work has been an inspiration and a source of ideas: Russ Conway, Roy MacGregor, Dick Irvin, John Davidson, Ken Daniels, Michael Ulmer, Douglas Hunter, Roy MacSkimming, Stan Fischler, Peter Gzowski, Jim Matheson, Al Strachan, Stan Fischler, Lawrence Martin, Michael Farber, Jason LaCanfora, Drew Sharp, Jim Taylor, Jiri Kolis, Lloyd Percival, Chris Cuthbert, and Scott Russell. Special thanks to John Keegan, Lionel Tiger, Harold Klawans, John Hoberman, and Robert Ardrey for their insights on non-hockey topics.

My gratitude for the cooperation and patience of Phil Dugas and the CBC Radio Sports team, both in Toronto and Nagano, would fill the atrium at CBC headquarters. Thanks also to the friendly staff at The Legal Index in Toronto for keeping me updated on legal and corporate hockey matters over the years.

Thank you to Gary Ross of MW & R for the idea and the editing, and to the people associated with the publishing house who helped realize this sprawling project. Wendy Thomas deserves special gratitude for her careful copy-editing.

Finally, the completion of this work reflects the indefatigable support I've always received from my wonderful family: Meredith, Evan, Rhys, and Clare—you are my true work of art.

B.D., TORONTO, JULY 1998

INTRODUCTION

*"Conscience and reason will have the last word, but passion...
passion will have the last deed."*

SIGMUND FREUD, HOCKEY FAN

"A HOCKEY GAME ON RADIO," sniffed the veteran NBA coach Gene
Shue, "is like listening to one long mistake." There's a grain of truth in
his complaint. If hockey counted turnovers with the same zeal that the
NBA does, they'd run out of paper before the end of the first period. In
the 1970s it was estimated that a puck changed teams as often as six
times a minute, more than 120 times a period, more than 400 times a
game. In the speeded-up game of today, with turnovers caused by neutral-zone traps and left-wing locks, that figure has increased
exponentially. Turnovers in today's NHL would have to be catalogued
in numbers best left to auditors and player agents. As the Soviet star
Sergei Makarov observed after playing in the NHL, "In Europe we try
to build plays. Here they try to break them up."

By its nature hockey is a constant improvisation, a five-man rhap-
sody of assault and recoil that only works — as Gene Shue contends
when someone makes a mistake. The coach has the wrong line combi-

nation on the ice, the forward lets up on the backcheck, the defense-man goes for the deke, the referee misses the trip, the goalie guesses high when the shooter goes low.

"He scores!"

At last, blessed relief for the Gene Shues of the world.

Sadly for Shue and other attention-deficit observers, goals in the modern NHL are governed by laws of scarcity. Michael Jordan will create a dozen or more points with the basketball in six minutes on the court; sixty minutes of 1990s-style NHL hockey will net you six or seven scores if you're lucky. The rest, as Shue observes, is futility. And fights.

Several years ago, the American political pundit George Will created a Cartesian model of baseball in his book *Men at Work*. Baseball is open to these flights of scholarly introspection. It once had an Elizabethan literary scholar as commissioner (while hockey was run by a Nuremberg war crimes lawyer). Metaphors and symbolism can be slathered on the sport as easily as pine tar on the bat.

Will decided to take a naïf's tour to discover how the game was played at its highest level. Reading his dissection of the inner game of baseball is not unlike opening the hood on a performance car. There are enough wires, belts, hoses, fuses, systems, linkages, and valves in base-ball to keep the idler fascinated for months. Will tweaked and fiddled with these contraptions long enough to declare that baseball is circum-scribed by minutiae, ruled by numbers and statistics.

By comparison, popping the hood on hockey is like looking into the cool icy rods of a nuclear reactor. There is little to suggest the unimaginable force and power locked in those sleek, functional tubes. All you see at first is some heavy water and a lot of expensive metal. Ten seconds will satisfy the George Wills that they have seen all there is to see. Hockey abhors complication the way nature abhors a vacuum.

Not that numbers aren't important in hockey, too. Former NHL coach Gene Ubriaco quantified it this way. "In hockey, goaltending is 75 percent of the game. Unless it's bad goaltending. Then it's 100 percent of the game, because you're going to lose." But numbers offer only a partial explanation of why one team loses and another team wins. Hockey's immeasurable qualities have much to say in the determination of a winner. "A hockey player must have three things planted in his head—hate, greed, and jealousy," said former Bruin star Derek Sanderson. "He must hate the other guy, he must be greedy for the puck, and he must be jealous when he loses. Hockey players without those traits don't survive for long." These intangibles—which form a mantra for Canadian players—have achieved mythic status among Don Cherry's blue-collar fans, too.

Among the major team sports in North America, hockey has most often been compared to football because of its brute territoriality, its speed, its willingness to sacrifice the body. As hockey has evolved, with larger players creating a more static game, the two sports have seemed more connected than ever. But in football, there is considerable deliberation; players pause to draw up plays and consult coaches, heal wounds and mug for the TV camera. Football's flow is episodic while hockey's is virtually constant.

There are many books about how people came to be NHL stars, countless evocative descriptions of small Quebec mining towns, frozen sloughs, long bus rides on the way to the top, stories with moms and dads in parkas, their steamy breath clouding the night air, with Foster Hewitt's voice calling across the generations, with Walter's little boy beating the big kids. This will not be one of them. This book is about craft, the inner workings of the hockey reactor. There has been remarkably little investigation of the craft of the game in print and on TV, little that specifically looks at how the best perform the job of hockey. Yet there is considerable evidence that talking about craft, dissecting a game, leads to improvements in the performance and understanding of that game — the so-called Wimbledon effect. Tennis pros around England have noted that the play of amateurs improves dramatically in the weeks following Wimbledon. Watching TV experts analyze tennis on the lawns of the All England Club for a fortnight apparently gives everyone a better topspin lob.

Hockey has been a bulwark against such notions. In the 1950s, Lloyd Percival attempted to reason with hockey, using research to define the sport. He was laughed at for years, then shamelessly imitated. In the 1960s, the Soviets tried to expose the NHL to beauties in the game and its strategy that had been ignored or forgotten. They were first vilified, then signed to contracts for millions of dollars by the clubs that had ridiculed them.

Howie Meeker flirted with the nuances of craft for a while on "Hockey Night in Canada." But his video chalk talks ("Could you take the tape back just a few frames, Mike?") seemed to offend the sizable segment of the population that experiences hockey the way opera fans absorb Wagner—through the pores. It was with some national relief that Don Cherry succeeded Meeker and re-established a bully pulpit of machismo and Reform politics.

Yet who hasn't watched the wonderful athletes in these pages and wondered, "How did he do that?" Fans who've been away from the game for a decade or more are amazed at the dizzying pace and sheer athleticism of today's players. There are many great athletes and some wonderfully skilled stars in the NHL, more than ever. Does their genius spring from some shrouded secret deep in the subconscious, or from something more quantifiable?

I've divided the game into four essential roles: forward, defenseman, goalie, and coach/general manager. In each of these roles I've chosen a figure who personifies the discipline. Dominik Hasek of the Buffalo

Sabres is the best goalie in the world these past five years—an Olympic gold medal and two Hart Trophies require no further explanation. Steve Yzerman, captain of the two-time Stanley Cup champion Red Wings, has a unique blend of skill and leadership that few in the game can match. I selected three-time Norris Trophy winner Chris Chelios as the defenseman for his combination of scoring and scaring, the keystones of all great defensemen. And Glen Sather's record as coach or general manager of five Stanley Cup champions and two Canada Cup champions makes him a natural as the guy in the Guccis.

In some ways this book is also, I hope, about the tribal, self-deprecating Canadian identity that shaped the game and that now seems threatened by all manner of forces out of our control. "Hockey's where we finally got it right," wrote David Adams Richards in his book *Hockey Dreams*, "but we're not allowed to tell anyone that we have. So what do we do within the National Hockey League and the international hockey community—we tilt the mirror till we are out of focus again."

Canada was settled by Scots and Irish and French, and the heart of hockey is a Celtic and Gallic passion play of heroism and cowardice, loyalty and betrayal, obedience and will. It remains a game where the honor of conduct is still supposed to matter the way it did when the game was played with hurleys and frozen clods of dirt. Perhaps, as many Americans have suggested, hockey would be better off without the fighting, or on a larger surface, or without a center red line. But a game now mainly owned and run by Americans is still captive to a Canadian imperative.

"It's their game," says Chelios, an American who has played both junior and NHL hockey in Canada. "Americans don't have the same pride in baseball, their national game, that Canadians have about hockey. They're proud. I learned to love hockey because I was up there."

It's their love of hockey that binds the subjects of this book. It's their mastery of craft that led me to write about them.

Steve Yzerman
NATURAL
LEADER

"I've been through it all. After you go through everything you learn to deal with failure and not fall apart."

STEVE YZERMAN, DETROIT RED WINGS

HE SKATES CAUTIOUSLY across the ice at Joe Louis Arena, precious cargo in hand. Though he rarely smiles during games, his megawatt grin this day packs the candlepower of the TV lights in the rafters above. Looking up from his happy payload, Steve Yzerman can see the pennants marking Detroit's Stanley Cup triumphs and honoring the retired numbers of such immortals as Howe and Lindsay and Sawchuk, the glory years of the 1950s when Detroit ruled the NHL. Yzerman has played beneath those pennants his entire NHL career; they are constant reminders of the legacy handed down to the team's longest-serving captain.

In his bulky pads, Yzerman glides across the frozen motto at center ice — "Hockeytown," it proclaims in bold black and red script. It's no idle boast. The sport in all its incarnations is bred into the bone of Detroiters. From the Red Wings down to teams of atoms, this city on the St. Clair River loves its hockey. The fans know its traditions; they understand longing, they savor vindication. "Hockey holds a special place in metro Detroit hearts," says Michael Bernacci, a professor of sports marketing at the University of Detroit Mercy. "There isn't another of the original U.S. NHL cities that could ever be called Hockeytown."

The Red Wings' first Stanley Cup in 42 years has vaulted the 32-year-old Yzerman to the summit of the city's sports heroes, alongside Joe Louis, Bobby Layne, Isiah Thomas, and Mr. Hockey himself, Gordie Howe. For Yzerman, this is completion. After all the injuries, the coaching changes, the near-misses in the playoffs, the Wings' long-awaited championship allows him to dwell contentedly in this instant, in this special building, in this hockey-mad town. He's enjoying his moment of redemption.

"Shouldn't she be wearing a helmet?" calls Yzerman's wife, Lisa, from the players' bench. Yzerman looks up from his daughter as they carefully make their way across the ice. Nearby, Igor Larionov's daughters turn from their figure skating to watch Steve and four-year-old Isabel.

"She'll be okay," says Yzerman. "I'm right behind her." For a reluctant public figure, this is a precious moment. His pride and jubilation at his young daughter's tentative strides are not so far removed from the exultation he felt on this same ice surface four months earlier, June 7, 1997, the day he carried the Stanley Cup aloft to the delirious cheers of Red Wings fans. Again today he wears the smile of a winner; the missing front tooth — courtesy of a Theo Fleury butt end — merely adds to his boyish quality. "Trade Yzerman?" his former coach Jacques Demers once snorted. "That's like asking me if I want to trade my son Jason for the kid next door."

Fulfillment has been a long time coming for Yzerman. Teammates and opponents speak of him in glowing terms — Pavel Bure called Yzerman and Mario Lemieux the two greatest players in the world — yet he has long toiled in the shadow of his more celebrated peers, just as he played season after season in the shadow of those pennants dangling overhead. When *The Hockey News* drew up a list of the top 50 players of all time in early 1988, Yzerman's name was inexplicably absent. Stan Mikita, Bryan Trottier, Dave Keon, and Marcel Dionne were there. Given three or four more healthy seasons, Yzerman will finish ahead of almost all of them, among the top half dozen goal scorers, and the top four point getters in NHL history. How could a player of his obvious gifts, statistics, and stature have escaped acclaim for so long?

For starters, an almost pathological shyness has obscured his achievements; Yzerman has never been one to draw attention to himself with clever quips, emotional speeches, or jocular TV commercials for potato chips or breakfast cereal. And Detroit's many playoff frustrations kept him out of the media limelight at the time of year when his peers became household names. As his teammate Brendan Shanahan points out, "Being a center in the era of Gretzky, Lemieux, and [Mark] Messier — three of the greatest centers in the history of hockey — was just tough luck for Steve."

Then there was the Mike Keenan factor. Coaching kreigmeister Keenan appeared to question Yzerman's heart by not selecting him for either the 1987 or 1991 editions of Team Canada. "They said he didn't have the make-up to really sacrifice himself in that kind of tournament," remembers Rangers general manager Neil Smith. "He was small, he was weak and not very good defensively, he's never won anything. It's hard to believe today that that talk was true, but it was." At the time, the Detroit team he led was widely disparaged as lacking defensive discipline or chemistry ("Too many Russians," huffed Don Cherry). Indeed, each playoff year brought greater heartbreak, none more so than 1996 when the club set an NHL record for wins in a regular season (62) before being swept aside by New Jersey in the finals. Could Stevie Y not boot home a sure winner?

Yzerman quietly answered Keenan with his fine performance on Team Canada at the 1996 World Cup (he was perhaps Canada's best player, and his overtime goal beat Slovakia 3–2). Then, in 1997, the Red Wings demolished the bigger, more powerful Philadelphia Flyers in four straight games to win the eighth Stanley Cup in the team's history. His example at both ends of the rink — scoring two game winners, controlling important face-offs, falling in front of shots while killing penalties — clinched his eventual place in the Hall of Fame and consolidated his reputation as one of the great players of his generation. His beaming smile as he hoisted the Cup became hockey's iconic image. Talk about sweet vindication.

He may not have the other-worldly anticipation of Gretzky, the masterful sleight of hand of Lemieux, or the laser shot of Bobby Hull, but even a cursory look at the record books shows that Yzerman ranks with the very best. Among players to wear an NHL jersey for at least 500 games, only Gretzky, Lemieux, Orr, and Mike Bossy have a higher average points per game than Yzerman's 1.28. In five straight seasons, he scored 50 goals or more, and in two of those seasons he counted 60 or more. His 18 games with three goals or more place him behind only Gretzky, Hull, and Jari Kurri among current players. Since notching 39 goals and 48 assists in 1983–84 as a rookie (he was runner-up for the Calder Trophy, won by Steve Larmer of the Blackhawks), he has recorded six seasons of 100 points or more, and he's one of only four NHL players ever to record more than 150 points in a season. He's just the thirteenth player to crack the career 1,400-point mark. This prodigious scoring was achieved against teams that, until the arrival of Shanahan and vaunted Russians like Sergei Federov and Larionov and Vyacheslav Kozlov, keyed on Yzerman as the Red Wings' principal offensive threat. Still he found a way to produce at levels reached only by Lemieux and Gretzky. Like them, he has also inspired a long list of wingers, from

John Ogrodnick to Darren McCarty, to heights they'd never have reached otherwise. "It made my career to play with Yzerman," says Gerard Gallant, a feisty, modestly talented P.E.I. native who racked up 207 goals and 260 assists skating alongside Yzerman from 1984 to 1992.

With the likes of Eric Lindros, Paul Kariya, Jaromir Jagr, Teemu Selanne, and Brett Hull around to terrorize them, NHL goalies don't consider Yzerman Public Enemy Number One these days. And while each of those players has certain skills superior to Yzerman's, none presents a more complete package. Indeed, it's hard to think of a player with his career numbers who's got a comparable all-round game — maybe Joe Sakic or Peter Forsberg in Colorado, if they last another five or six years. Doug Gilmour, also a gifted defensive player, entered the NHL the same year as Yzerman but has 200 fewer goals. Ron Francis? Maybe. Yzerman's Detroit teammate Sergei Federov? Perhaps. The point is, it's a very short list.

Many describe Yzerman's style as European — skill with the puck, a vivid hockey imagination, great skating. His opponents know what's coming, they just have problems stopping him. "He's got this move where he comes down on his off side and curls up at the blue line," says veteran defenseman Jeff Brown. "As a defenseman you've got to step up to him, but then he twirls and goes by you. You just try to contain him, not overplay him and especially not to look silly." Former NHL forward Pat Flatley adds, "You've got to get on him as soon as he gets the puck or else he'll turn his body and protect it. He'll make a great play on the puck every time."

Yzerman's quietly fierce competitive nature, the one implicitly maligned by Mike Keenan, inspires teammates and intimidates opponents. "There are guys who'll get mad during the game and raise their play," says one opponent, who requested anonymity. "Yzerman starts the game mad. There are certain players who get a look on their face and you know you're in for a long night. That's Yzerman. He won't accept being covered. Whether it's an elbow or a chop, he just won't accept it." Says former Detroit teammate Slava Fetisov, "You can see how he is willing to compete and fight on every shift on the ice. Even when he makes a mistake, you can see the expression on his face. Everyone knows he is unhappy and will fix it."

Those who remember Scotty Bowman's great Montreal teams in the 1970s find a remarkable similarity between Yzerman's game and that of Jacques Lemaire, until recently the coach in New Jersey — the quick, accurate shot, the ability to make others around them better. But Lemaire — while popular and a key part of some great Montreal teams — never possessed the natural leadership of the Detroit captain. Further, in an era of player transience and contract instability, Yzerman's unbroken tenure of 15 seasons with the Red Wings is a testament to his character, his priorities, and his staying power.

Perhaps Yzerman's most notable accomplishment, however, is the least noticed. Faced with a choice between personal glory and team success in the back half of his career, he has gradually reinvented himself as a consummate two-way player in Bowman's championship scheme in Detroit. "We went to Steve, and he seemed to be a natural for that style of play," recalls Bowman. "We discussed the fact that his scoring and everything might be reduced. It's pretty tough on an individual player, because the financial people are going to throw stats at you. But if you have a good team and you win, of course, everybody is going to benefit by it."

"He's changed his game a lot," acknowledges Chicago defenseman Chris Chelios, who'd rather chew ground glass than praise the enemy. "He doesn't try to beat you one on one anymore. He moves the puck a lot more. His goals are down, but he's more of a well-rounded player." Flatley, who played against Yzerman for 14 seasons, goes even further:

"Defensively and in his offensive ability, he's probably one of the most complete players to ever play."

STILL, IT IS THE ABILITY TO CREATE OFFENSE that lies at the heart of Yzerman's genius and that of every great forward in NHL history. What do they do with the puck, and how do they do it? Rocket Richard, the scoring machine of the Canadiens in the 1940s and 1950s, drove to the net on pure impulse. His strategy was the quintessence of *reductio ad absurdum*. "If you don't know what you're going to do," he once remarked, "how can the defenseman?" But in Richard's madness there was method. A left-handed shot playing right wing, he scored nearly half his goals with his quick, accurate backhand as he crashed toward the net. With his left — or lower hand — he used to fend off defensemen, and then with his stronger right hand he would steer the puck past the goalie. Richard also had great strength in his hands that allowed him to hold his stick higher up the shaft. That gave him a quick, heavy wrist shot. But the Rocket's repertoire went unreported in his day.

Technical analysis of offensive hockey — of why goals are scored and not scored — was not seriously undertaken until the late 1940s and 1950s, when the Canadian sports scientist Lloyd Percival sought to reduce the game to its composite parts through statistics and data. Using these data, Percival — also a world-class track coach — felt he could develop better training techniques and exercises for players. He believed that only perfect practice made perfect.

Anatoli Tarasov, who pioneered hockey in the Soviet Union, considered Percival a genius. "Your wonderful book which introduced us to the mysteries of Canadian hockey, I have read like a school boy," he wrote in his own book *Road to Olympus*. Many NHL people, such as Hall of Fame coach Dick Irvin Sr., were less flattering — "the product of a three-year-old mind," he opined. But Percival was decades ahead of his time. He used studies of NHL and amateur games to determine tendencies and create successful strategies. Reading *The Hockey Handbook* today, one is struck by its voluminous detail and the careful scrutiny Percival applied to the sport.

Why did players fail to score? Based on observations of 70 players — many of them Maple Leafs — Percival determined that 25 percent of shots were taken from too close in, 24 percent missed the net, 4 percent were fanned, and 20 percent were directed right at the goalie. Twelve percent were well aimed, but too weak to fool the goalie. On the remaining 15 percent of failed shots, the goalie made a good save.

How and where did players score from? In Percival's test of 100 goals scored — often in NHL play — 74 percent came on Yzerman's preferred method, the shot, and only 26 percent on dekes (or fakes). The majority of goals (62 percent) came from in front of the net at a distance of between 10 and 25 feet; 29 percent were from slight angles right and left, 6 percent from well-angled shots and 3 percent from sharp-angled shots. Of the 100 goals studied, 69 percent came on shots below the knees; 82 percent came on the forehand and 18 percent on the backhand.

By the mid-1950s, Percival had used these data to create drills and conditioning exercises, and much of his program was later adopted by the Canadian national team of Father David Bauer in the 1960s. But it wasn't until the study of videotape became widespread in the NHL 25 years later that Percival's findings were confirmed and his approach adopted by the hidebound thinkers of the league. Now it's common to hear assistant coaches bandying about the arcane statistics of their craft, data gleaned from studying tape or watching games on satellite TV dishes. Few of them even know of Percival's seminal work.

The question of what makes a player great has as many answers as there are great players. Mario Lemieux, for example, combined size and skill in a way nobody ever had. When healthy and motivated, no one controlled a game like the Pittsburgh center; the problem was keeping him healthy and motivated. "I like that open, artless smile on his face," wrote Tarasov. "You hardly believe that such a tall and seemingly heavy athlete can so deftly and swiftly carry the puck.... I am convinced that the one who taught Lemieux hockey, not for one iota destroyed what the kid was endowed with by nature. And how that sort of ease and nonchalance of movements pleases the eye!"

Opponents, too, could only marvel at Lemieux's size — at 6-foot-4 and 225 pounds he was a major load to move — and dexterity. Four inches taller and fifty pounds heavier than Gretzky, he could stay in heavy traffic longer, out-muscling defenders if necessary. But it was his wizardry with the puck that won him the sobriquet Mario the Magnificent. Defensemen still shudder at how he toyed with Ray Bourque in a playoff game in 1992.

The fast-breaking Lemieux escaped his end of the rink by pushing the puck into the feet of the fast-retreating Bourque, waiting for the moment Bourque switched skating from forward to backward to snatch the puck from its hiding place. The two great French Canadian players were locked in this puzzle ring from the Penguins' blue line to the Bruins' blue line. As Bourque finally spun around and started his furious back-pedal, Lemieux plucked the puck from safekeeping between the blades of the startled Bourque, swooped past him, and mesmerized Bruin goalie Andy Moog with a shot to the top of the net. If Lemieux could do that to one of the best defensemen of his generation, what might he have done to a mere mortal?

Yzerman was among the impressed. "He would come in on the defenseman and take the puck way to the outside," he says, spreading his arms in the Red Wings' dressing room to emulate Lemieux's boarding-house reach. "The defenseman had no choice but to go with him. But as soon as you reach for the puck, the big guy is going to lean in the other direction and go around you. That was the disadvantage for goalies as well as defensemen."

One hundred fourteen different goalies failed to stop Lemieux during his NHL career. His all-time NHL mark of .823 goals per game puts him ahead of Mike Bossy's .762, Bobby Hull's .717, and Gretzky's .626. Only Gretzky — the greatest playmaker of all time — surpassed Lemieux when it came to passing (Gretzky has 1.38 assists per game lifetime, compared to Lemieux at 1.18, Orr at .982, Adam Oates at .876, Paul Coffey at .859, Ron Francis at .807, Peter Stastny at .808, and Yzerman at .770).

Lemieux was at his most diabolical on breakaways or uneven rushes. He nailed six of eight lifetime penalty shots and had the uncanny knack of getting the puck up over the goalie's pads into the roof of the net from in close, the glaring weakness of the butterfly goalie. Lemieux did this by maintaining separation between himself and the goalie while making room for his shot. But he wasn't limited to one approach. Often he'd fake the shot, get the goalie to move, then slip the puck between his legs. "Mario Lemieux did that better than anyone else," says San Jose goalie Mike Vernon. "A guy like Mario," adds goaltending coach Francois Allaire, "even if he's got one second, he's going to pick a corner, and most of the time he's going to have it. But there aren't too many Marios in the NHL."

Although Lemieux was a right-handed shot, many compared him to an earlier French Canadian star, Jean Beliveau, who shot left. Both were big men and the preeminent stickhandlers of their day. While Beliveau protected the puck better by keeping it close to his skates, Lemieux probably had the edge when it came to speed, especially in his first years in the NHL. "Lemieux has the greatest hands on a big man I've ever seen," Hall of Fame defenseman Harry Howell told Michael Ulmer for his book *Canadiens Captains*, "but Beliveau's hands were awfully close."

Lemieux's first NHL goal cemented the comparison with Beliveau. Swooping in off the left wing against Boston at the Garden in 1984, the lanky rookie undressed a Bruins defenseman before drawing the puck from his forehand to his backhand — an enormous distance — and flipping it past Pete Peeters. He then crashed into the end boards. It was the first of countless goals Lemieux scored using the same move.

"I think most of the good guys have a repertoire of two moves to the forehand and one to the backhand," says Yzerman. "Jimmy Carson [a former Red Wing center who scored 275 NHL goals] and I used to talk about what we did. I'd start to the outside and cut back inside. Jimmy used to do the opposite. He'd come down on the left wing on the forehand, move outside to the backhand, then cut back inside to the forehand. I could never do what he did."

Back in the 1950s, Percival noted that players unconsciously had a "hot spot" on the ice they returned to, and that their shots were almost always the same height and location. They did not seem to recognize their own pattern, even when informed of it. When it came to deking the goalie, Percival noted a similar pattern of unconscious repetition. A player's biggest mistake — even in the NHL — was getting in too close before making his move or shooting. In his studies, Percival observed that the element separating amateurs from NHL players was the pros' tendency to get themselves into their "hot spots" when the opportunity arose — a point underlined by Gretzky's use of the area behind the net, or Lemieux's positioning just off the lower face-off circle on the power play. Videotape study and better coaching have made players more conscious of their patterns, of being too predictable; even so, as Yzerman notes, "Every player has a couple of favorite things to do when he gets in close."

Goal-scoring styles bear the signature of their creators, ranging from the 5-foot-6, 155-pound Theo Fleury in the flyweight class up to Eric Lindros at 6-foot-4 and 235 pounds in the super heavyweight. Their hot spots can vary from the edge of the crease, where buffalo such as Lindros and John LeClair roam, to the mid-range, where sniper Brett Hull is king, to the margins, where the likes of Yzerman, Paul Kariya, and Teemu Selanne rule with speed and savvy.

Kariya perhaps comes closest to the young Yzerman in his offensive package. Both men are 5-foot-11; Yzerman now weighs between 183 and 187 pounds but he began his career at 175 pounds, the same weight as Kariya. Neither steamrollers defensemen on his way to the net. They both became captains of their teams at young ages: Kariya was just 22 when he got the "C" in Anaheim, Yzerman a year younger when he became the youngest captain in Red Wings history. Both are masters of exploiting movement on the edge of the offensive zone to get free for a shot on the net. One of Yzerman's specialties is the art of cycling on the boards. A tactic developed in the more spacious rinks of Europe, cycling involves two or three teammates skating in a loose circle close to the boards, controlling the puck, trying to create interference or confusion among the defenders to set one player free for a good chance. Yzerman's uncanny ability to bob and weave and backtrack in this fashion is reminiscent of another Detroit sports legend, Barry Sanders of the Lions.

Yzerman may be the better passer, but Kariya has great speed, which allows him to jump into seams more quickly. And while neither is in Gretzky's class, both possess the anticipation to size up opportunities before they develop fully — a trait learned from an early start in the game and refined by endless hours of watching tape. Kariya has another gift: perhaps no young player since Gretzky has been as aware of the geometry of the game. "I think Kariya can anticipate better than anyone in the league," says Dallas coach Ken Hitchcock. "He knows how and when to commit himself on both offense and defense."

Former NHLer Ryan Walter, now a broadcaster, points to the little things in Kariya. "If you're watching him, notice how he always carries his stick with his gloves close together. In other words, he's way up the stick. And what he does, he never lifts the blade off the ice. He's always in position to get the puck and he wants it all the time. He shows everybody on his team, 'Hey, I want the puck.' He's become more of a leader."

Kariya's anticipation, and the best burst of speed in the NHL, allow him to exploit the transition game to perfection, taking the pass in stride to create uneven rushes. "The key with Kariya is to get up the ice and not let a gap develop," says Chris Chelios. "If there's a gap between him and the defender, he's over the blue line and in. You're going to have to give him the shot from outside, because you can't stand a kid like that up. That's what he's learned: the first year he didn't shoot enough. You backed in, he tried to go around you and ended up behind the net. Now he's changed his game, started shooting from out far. And he's got a great shot."

"Hockey Night in Canada" put a stopwatch on Kariya during Anaheim's 1997 playoff series against Phoenix; he started behind the Anaheim net, carried the puck up ice and scored a goal, all in a remarkable six seconds. Perhaps only Pavel Bure and Teemu Selanne can match him at taking the pass and turning the corner on a defenseman. Selanne, possibly the NHL's strongest player on his skates, brings his "A" game to the rink more consistently than Bure and has stayed healthier than the injury-prone Kariya. Still, "Kariya will be the best player over the next ten years if he stays healthy," says former NHL coach Michel Bergeron emphatically. "He's so fast, he's so smart. He reminds me of Guy Lafleur, with great breakaway speed. When he gets the puck in the middle, he's going to beat you easily."

It has greatly helped Kariya, of course, to have Selanne on his opposite wing. "They just feed off each other," says Trevor Linden of the Islanders. "They read one another and have fun playing together. It's a deadly combination." Selanne has had to do without Kariya for lengthy periods of time, but as Selanne's prolific scoring during Kariya's injuries and contract hassles in 1997–98 showed, he can work alone. "My sense is that, all by himself, Kariya would have a tougher time," observed Ryan Walter, "because lines could easily be aggressive on one player and not have to watch out for another player on the line. My question about Paul is: Playoff hockey is inside hockey. You can't play on the outside. For him to get to the inside, what kind of price will he pay?"

In the first playoff test for Kariya and Selanne as linemates, in the spring of 1997, the Ducks prevailed over Phoenix in a bitter seven-game series. Kariya keyed the win in game six, scoring two goals. On the winner in overtime, he beat Coyotes goalie Nicholai Khabibulin from a bad angle with a sensational wrist shot to the top corner — this after controlling a high lob pass from his defenseman Dimitri Mrionov with his feet. That goal sent the series back to the Ducks' home ice. In the rink that Disney built, the Ducks got a 3–0 shutout from Guy Hebert and a power-play goal from Kariya to seal the comeback series win. If great players win for you in the playoffs, Kariya staked his claim as a great player.

He and Selanne weren't enough to save the Ducks against Yzerman and the Red Wings in the next round. Surprisingly, the Ducks had owned Detroit during the regular season, winning three of four with a tie. And if a four-game sweep can be close, Kariya and the Ducks made it very close. "Think of it," says Yzerman. "Two of the games went to double OT, one to triple OT. What if we'd had the shootout like they do in the Olympics? With Kariya and Selanne shooting, we could easily have lost that series four straight."

The problem for the Ducks was that, as Yzerman knows, playoff hockey demands that you guard your own end first. Kariya was a minus 4 that series, Selanne a minus 3; by comparison, not one Detroit regular had a negative plus-minus figure. That was why Yzerman, not Kariya, was the captain who ended up hoisting the Stanley Cup in 1997.

Kariya shares another trait with Yzerman: the two men are reserved, and Kariya's reputation for zealously guarding his privacy (as Yzerman does) has some NHL people worried about whether he will grow into the job description of NHL messiah being vacated by Gretzky. While Yzerman's contracts with Detroit have almost always been done with little fuss (he's contracted through the 2000–01 season and will earn more than $5 million in 1998–99), Kariya used his first major deal to take a stand. He was a restricted free agent, but no team was willing to surrender seven first-round draft picks or invoke the financial wrath of the mighty Disney Corporation. He missed the start of the 1997–98 season, which included a trip to Japan for a series against Vancouver; the NHL was hoping Kariya (of Japanese Canadian descent) would create a sensation in Japan as it readied to host the Olympics in Nagano. Instead, Kariya stayed home, a holdout.

The money fight was messy: he was pilloried in the press for shouting at reporters who sought him out at his Vancouver home and for refusing to answer touchy questions when "Hockey Night in Canada" finally purloined an interview. Hockey fans wondered aloud how many millions a 24-year-old kid needed, but Kariya knew that as a franchise player he was setting a benchmark for everyone else. Many of his peers — including Lindros — silently cheered.

Kariya held out till December before he finally got a $14-million, two-year deal from Anaheim (he donated the portion of his salary covered by his holdout to charity). He quickly lived up to his lofty new status with 17 goals and 31 points in his first 22 games. The Ducks started winning. The Olympics beckoned. Life was good. Then, a week before he was to report to the Olympic team, he was crosschecked in the face by Gary Suter after scoring against Chicago. He went down with a concussion, the fourth of his young career. Durability is another component of greatness, and Kariya has yet to prove that he, like Yzerman, can stand up to year after year of NHL punishment.

YZERMAN NOW LIVES MOST OF THE YEAR in affluent Grosse Pointe, a Detroit suburb, but he retains a deep attachment to the Ottawa area, where he played minor hockey, where his family and friends still live, and where the arena in Nepean is named after him. Unfortunately, because the Red Wings play in a different conference, they visit Ottawa but once a year, and then they are usually in and out within 24 hours, leaving little time for Yzerman to see people he grew up with. This year, however, the schedule maker was kind. The Red Wings have a day off after their game with the Senators, and Scotty Bowman — who generally speeds back to Detroit after games — has decided the Wings will practice in Ottawa before leaving town. There will be time for visits, for talk about the baby Steve and Lisa are expecting in early summer and about the prospect of Steve's father making the trip to Nagano if Steve makes Team Canada's Olympic roster.

First the business at hand: playing the Senators. Almost everyone has criticisms of the Corel Centre location in the extreme west end of the city. It's too far for many to drive, the access road is pitifully inadequate, it's an arena waiting for a community to spring up around it in the farm fields. But it's just minutes from where Yzerman grew up in Nepean, and he finds it a comfortable place to play, more so than the old Civic Centre downtown, where the Senators began NHL play and where he played against the home-town junior club, the 67s. "For some reason, I never played well at the Civic Centre," he recalls. "But since the Senators moved to the Corel Centre, we've done a lot better." (In part the reason may lie in the smaller ice surface at the Civic Centre, which restricted Yzerman's mobility.)

His success at Corel continues this night. He personally buries the

Senators, a team waiting for one of its young players to emerge into NHL stardom as Yzerman did in the mid-1980s. With Team Canada assistant general manager Bob Gainey scouting him for the Olympic team from the press box, Yzerman wins a face-off from Alexei Yashin in his own zone early in the first period, drives down the right wing, and from the top of the circle unloads a low screamer to the far side that just catches the post behind a startled Damian Rhodes. 1-0 Detroit.

Nine minutes after that single-handed score, Yzerman makes a Gretzky-like feed between the legs to Brendan Shanahan. Shanahan finds Darren McCarty at the top of the crease; McCarty completes the geometry lesson by tipping it past Rhodes. 2–0 Detroit. The Senators rally, but the Red Wings never let them seize the momentum. With Ottawa down 3–2 late in the third and Rhodes on the bench for an extra player, Yzerman calmly deposits an empty-net goal to clinch the win. While no one wants the home team to lose, the applause for Yzerman's bravura performance is enthusiastic and genuine. After the game, friends, family, and local press seek him out for comment on the return of the native. Anyone looking for hyperbole and braggadocio is sadly disappointed. Yzerman shakes many hands, signs autographs, then quietly slips away to join his family.

Yzerman's fine performance against the Senators is typical — highly effective, but in a subtle, almost elusive way. What is it, exactly, that makes him so good? His gift, like that of most great athletes in his sport, owes something to genetics and something to what's known as the canary factor. Other birds must hear a song in the first few months of life or they will never learn it; the canary is the only bird that can learn to sing once it gets past infancy. Yzerman was clearly born with inherent genetic advantages (he himself believes that "about 80 percent" of his skating ability was likely inherited), but then the great players are almost all exceptional athletes. When Gretzky's tests for recuperative abilities were measured in the 1980s by exercise physiologist Dave Smith at the University of Alberta, Smith thought the cardiovascular machine had broken. Gretzky's results went off the dial. Though he couldn't bench press his own 160 pounds, Gretzky was the fittest man on his team.

If so much is in the genes, why do coordinated kids who get a late start in a sport not catch up to their peer group? What's to say an athletic soccer player — as Yzerman was — couldn't switch to hockey at age 16, say, and become successful? In effect, imitate the canary and learn to sing a song after childhood? The answer lies in the unique developmental pattern of humans. A turtle is born knowing it must swim out to sea to survive; a baby kangaroo instinctively crawls into the mother's pouch. Humans are born virtually helpless. Seventy-five percent of the human brain's growth — its ability to acquire and hone fine motor skills — occurs after birth. The so-called "action-releasing mechanisms" of the central nervous system are open, not already decided, as they are in animals. We learn virtually everything outside the womb. As Joseph Campbell noted, the human animal's learning and reasoning skills "are engraved, as it were, upon its nerves" after birth.

Apparently the skills that make a great player must — like the song of the bird — be imprinted at an early stage. For the first 16 or 18 years of life, the elasticity of the brain allows for all manner of engraving. Within this growing phase, there seem to be windows of enhanced opportunity for learning, when the brain is able to absorb skills at a prodigious rate. Miss them and you can never recover this optimum period of absorption. In Yzerman's case, the engraving of hockey motor skills was given an early start. When his older brother, Mike, was starting hockey in Cranbrook, British Columbia, where Steve was born in 1965, neighbors asked their dad if he'd coach the team. Ron Yzerman had one condition: that they let Steve start playing a year early. Yzerman thus had a year's head start on his peers.

Gretzky, of course, also started learning many years earlier than his peers. As everyone this side of Mars already knows, Walter Gretzky gave his precocious son an intense schooling in the skills of the game from the time he could stand up on the family's backyard rink in Brantford, Ontario. The drills emphasized balance, dexterity, and accuracy, not intensity and brawn. "When the Russians came over here in 1972 and '74, people said, 'Wow, this is something incredible,'" Gretzky once remarked. "Not to me it wasn't. I'd been doing those drills since I was three years old. My dad was very smart."

Also participating in the Walter Gretzky Backyard Hockey School was another future NHL player: Greg Stefan, who played goal behind Yzerman in Detroit. And a third youngster from Gretzky's novice days with the Brantford Steelers, forward Len Hachborn, also cracked the big time with Philadelphia and Los Angeles (Hachborn scored 111 goals playing on Gretzky's novice team; Gretzky scored 378). Was it coincidence that three young men from such a tiny sample group in a small Ontario town bucked the odds and made it to the NHL? Or did Walter Gretzky's innovative coaching imprint itself on more than just his son Wayne?

Gretzky himself told Peter Gzowski for the 1982 book *The Game of Our Lives*: "Nine out of ten people think it's instinct, and it isn't. Nobody would ever say a doctor learned his profession by instinct; yet in my own way I've put in almost as much time studying hockey as a medical student puts in studying medicine." As Coleman Griffith, the father of sport psychology, once observed, "Skill at anything is only a group of correct habits formed through practice of correct technical principles."

While no one is able to predict precisely when these windows of athletic opportunity open, it is generally believed that if a young hockey player isn't nurturing specific skills early, he hasn't got a Zamboni's chance of playing in the NHL. And even with ideal training, a hockey player who's not showing NHL-level skills by age 18 is highly unlikely to develop them later.

Elite athletes are like mathematicians, physicists, and lyric poets: they tend to peak in their late twenties and then experience a steep decline in the skills that set them apart. According to Dr. Harold Klawans, an American neurologist, parents looking for a long career for their kids should direct them toward being novelists, philosophers, or historians — they peak in their forties and fifties. In his book *Why Michael Couldn't Hit* (a study of why Michael Jordan failed in his attempt to become a major league baseball player), Klawans points out that the brain's capacity to re-do its circuitry at a young age is amazing. He cites many cases of children changing handedness without problem before the age of 15 or 16. If the brain suffers an injury to its left side — the side that controls the right side — before the mid-teens, it can switch this function to the right side of the brain. With a little therapy the child becomes left-handed. Yet no matter how much therapy they attempt, adults who've suffered brain damage from a stroke cannot emulate the same smooth transition in handedness.

Yzerman — like Gretzky and the other great players — was clearly a product of the right genes and proper training at optimum developmental stages. Despite his early start, though, he was not an immediate prodigy (unlike Gretzky, who scored 650 goals in his five-year novice career). His father remembers Steve as a poor skater when he began. "He dragged his left foot behind him when he skated," chuckles Ron Yzerman, demonstrating a pigeon-toed technique with his left foot. "His older brother was a much better skater. But even then Steve had a tremendous intensity to get better."

Yzerman himself recognizes the advantage of his early start as a key to development. "You get a few players who are late bloomers," he says. "But most guys were strong all along. You just played and didn't think about it." Played a lot, in fact; first in Cranbrook, then in Nepean, where the family moved in 1975 when Ron Yzerman took a job as a bureaucrat with the department of Health and Welfare in Ottawa. Once more, the burning desire impressed coaches and friends. "He is the most intense kid I've ever seen in my life," his bantam coach Ron Goddard told Scott Russell for the book *The Rink*. "He was better than anybody in the city. He had pro written all over him from the time he was 13." As he grew up in the Nepean hockey system, Yzerman captained every team he played on. His peewee team won the provincial championship. His name and his exploits became common knowledge around Nepean.

While many hockey parents are convinced that their progeny is predestined for stardom, Ron Yzerman was less certain. "If you asked me did I think he'd be a pro, I'd say I never thought about it till Steve was in junior. If you asked me if he'd be a star in the NHL, I never would have guessed." It was, remembers his dad, almost scary at times to see how Steve drove himself to be better. Once he quit when the pressure became too great.

Singlemindedness at a young age is another key element in the development of a great athlete. While friends are broadening horizons, exploring and experimenting with the wide variety life has to offer, a young player is narrowing his focus. In Yzerman's case that meant cutting back on soccer. "I was 15, in Tier II junior with the Nepean Raiders, and I quit soccer that spring because I didn't want to get hurt. To this day, I'm disappointed about that. You miss out on things. I don't know if priorities is the right word, but hockey does become the main thing in your life." Still, the soccer training he did receive has come in handy in the NHL. Anyone watching Yzerman play the puck with his feet along the boards or shielding the puck with his body while holding off larger defenders can see the benefits.

Unlike most of the young men he would compete against in the NHL — sure-fire prospects from an early age — Yzerman was largely oblivious to the possibilities his early prowess held out until he hit puberty. "It comes upon you pretty quickly. You're just thinking of the next tournament or game. Then I was 14, playing bantam, and on the way home my dad mentioned the midget draft was the next year. I said, 'Oh yeah?' It was the first time it dawned on me that I was going anywhere."

WHERE HE WENT WAS to the Peterborough Petes of the Ontario Hockey League. For a young man looking to a pro career, the Petes are the MIT of junior hockey programs. Since the inception of the NHL entry or amateur draft in 1967, 139 products of the Peterborough hockey program had been selected by NHL teams through 1997. That total is not only the most for any OHL or CHL club, it is the most of any single source in the world. Mickey Redmond, Danny Grant, and Bob Gainey are among the famous alumni of the Petes. Former Petes on current NHL rosters include Larry Murphy, Chris Pronger, Mike Ricci, Bob Errey, Kris King, Tie Domi, John Druce, Terry Carkner, Jaime Langenbrunner, and Randy Burridge. From stars to role players, the Petes have always given young players a great grounding in NHL skills, perhaps because the list of excellent coaches and teachers who emerged from Peterborough is similarly impressive. Scotty Bowman, Roger Neilson, Mike Keenan, Gary Green, Dick Todd, and Dave Dryden all coached the Petes.

In the little city on the Trent, the slight, driven 16-year-old Steve Yzerman was married to a hockey discipline. "Peterborough has always been known as a pretty good defensive hockey club," he recalls. "I'm not sure other teams spent that much time on it, but it really benefited me a lot. It was the first time we spent on conditioning, backchecking, picking up guys — let the defenseman take the guy with the puck. Dave Dryden was my coach and he introduced me to a lot of videotape. It was also the first time I saw that."

The NHL prefers that its prospects be tested and trained in junior programs like Peterborough's for many reasons. The advanced skill level, the coaching, and the sheer visibility are foremost. But it is also the first time a young player is exposed to the rigors of travel and the long, draining schedule he will encounter in the NHL. Unlike American collegians or European prospects, who play perhaps 40 or 50 games a season — many close to home — a player in the Canadian Hockey League will normally log more than 100 exhibition, regular season, and playoff games.

Many NHL prospects must choose between junior hockey and the U.S. collegiate system. The NHL has made it abundantly clear where it stands. After the league's brief flirtation with drafting U.S. collegiate players in the late 1980s, when college players made up about 20 percent of draftees, that proportion has dropped to as low as 2 percent in 1995. Likewise, U.S. high schoolers, who represented nearly a quarter of players drafted in 1990, dropped to less than 1 percent in 1995. The number selected from junior teams, meanwhile, has rebounded everywhere but in Quebec.

Hockey's development scenario has remained unchanged for generations. A prospect who thrives in spite of the bad food and long bus trips across the endless night of the Prairies or northern Ontario will probably develop the mental toughness to survive the gypsy life of an NHL career. No other team sport requires as much sacrifice at a young age. While teenaged football, basketball, and baseball players can pursue their training close to home with a high school or civic program, hockey prospects face an awesome upheaval when they reach their mid-teens. A young man who dreams of a pro career must subject himself to being drafted and told where to play. A young anglophone from the Maritimes may end up in a Quebec town where only French is spoken; a teenager from Vancouver Island may find himself in a boarding house in Brandon, Manitoba.

"If you ask me," says Bernie Nicholls, now with the Sharks, who left Haliburton, Ontario, at 15 to move to Woodstock, "the most difficult part of our business was having to leave home at a young age and being away from your parents in your mid-teens. I found that real tough. I know of a lot of young kids with great talent who can't seem to leave home for such a long time, because they get homesick."

Mark Recchi of the Montreal Canadiens echoes that sentiment. At the age of 17, he moved from Kamloops in the British Columbia interior to New Westminster on the coast. "This was my first experience away from home, and it was tough," he remembers. "I mean, when you're close with your brothers and your family the way I was it's tough to be a seven-hour drive away."

Nor is there any guarantee that a junior hockey player will not be traded to another city, another school, midway through the season. Paul Coffey was brought up near the airport in northwest Toronto, but at 17 he was drafted by the Greyhounds in Sault Ste. Marie, about 700 kilometers away. Twenty-three games into his second season in the Sault, he was traded to Kitchener, near his Toronto home. Coffey remembers crying when he got the news.

Castlegar, B.C., native Travis Green of the Islanders was traded from one country to another. Midway through his fourth junior season, he was shipped from Spokane, Washington, to Medicine Hat, Alberta. Sudbury native Dave Hannan — now with Ottawa — was traded halfway through his rookie season in the OHL from Sault Ste. Marie to Brantford. And Montreal's Stephane Richer was shipped from Granby in Quebec's Eastern Townships to Chicoutimi on the shore of the Saguenay in northern Quebec.

At least these players can console themselves with having made the big time. After all the loneliness and sacrifice, the vast majority of juniors end up with no NHL career and little education (though the CHL now puts money toward a player's post-secondary education after he finishes junior hockey, the catch being that he cannot obtain the funds if he signs a pro contract). They play for $100 a week and all the dreams they can conjure. "The most successful salary cap in all sports is in junior hockey," notes former NHL star Carl Brewer, who toiled for the Toronto Marlboros in the 1950s. "The kids are being paid today what we were paid back when I played. And it's not because the teams today are not profit-making businesses. The last expansion teams in the OHL sold for $1.2 million each. Someone's making money, but it isn't the players."

The sense of dislocation can also allow a coach to prey upon vulnerable young players far from home. One of Graham James's victims, Sheldon Kennedy, moved from his home in Elkhorn, Manitoba, at age 14 to advance his career under James's tutelage in Winnipeg, then followed him to Swift Current, Saskatchewan, to play junior. Less publicized are the effects upon impressionable young men of being exposed to alcohol, drugs, and the inherent violence of hockey without family and friends to modify the messaging. One recent top prospect — who'd moved from Newfoundland — sank in the first round of the 1997 draft because of whispered allegations of drinking problems. The whispers were later confirmed by a drunk-driving conviction. The many stories of hazing and sexual violence in the past few years also speak to a system whose values need close scrutiny.

"It's tough for a dad to see his son go at that age," says Ron Yzerman. "But we're thankful, because he couldn't have gone to a better situation than Peterborough. They encouraged education, and Steve boarded with some wonderful people. Still, it makes me shudder when I think of the things that happened to other people." (Needless to say, many fine people act as guardians and tutors, and most junior players have enjoyed their homes away from home.)

There have been attempts to improve the prospects of young men looking to a hockey career. A commission in Quebec in 1988 recom-

mended the shifting of hockey development from community organizations to the schools. That task force, headed by Robert Therien,
also proposed the virtual elimination of competition before the age of
12. The task force was pilloried by many in the hockey establishment
as impractical, and its recommendations have never been resurrected.

Perhaps the experiment underway at St. Michael's College in
Toronto will be a model for marrying education and sport. St. Mike's
was once a junior hockey power, turning out Catholic boys with schooling and a hockey education to boot. But St. Mike's dropped out of the
junior system in 1962, the year it won the Memorial Cup. School and
hockey had become increasingly incompatible, and the Basilian fathers
would no longer be party to this commerce in teenaged boys.

St. Mike's returned to junior hockey in 1997–98. The idea is again
to integrate hockey development with an education. How this experiment will work when competing with junior operations that make
money and offer lip service to education is unclear. In the ideal paradigm, St. Mike's will be a blueprint for the future, offering fewer games,
better training, and an educational setting for impressionable young
men. With the encouragement of such progressive thinkers as Leafs
president Ken Dryden, it may become more than a novelty.

As it stands, the Canadian development system of community-based
teams is not cost-effective. For the amount of spaghetti Canadians throw
at the wall, very little sticks. As Toronto's director of scouting, Anders
Hedberg, himself a great Swedish player, pointed out, "If Canadians took
skill training as seriously as Europeans do, they'd beat the world by nine
or ten goals every game." It's instructive to compare the Canadian model
to the manner in which the Soviets turned out great players from Valeri
Kharlamov and Alexander Yakushev to Fetisov to Bure. Instead of con-
signing their prospects to a far-flung junior system run for profit at the
whim of local operators — as we do in Canada — the Soviets brought

their young players to state-supported schools dedicated to conditioning and skills development by the best coaches available. Canadian prospects are exposed to coaching that ranges from excellent to terrible; to improve they must often supplement a winter of games and tournaments with power-skating schools and other skills development.

Instead of channeling most of their best athletes into hockey — as we do in Canada — the Soviets first determined which athletes were best suited to the sport using comparisons of cardiovascular abilities and "quick-twitch" versus "slow-twitch" muscle analysis. Instead of confining practice and skills development to infrequent pauses in an endless schedule of games, the Soviets gave practice equal footing. Instead of allowing young men to exist on takeout food and snacks, they stressed diet and nutrition.

Tod Hartje, an American who played a season at the Soviet elite level, remembered how deceptive his first impressions were. "They had the gulag look, sunken, drained," he wrote in his book *From Behind the Red Line*. "There was no shine to their hair, they had blanks in their eyes.... They projected not energy but lassitude. As a full blooded, sports-mad American, I know I looked in better condition, more healthy, gave off more energy. But I soon found new meaning in the cliché about looks being deceiving. I could barely keep up." The Russian-trained players have helped raise the conditioning standard to new highs in the NHL, but the feeder system in Canada is still not keeping pace in producing the same level of fitness in its prospects.

Of course, no one is advocating the realpolitik baggage that came with the Soviet system, or the drug regimes that supplemented legitimate training. But as Canadian minor hockey coach Brian Proctor — who took Canadian teens to train in Minsk every summer — asked, "Can you imagine the type of athletes we could produce in North America if we identified talent scientifically around the age of 12 and nurtured these teenagers through maturity at sports camps, making sure their diet, training, mental attitude, and competition were all finely tuned?"

It's not just outsiders who have novel ideas for reforming the NHL feeder system. Edmonton president and general manager Glen Sather was proposing such ideas back in 1985. "Put them in a training facility like the Banff School of Fine Arts where they can get everything — gymnastics, dance, and a great academic course with the teachers in that town," he proposed. "You could go through all the hockey and cross-country skiing, all the off-ice training you would need to develop some elite athletes." Sather's ideas largely fell on deaf ears.

The minor system in Canada — with its bantam, midget, and junior drafts — is not wrong or evil by design, merely flawed in such a way that games — and dollars — are deemed more important to the young hockey player than skills development. It evolved to develop NHL prospects, not well-adjusted student athletes. Ordinary kids became filler for the prodigies to practice their skills against, then were cast aside. Meanwhile, NHL owners paid little for the products that emerged from this system, and — as happens when a commodity is cheap — cared even less about the human casualties of the process. The contemporary Canadian system turns out sounder technical players with more game experience than it did before 1972, but it still fails to turn out stars who transcend the game as Orr and Gretzky once did — and as Jagr and Bure and Selanne and Federov do today. The profit-driven system leaves little time for the improvisation that encourages genius, and the detailed training that hones it. "To the extent that Wayne Gretzky was made, not born," observed Dryden and Roy MacGregor in their book *Home Game*, "it happened far more in his backyard and side yard than in all the arenas of Brantford."

"I don't think there's enough practice time," says Sather. "My own kids' experience in Edmonton, they were playing games every second or third night, they hardly ever had practices. People put so much emphasis on games and standings that they don't ever practice." Or play pick-up hockey, where creativity and love of the game are engendered. The story of Gordie Howe playing on three separate teams as a boy in Saskatchewan is well known; what's less well known is that, even then, Howe played fewer than half the games in a season that a 12-year-old boy now plays in the Toronto minor-hockey system. The rest of Howe's time was spent on sloughs and ponds, honing his skills.

Why do junior teams need to play 80 to 100 games a season to legitimize their position? For years, junior hockey was a losing financial proposition. Many owners kept going for the love of the sport or the ego rush of having a stake in the game. Small-time business people, they had neither the wherewithal nor the nerve to insist on adequate payment from the NHL for the players they developed. To push too hard was to risk losing that foothold on the hockey ladder, the status that it brought. To suggest to the omnipotent Clarence Campbell, president of the NHL from 1946 to 1977, that teams should shell out more money for the next Bobby Hull or Bobby Orr was to risk sanction. And so the cycle of poverty dictated games, games, and more games to turn a cheap buck. When money was tight, perhaps a full schedule was conscionable. Nowadays, when junior teams change hands for considerable sums, profit has superceded every other motive. Junior hockey is sold in metropolitan areas as an affordable alternative to the high-cost NHL; the development and education of young men are clearly secondary.

The latest challenge for hockey development is the growing influx of European players into the Canadian system. In 1997–98, an estimated 350 imports played midget, Junior B, or Junior A hockey in Canada. This invasion is fed in part by the perception that these players will not be rated as highly for the NHL draft if they don't showcase their skills in North America. In part, it compensates for the dearth of skill players emerging from the system in Canada. And in part it is fueled by the profit motive among junior owners who want to attract ticket buyers with the best possible team.

"I blame the agents," says Bob Nicholson, president of Canadian Hockey. "They're bringing their clients over early so they can be drafted higher and get more money when they're drafted." Glen Sather sees it differently: "To me, it's the people who are running junior hockey who have to take the responsibility. Junior hockey has become a big business and these guys want the best players so they can make lots of money. In doing that they're pushing Canadian kids out of their own system."

The pillaging of the European development leagues and the loss of high-caliber spots for Canadian players pose dangers for hockey. The downside for the Europeans is that the best young players are skimmed off and the competition in those countries diluted. According to George Kingston, the former NHL coach who now coaches the German national team, the programs in that country are being gutted as Canadian imports overwhelm the German pro league while the best German prospects are siphoned off to Canada's junior leagues. (The European country that protects its prospects most zealously, Switzerland, is taking the biggest steps of late.) If the Canadian development system were doing a good job of skills development, this wholesale airlift of fast-skating, technically gifted foreigners would be moot. But given the inferior training of many Canadian players, the invasion is entirely understandable. Highly drafted European junior stars such as Martin Skoula in Barrie, Jiri Fischer in Hull, and Michal Roszival in Swift Current sell tickets. Unfortunately, they also relegate Canadian prospects to second-rate status. It's not unlike the way superior American football training effectively wiped out Canadians at skill positions in the CFL.

The House of Commons committee investigating the hockey industry has met with cynicism from hockey traditionalists. The committee

— led by MP Dennis Mills, himself the father of an NHL player — has been accused of meddling and grandstanding to get more money for rich NHL owners and players. Yet the probe can — and should — focus on how resources are directed in the sprawling, uncharted territory of minor hockey. In Canada, where hockey is part of the ethos, we have the resources to improve the way young players are developed, but there seems little inclination to change the system. When Toronto native Eric Lindros balked at going to Sault Ste. Marie in the junior draft, wanting to stay close to home at a crucial stage in his hockey, academic, and personal development, he was not applauded for his admirable priorities; he was condemned for wanting "preferential" treatment.

THE RED WINGS DRESSING ROOM at Joe Louis Arena is almost empty. Many of Steve Yzerman's teammates have changed and gone home. He's seen many faces come and go in his 15 years with the team. Some — such as current Detroit GM Ken Holland — stayed only long enough to unpack their gear. Others — like Joey Kocur — have left for a time and then come back for a second stint. This is clearly his room; his daughter rummages contentedly through a box of granola bars nearby. With the carpeting at his feet, the subdued lighting, the rich wood of the lockers, and the techno-beat pumping through the sound system, it could almost be his rec room in Grosse Pointe.

Yzerman is mulling a reporter's question: What's the most satisfying goal he's ever scored? He pauses. Clearly, asking Yzerman to sort through thousands of hockey games for a single goal is like asking Imelda Marcos to select a favorite pair of pumps. "Honestly, not that many stand out. Probably scoring in double overtime in game seven to eliminate St. Louis," he ventures after a pause. A heavily favored Detroit team was rescued (temporarily) by its captain in 1996 when Yzerman ripped a laser from inside the blue line. Blues goalie Jon Casey hardly budged as the puck went by. On the videotape, an exhausted Yzerman seems to be turning back to the bench for a change after launching his long prayer. But the prayer was answered with a ringing flourish as the puck pinged in off the crossbar.

What was so satisfying about that goal? "There are only a few guys — Hull, Sakic, Lindros — guys who have really hard shots who actually pick the corner and just score there. Most of us just shoot. So every now and then, when you come down the wing and aim there and really get some heat on it...I feel good about those ones.

"I never really considered myself an explosive scorer in junior," he recalls, stripping off his green practice jersey. Maybe so, but in Peterborough — just 90 minutes from Nepean — Yzerman flourished where other talented teenagers stalled in their development, or were defeated by the challenges of making a million-to-one shot come true. In his final year with the Petes, he scored 56 goals and 98 assists, numbers dwarfed, as he suggests, by Pat Lafontaine's 104 goals and 234 points, but impressive nonetheless.

The Red Wings, who'd missed the playoffs in 12 of the previous 13 seasons, had the fourth pick overall in the 1983 draft. They were the epitome of ineptitude, having survived the deleterious ownership of Bruce Norris and presidency of John Ziegler only because Detroit is a great hockey city. An attempt to trade for the third pick (owned by the Islanders) had failed, and with it new owner Mike Ilitch's hopes of selecting the Detroit product Lafontaine. For his part, Yzerman, a long-time fan of the Islanders, had been hoping that the New York team would select him. In this unpromising fashion, Yzerman became a Red Wing.

Yzerman and new general manager Jimmy Devellano, who'd helped build the Islanders' dynasty as chief scout, ushered in a new era for Ilitch, revitalizing the team and the marketing of hockey in Detroit with an innovative approach and exciting play. The Red Wings' return to respectability, and then to excellence, coincided with Yzerman's evolution into an explosive scorer and then — under Bowman — a fine two-way player and team leader. He admired the Islanders' great center Bryan Trottier, and wore number 19 because it was Trottier's number. Winner of six Stanley Cups, Trottier combined speed and finesse with a hard, accurate shot, great instincts, and a bulldog determination at both ends of the rink, a combination of skills Yzerman came to emulate.

While the complete package of skills took time, Yzerman has always had a fine shot. In practice, while his teammates gather at the bench, he'll often move off to the side and practice his shot against the boards, the glass, a goalie — anything will do. As befits a man who loves to shoot, Yzerman is always tinkering with his stick. During the 1997–98 season he switched from a Victoriaville stick to a new Easton T-Flex shaft with a graphite blade. The company makes individual molds for him for each blade it makes, allowing him to modify his sticks continuously; the shaft is thinner and lighter than a wooden one. Assistant coach Dave Lewis says Yzerman is shooting better than ever.

"A lot can go wrong when you deke," he explains, slipping off his shoulder pads. Away from his teammates, he seems taller, more substantial than he appears alongside the likes of McCarty and Shanahan. "But if you come in and see a spot and then hit it, the goalie isn't going to stop you."

Shortly before Yzerman began his NHL career, former Peterborough coach Roger Neilson popularized the use of videotape, and Yzerman made abundant use of it in his early career. "I'd watch a lot of the times when I'd miss — if I had a breakaway, I'd come in the next day and try to see where the goalie was standing and how I came in on him. I always felt there were certain spots on a goalie that came from their style. If they dropped down, you could get them above the ankles, for instance. I observed where goals went in on guys.

33

"You know, you hear guys talking, 'Where do you go on this guy? Where can he be beat?' But I haven't heard of a goalie yet who can't be beaten through the legs. So you can over-analyze. I know I did. Now the coaches break it down for us. If we're going well, they'll show it to reinforce something we're doing well. And if we have a stretch of really bad games, they'll show us the breakdowns."

Those video clues often yield better ideas for breaking down an opposing goalie. Typical of the goalies Yzerman has scrutinized is Patrick Roy, the 6-foot-1, impregnable wall in the Colorado net. "He makes a lot of plays look easy. Coming in on the deke, he simply won't give you between the legs. He's relaxed, not hyper in front of the net. He just seems to be trying to stay in front of the puck, to let it hit him. He's not going to watch your body or anything. Other guys get distracted and you can put it through their legs, but not Patrick."

Of course, before you can get to the goalies, there's the problem of circumventing the defensemen. Who are the best? The stars such as Chelios, Bourque, Adam Foote, and former teammate Vladimir Konstantinov, of course. But Yzerman also includes journeymen such as Craig Ludwig, of Dallas, and Dave Lewis, the assistant Red Wings coach, on his personal list of immovable objects. They employ the boxer's technique of cutting off the ring, taking the player wide, thereby limiting the angles and reducing the ice surface.

"After all these years, you'd think you'd be able to beat these guys," says Yzerman. "Just take 'em wide, but you can't do it. They angle you off. And the best are pretty good backward skaters. They'll put you in the corner of the rink and give you the shot from outside." So how do you get around today's Goliath-sized defensemen? "The only times you beat them is when they've had to commit, and you made them get from one spot to another," he says, running his thumb down the blade of his skate, cleaning it of ice and snow. "Occasionally you can get wide and down low and round the outside when you have a step, but it doesn't happen very often, because generally he's playing the body."

This whip-around-the-defenseman technique was a favorite of Henri Richard, the Rocket's little brother, who has more Stanley Cup rings than any player in NHL history with eleven (four more than brother Maurice). The Pocket Rocket stood just 5-foot-6, four inches shorter than his more powerful elder sibling, and needed a little help in beating the defenseman to the corner. When Richard attempted to go around a defenseman, he'd lean in as he pivoted and grab the opponent's knee. This gave him a slingshot effect as he made the turn, propelling him past the defenseman. If he was unable to make the turn successfully, he'd often go to the ice, clutching his opponent's knee. To many referees, it looked as if Henri was being taken down by the defenseman. "I'd get a penalty for holding," lamented Fernie Flaman of Boston, "because it was impossible to see what Henri was doing. It used to drive me crazy."

In the modern NHL game, this sort of one-on-one confrontation has virtually disappeared, swallowed up by traps and locks and dump-and-chase. Most players get ridden off into the boards before they can cut to the net for a scoring chance. Or they simply forgo the individual challenge and dump the puck into the corner. "Unless you've got huge reach and strength, like Mario," shrugs Yzerman, "you're just not going to get around them."

Except for a period in the 1960s and 1970s when the slapshot overwhelmed goaltenders — in effect, stretching the prime scoring area back 10 or 15 feet — scorers have needed to get close to maximize their opportunities. Today, the goaltenders' improved equipment makes it difficult to score from anywhere but the prime scoring zone. Even then, top goalies such as Roy, Dominik Hasek, and Martin Brodeur are rarely beaten on the first shot unless they are screened.

Adding to the difficulty of scoring these days is the religious conversion to team defense in the NHL. Checkers have always been employed to hobble stars, of course; Detroit's Bryan Watson clung to Bobby Hull in the 1960s like a barnacle to a boat, and Esa Tikkanen virtually shared the uniform of the man he was shadowing for the Oilers in the 1980s ("Don't worry," Tikkanen reassured Craig Janney back in 1990. "I brush my teeth every day"). But the league-wide emphasis on smothering scorers is new. "In the last few years I heard people say, 'We don't want you to score,'" points out Pat Flatley, who often checked the other team's top scorers. "I'd never heard that before. They said, 'We have guys to score. Your job is not to get scored on.'"

The paltry scoring levels of the 1950s are back. Hasek rings up shutouts like Shakespeare turned out sonnets. Whether this is progress — whether low-scoring hockey represents the zenith of the team game or the nadir of individualism — is debatable. But Yzerman's declining scoring totals in recent years do not indicate a waning of talent so much as a recognition of the new realities in the NHL and a deliberate undertaking to adapt his game accordingly under Bowman. "Scotty puts a lot of emphasis on the little things, he concentrates on them, and he makes the players aware of them," says Yzerman. "We've become very conscientious and personally I've done the same."

Yzerman excuses himself. Hockey players learn to talk to reporters while undressing; their comments are often issued with little more than a smile to protect their dignity. Yzerman has a calm, unhurried sort of dignity even as he pads naked from the shower to a media scrum. Though he appears slight on the ice, he has a compact, muscled body and surprisingly trunk-like thighs; his superbly toned body has only about 8 percent body fat. A workout warrior, he's always the fittest player on the Wings.

And while some players develop a big head from celebrity, Yzerman has got bigger feet. "When I came into the league, I wore a size seven skate," he laughs after his shower, lacing up cross trainers. "Now I'm up to eight and a quarter. I may go even bigger, because they're a little tight right now. I have a fat foot and I don't like the laces getting too tight, because you lose some of the support. So I get the skate maker Easton to make mine extra stiff and I cut the lacing back, making it a little bit wider. It's funny, some guys used to jam their feet right in. I can understand them doing that, but they do look funny."

Perhaps the most famous skate-stuffer is Yzerman's old Red Wings teammate, Paul Coffey, now with Chicago, who crams his feet into skates two sizes smaller than his shoes. Coffey calls his skates "the most important part of my equipment. If my skates are not quite right, I feel very below average as a player. But if the fit is good, I feel as if I can do anything on the ice." Doug Gilmour of the Devils was also famous for jamming his feet into undersized skates during his days as a Leaf, but he developed a bony irritation in his foot and was forced to move up in size.

Coffey contends that properly fitted skates help sustain his speed when he makes the transition from defensive zone to attack. Well-fitted skates transfer the energy most efficiently from the legs through the boot and into the ice. Yzerman's skates, like most players', have a rocker blade, a back-to-front bow. This works well in the stop-and-start game employed by forwards and stay-at-home defensemen. But Coffey's rushing style stresses speed and acceleration with fewer stops and starts, and his long, flat blades — more like a speedskater's — help him maintain top speed. He also has the equipment man sharpen his skates with a distinct hollow between the edges to give him traction for quick moves to either side. Ray Bourque and Brian Leetch also employ flatter blades, like Coffey's.

The skate has undergone many changes since the humble days of leather boots and tube blades — all of them designed to make the skate lighter without sacrificing support or stiffness. According to Jim Gary of Bauer — which has about 65 percent of the NHL market — pro players look for a stiffer boot than the average consumer. Bruins great Rick Middleton remembers that he used to pop the rivets on his skates from the stress he put on them. He needed a stronger, stiffer product to absorb the stress. The first solution from the industry was the plastic boot, like a modified ski boot; now boots are made of space-age nylons and other synthetics more suited to the unique rigors of skating.

Weight is also key. A player like Yzerman lifts his leg approximately 2,000 times during a game, and a lighter skate can only give him fresher legs in the third period. The new ultra-light Bauer "Vapor" skate is drawing raves from players and trainers alike. The only parts of the boot that are still leather are the heel and the eyelets; the rest of the boot is made of materials common to bullet-proof vests: Kevlar, graphite, and ballistic nylon held together by strong glues. In the past, defensemen wore skates with more padding than those worn by forwards; the new materials mean that everyone except goalies wears the same skate. Other small touches these days include the positioning of the eyelets further down the boot and over the blade, and a flattening of the top surface of the boot so that the eyelets lie flatter.

Yzerman doesn't wear the smallest skate in the NHL; Brian Bradley of Tampa Bay wears a 6 1/2. At the other end of the spectrum is Derian Hatcher of Dallas, who wears a size 12 boot. But extremes represent only a small percentage of the NHL market — only 5 percent, according to Gary — as do players who wear no socks. Where once a large number of NHL players, inspired by Bobby Orr's example, went barefoot in the boot, now 95 percent wear socks.

There are new cosmetic options, such as the choice of white or black blade holders. And the move from full sole to waffle sole has given some players a sleeker look. The cosmetic and technological secrets of skate makers are jealously guarded as they fight for a greater share of the lucrative, and growing, skate market. Getting Gretzky or Yzerman or Hull to endorse the product is the goal of marketing departments, since the tastes of the stars are watched closely by the young players hoping to emulate them.

The other significant change in skates has been the move away from tube blades fixed to the boot through steel posts, to carbon steel or stainless-steel blades slotted into a plastic holder. Most NHLers use a stainless-steel blade because it holds an edge better than carbon steel and is harder. These blades can also be replaced more easily behind the bench when a player has skate problems. There is considerable experimentation with different alloys that produce strong blades with less bend. For some time, Tuuk has had a patent on the blade holder. With that patent now up, changes are expected in the next two years. Most new products being tested are aimed at easier removal, and a lighter blade. One new blade in development is only about the width of a hacksaw. Eventually consumers will be able to create a personalized template, then order blades from the manufacturer with their favorite hollow and sharpness, ready to slip into the blade holders.

Skating, of course, is the foundation of hockey. To misquote Corinthians, "And now abideth speed, toughness, and character, but the greatest of these is speed." "If you can't skate, you can't play at the NHL level," says Kings coach Larry Robinson, echoing a familiar sentiment. "Great skaters can last in the league without a shot or a mean streak. You can't say the same vice versa." Coffey, widely held to be the best pure skater in the NHL over the past decade, generates his speed in the corners behind the net, using four or five dynamic strides to get up to cruising speed for the trip through the neutral zone. Coffey — who's also one of the most eloquent students of the craft of hockey — has observed that other great skaters like Sergei Federov use this same technique of building speed in the corners.

The thorough Lloyd Percival quantified exactly what skating meant to the sport. According to Percival, players skate an average of two to three miles in a game — and as many as four miles when poor line changes are used. "Skating is to hockey what throwing is to baseball, what tackling is to football, or what footwork is to tennis," he wrote in his *Hockey Handbook*. "It is the most important fundamental."

Percival recognized that much of skating then — as now — was haphazardly taught in between games of minor hockey. Hidebound by tradition stretching back to the beginning of the NHL, skaters were locked in an "unconscious skating complacency" that took a lot of selling to change. He noted that Canadian players failed to get enough hip action into their stride, spoiled efficiency through needless tension in their muscles, and lifted their feet too high in the backward motion at the end of the stride. He urged skaters to develop proficiency in three areas: free skating, agility skating, and backward skating.

Another who dissected skating technique was Anatoli Tarasov. He was dismissive of the Canadian method, writing that "it is completely wrong to teach the kids to skate in the Canadian way — with their skates straddled wide." Tarasov had studied the matter and concluded that a proper skate technique "will leave a drawing. If it is the 'herringbone style,' it means the athlete is skating in the most economical way....It is important that his legs be half bent, his takeoffs be powerful, which predetermines strong feet and hips, for the trunk to be unstrained and the hands, holding the stick, feel free and easy."

Of course, we have seen only the cream of the crop from Russia. Still, it's hard to remember a mediocre skater in the bunch, a tribute to the thoroughness of Tarasov's philosophy. In his book, *The Game*, Ken Dryden recognized the Soviets' "short, choppy, wide-gaited stride" and their almost impregnable base of legs and skates. "Their smaller bodies were strong enough, tough enough to stand up to the game, to wrestle for the puck, to get it and move it, if rarely to punish." That's equally true today, even if Soviets named Krutov and Maltsev are now Russians named Bure and Federov.

Since the epiphany brought on by Tarasov's Soviet disciples in the 1970s, many have begun following Percival's principles in power-skating schools and hockey programs across the country. Cindy Bower, daughter of former goalie Johnny Bower, teaches one of the most respected programs. The problem has been to integrate these teachings into a system obsessed with games and tournaments. Cindy Bower receives a continuous stream of students — many of whom have played hockey at the pro level — who have little idea of how to maximize their skating abilities, even though speed is the sport's supreme tactical weapon.

EARLY IN THE 1997–98 SEASON, the St. Louis Blues are in Detroit to flex their muscle against the defending Stanley Cup champs. It is the first game of real significance for the Wings; St. Louis is a division opponent and a bitter rival. Besides the critically injured Konstantinov, nearly killed in a limousine accident not long after Detroit's Stanley Cup victory, the Red Wings are missing Shanahan (sore back), Federov (unsigned free agent), and Kirk Maltby (separated shoulder), as well as Mike Vernon and Tomas Sandstrom (new teams) from the club that won the Cup just 17 weeks earlier. The Blues, of course, have Brett Hull, and they're off to a fast start.

What Paul Kariya is to speed in the NHL, Brett Hull is to power. If a significant part of hockey skill is inherited, Brett Hull got all the right genes from his father. Bernie Geoffrion and Andy Bathgate perfected the slapshot, and Gordie Howe was the first true power forward in hockey, but Bobby Hull married the two attributes in a package so awe-inspiring that many goalies cite him alone as their reason for adopting a mask. Hull virtually created the notion of a power player in the NHL.

Brett does not have his father's Olympian frame; indeed, he has confessed to being a tad soft around the edges at times earlier in his career. And he has never been accused of having a type-A personality. "I'll be sad to go, and I won't be sad to go," he mused when trade rumors cropped up in St. Louis. "It wouldn't upset me to leave St. Louis, and it would upset me to leave St. Louis. It's hard to explain. You'll find out one of these days, but maybe you never will." (Hull signed with Dallas in the summer of 1998.)

Hull may not be intensity personified, but when goalies and coaches talk of quick release, accuracy, and power, it's Hull they mention first. His 554 lifetime goals — including 86 in 1990–91, third most in a single NHL season — attest to his superb timing and accuracy. "It's kind of like we carry the instruments, and he's the lead singer," former teammate Glen Featherstone said, summing up Hull's place with the Blues. "If you keep Brett Hull off the board," observed former NHL defenseman Brad Marsh, "it's more a case of him having a bad night, not so much what you do against him."

While Teemu Selanne scores many of his goals on the move, Hull rifles home many of his flat-footed, from the slot. To watch Hull in action is to see him constantly swirling in the opponent's end, probing for a gap in the coverage, setting up just away from the perimeter of the defense and goalie. He's adept at slipping to the off side of the ice on power plays, getting lost away from the play while the Blues overload one side of the rink. Left alone for a split second, Hull one-times the puck off a pass. This quick shot often catches the goalie opening his legs as he slides across the crease.

"I think it's the toughest shot," says Martin Brodeur of the Devils. "That's why they made the rule about the man not being in the crease, to help goalies get across the crease before the guy shoots it. But that quick shot, sometimes they catch you moving, that's what makes it so tough. Brett Hull's the best at it. And his shot's hard, too."

Hull uses a short stick, adding to his power by holding his hands up the shaft, creating a longer arc, the way a golfer uses a longer club to maximize club-head speed. Hull has even pushed the golf comparison a step further: he now uses a "bubble shaft" hockey stick from Easton, much like the graphite golf clubs with a bubble cavity halfway down the shaft to create balance.

Like Kariya, Hull keeps his stick on the ice as much as possible, ready to tip a shot or snap one by the goalie, especially when he's being tied up. Hull will allow his body to be immobilized but not his stick. This allows him to anticipate passes. "It's like in football where a quarterback can throw a pass to a receiver before he even breaks out of his cut," Hull says. "A good centerman knows his wings, and he can move the puck to a spot before you even turn to go there." While Hull scores more goals than most players on shots from beyond 45 feet, he is most dangerous in the 10-to-25-foot range, described by Percival as the prime scoring zone. It's Ryan Walter's "inside" game, the place where a price must be paid for the right to snipe.

Conventional hockey wisdom insists that revenge must be exacted for each and every slight received upon one's person on the rink, but Hull emulates Mahatma Gandhi when opponents hack away at him. Non-violence is his credo. "One thing that's important is learning to take a lot of abuse from the opposition without retaliating or yapping back," he says. "Sooner or later they forget about you." That extends to a little play acting in front of the net, too. The 5-foot-10 Hull is a solid 200 pounds, but tends to linger on the ice when knocked down, playing possum. Then, when he's become an afterthought, he's back, ready to shoot. (To help him unload quickly, Hull wears gloves with narrow six-inch cuffs. That minimal protection may have cost him when a Tomas Sandstrom slash sidelined him for six weeks in 1997–98, an injury that might have been prevented by larger gloves.)

Besides patience, Hull has a sense of proportion. "I'm not a grinder," he concedes. "If we had 20 guys like me, we wouldn't win five games all season." A look at his plus-minus stats underscores the point: he was minus nine for the 1997–98 season, despite being on the ice for 72 St. Louis scores in which he had a hand. By comparison, center Jason Allison of Boston was plus 33, sniper John LeClair of the Flyers was plus 30, Mike Modano of the Stars was plus 25, Bobby Holik of the Devils was plus 23, while Chicago's ace Tony Amonte was plus 21. On the other hand, if you had 20 players and no Brett Hulls, you wouldn't win five games either.

This night against the Red Wings, Hull displays flashes of brilliance, but it's Yzerman who makes the lasting impression. In the first period, Yzerman is cutting across the blue line when St. Louis forward Pavol Demitra flicks out his stick. The blade creases Yzerman's left cheek, cutting him. Demitra is banished to the penalty box and the Wings go on the power play.

Power plays have evolved considerably in the past decade, due in large part to innovations sparked by Gretzky and Lemieux. In the past, defensemen such as Bobby Orr keyed the attack from the point, searching for either a clear shot or an open man to pass to. Effective penalty-killing units defied this strategy using a "box" or "diamond-shaped" formation to crowd the middle of the ice, denying the slot or clear shooting lanes to the goalie. It became necessary then for power plays to open up this box or diamond by drawing defensive players closer to the boards, creating more two-on-one situations or isolating an open player on the opposite side of the action. Hull is deadly for the Blues in this situation, and Yzerman is masterful at creating chances on the Wings' power play from a position on the side boards.

In Pittsburgh, Mario Lemieux specialized in what is known as the "half-board" play — positioning himself halfway between the blue line and the goal line along the boards. As Lemieux handled the puck from this spot, he hoped to draw the defense to him, opening seams in the penalty-killers' zone defense. If the defenseman challenged Lemieux for the puck, the Penguins center had four options: slide a pass to Ron Francis in the slot or to Jaromir Jagr perched on the opposite side of the goalie's crease, send a pass back along the boards to his defenseman Kevin Hatcher on the point, or look for the second defenseman breaking toward the net off the other point. To emphasize the gaps in the defensive zone, Lemieux and his teammates spread themselves around the zone.

Of course, if the defense chose to leave Lemieux alone, he could take the puck to the net himself or circle behind the goalie and try to set up the same play on the opposite side. It worked again and again. Lemieux scored 201 goals on the power play in his career. Gretzky's variation on the theme was to set up behind the net or in the corner. The idea was the same; force the defense to chase him with the puck and leave other players open. With his extraordinary passing and vision, Gretzky was deadly from this position. Yzerman, too, is expert at drawing in a penalty killer and then finding the open man.

The other power-play positions have their unique requirements, too. The player who sets up in the slot must have a quick release and the ability to shed defenders. It helps if he can set up in the deep slot, pulling the defense away from their cozy spot next to the goalie. Brett Hull, Francis, and Kariya have excelled here. The man positioned at the edge of the crease must take abuse from defensemen and goalies, be a solid corner player digging for the puck, and possess a quick release off the pass. Jagr is a current master of this art, as is Martin Lapointe of the Wings, who nearly scores on the Wings' power play against St. Louis off a deft feed from Yzerman in the corner.

Blasting away was once the method of choice for point men, but NHLers learned patience from the Soviets; in a man-advantage situation, there's no point surrendering the puck for anything less than an ideal shot. Now, effective point men need a great shot (Al MacInnis), great passing skills (Brian Leetch), or a combination of both (Nicklas Lidstrom). To help them string out the defensive coverage, they have begun standing with their feet outside the blue line but with their sticks inside, gaining a bit more ice in the offensive area. They know that Hasek or Roy will likely stop anything they see, so they must get the goalie moving or screened. To do that, teams need to control the puck, keep it moving, and be constantly circulating themselves.

With Yzerman directing traffic down low, Lidstrom controlling the point, Shanahan shooting, and Tomas Holmstrom or Lapointe screening the goalie, Detroit has one of the best power-play units. The Wings twice come close against St. Louis while Demitra is in the box, but come up empty against Grant Fuhr, still acrobatic at 35.

In the second period, Demitra learns that Yzerman has a memory and a mean streak. The two men face off to the right of Fuhr in the Blues' net. Demitra considers the Wings captain, a man who never fights, and decides it's safe to go for the puck. Yzerman, who now sports a bandage on his cheek, goes for the puck too, drawing it back between his legs, but he allows his gloved left hand to follow through, across Demitra's jaw. Faster than you can say "Dukla Trencin," Demitra's team back home in the Czech Republic, he slumps to the ice. There's no penalty. Yzerman has bought himself a little space in the 22-year-old universe of Pavol Demitra.

"You can intimidate players," says Chris Chelios, "but you get some guys like Yzerman who'll give it back to you. I respect him more than anyone else in the league. He's tougher than people know. He takes it and doesn't let it affect his game. He's a leader."

Yzerman himself gets a good scoring chance in the third period against St. Louis, taking a pass from Nicklas Lidstrom on the fly and quickly unloading a shot that beats Fuhr on the far side, grazing the post. What happens inside the brain of the Red Wings captain when Lidstrom feeds him the puck? What allows him to receive the pass and go in for the shot on Fuhr? Human muscles work in a chain. Optical stimuli or messages — such as the arrival of the puck on Yzerman's stick — are received via the eyes in the neurons in the brain. From repeated experience, the brain recognizes the message of the puck's arrival. This recognition causes a complex involuntary message to be sent to the muscles through the nerves in the spinal cord. The message tells certain muscles to perform an acquired task, such as shooting. These are the messages Joseph Campbell described as "engraved on the nerves" through experience.

These acquired reflexes are a short cut for the athlete. If Yzerman were forced to think himself through the process of shooting a puck with a Blues defenseman draped all over him, he would be easily checked in the time it took to complete the action. Like attempting to juggle for the first time, shooting the puck while fending off a defender seems laborious and slow to the novice, almost impossible. It is an acquired skill that requires timing, coordination, and practice.

While most healthy people can learn to juggle or shoot the puck, only a few will learn to keep five objects in the air or to pick the far side of the net on Grant Fuhr while skating 20 miles an hour and being bothered by a defenseman. This is where long-loop reflexes come in. These are the motor responses to sensory stimuli that involve long loops of neurons in the brain. Doctor William Tatton, a neurologist at the University of British Columbia, has tested subjects for the long-loop reflex arc. Of all the people he has studied, Wayne Gretzky has the fastest long-loop reflex arc he has ever encountered. From the time Gretzky receives the message of an opening on the goalie's far side to the instant of shooting the puck, in other words, he's the fastest gun in the west. Yzerman, as his 600-odd regular-season and playoff career goals attest, is no slouch himself.

Doctor Tatton identified another outstanding neurological attribute in Gretzky, one shared by Yzerman. Hockey analysts have long raved about Gretzky's ability to "see the ice." Anatoli Tarasov wrote, "More than once I witnessed Gretzky, instead of taking a seemingly obvious shot, making a pass directing it not to his teammates in the attack, but backward, to one of the defenders. It might be possible that he has the capacity for 'seeing' through the back of his head." Gretzky himself claims to not have to turn his head to see teammates on his wings. This heightened peripheral vision allows him to detect motion most of us would have to turn our heads to see. It's a hereditary trait, but through diligent practice during the appropriate window of opportunity in his brain's development, he refined the gift.

Walter Gretzky probably didn't know a neuron from a nimrod, but he understood the value of this gift. Walter started Wayne — and all his sons — as defensemen, so that they'd get a sense of how plays develop from the deeper perspective at the back of the action. Gretzky trained neurons in his brain that let him see more of the ice than the average player, and thus, more opportunities for passes and shots. Players describe it as "knowing where you are at all times." Bronco Horvath, a Bruins sniper in the 1950s and 1960s, once demonstrated this knack to kids at a summer hockey school. Standing between the blue line and the center red line, talking about the importance of knowing where you are on the ice, he said, "Left post" and, moving back and forth while he was talking, blindly shot toward the goal behind him, more than 100 feet away. In five shots, without ever looking in the direction of the net, he hit the left post twice and came close twice more.

The former basketball star Bill Bradley once demonstrated this same concept — "court sense," as it's known in basketball — to author John McPhee. At Princeton University Bradley had an over-the-shoulder trick shot with his back to the hoop. He'd seen greats such as Oscar Robertson and Jerry West do it, and he "worked it out for himself. He went on to say that it is a much simpler shot than it appears to be and, to illustrate, he tossed the ball over his shoulder and into the basket while he was talking and looking me in the eye. 'When you have played basketball for a while, you don't need to look at the basket when you are in this close,' he said, throwing it over his shoulder again and right through the hoop. 'You develop a sense of where you are.'"

Gretzky may have hockey's best internal compass, but Yzerman also has a highly refined sense of where he is on the ice. (That innate sense might have a downside, too. It might explain why — in the short term — North American players are slightly disoriented on the larger international surface. The boards, the net, and other signposts are slightly out of place; the brain must now respond consciously to stimuli that are otherwise processed subconsciously.) And while Gretzky's long-loop reflex arc is unprecedented, Yzerman's is also extraordinarily fast.

One obvious manifestation of the long-loop reflex can be seen any time a linesman drops the puck. Controlling the face-off, of course, is key to controlling possession of the puck and the flow of the game. Its importance is magnified tenfold come playoff time. It's a part of Yzerman's craft that has steadily improved through his career; his peers have long considered him (along with Guy Carbonneau, Peter Zezel, and Mark Messier) one of the best in the NHL at controlling the draw.

Alyn McCauley of the Maple Leafs finds out just how good Yzerman is at Maple Leaf Gardens a few weeks after the Wings-Blues game (which finished with the undermanned Wings earning a 3–3 draw). The Wings are still adjusting to the role of defending champs when they play in Toronto, still dealing with the devastating accident that nearly took the life of Konstantinov, still working young players into a line-up scrambled by a rash of injuries. The Leafs hope to catch them on an off-night, maybe even write a signature game for their young season.

With the Gardens crowd cheering him on, Toronto goalie Glenn Healy holds the powerful Detroit offense to a single goal in the first 28 minutes of the game. Meanwhile, the Leafs even the score late in the first on a goal by Steve Sullivan. With a little luck, Toronto might pot another goal or two, then try to hold on for dear life. Eight minutes into the second, though, the Wings force a face-off to Healy's right. Yzerman has Darren McCarty on his left; newcomer Brent Gilchrist — who's never played with Yzerman before this season — is in the high slot on his right. Gilchrist, a left-handed shot, is looking for Yzerman to draw the puck back to him for a one-time shot.

Across the face-off circle, McCauley, a 20-year-old rookie, tries to calm himself as he anticipates what Yzerman might do and how he can counter. As he admits later, worrying about his opponent was his first mistake. McCauley is a left-hand shot up against the right-handed Yzerman. He has to be careful not to pull the puck back too hard or it'll end up in the vicinity of Healy. If he knocks it forward, he may set up a clear shot from the point for Detroit. Yzerman, meanwhile, can call on a repertoire of moves. "There's a half dozen things you can do depending on who you're playing against," he says later. "You don't want to lose it straight back. A scrum doesn't matter so much. I don't know him [McCauley] that well yet, so I stuck to what was working. You just hope he won't figure it out before the game ends."

McCauley sees Yzerman reverse the grip on his lower — right — hand, and thinks, "He'll try to draw the puck back — to Gilchrist, or to Nicklas Lidstrom at the point." McCauley decides to go to his forehand and sweep the puck toward the boards, away from both Gilchrist and Lidstrom.

The NHL has added lines on the ice in the face-off circle, where the player must place his feet. Before these lines were added, veteran players would stagger their stance in one direction or the other to give themselves leverage. "You could try to take the opponent's stick out," Yzerman points out, "but you can't do that now with the lines." The visiting player must put his stick on the ice first; only then does the home player commit his stick. These rules have cleaned up face-offs to a considerable degree; the incidence of players being tossed out of the circle for anticipating the drop of the puck or refusing to put their sticks in position has thankfully diminished.

Both Yzerman and McCauley spread their feet wide to gain leverage. Both sets of eyes fix on linesman Gerard Gauthier's hand. Some players claim they can see the skin on the linesman's knuckles go from white to pink as he readies to drop the puck, but both Yzerman and McCauley are going on first movement. Yzerman puts his stick at the line. "If I can get leverage and pick it clean," he thinks, "I can draw it back."

What happens next can be charitably described as a learning experience for McCauley. He will win his share of face-offs in his rookie year against the likes of Linden, Messier, Saku Koivu, and Joe Nieuwendyk, but no sooner is the puck on the ice than Yzerman has it on his back hand. McCauley is left to sweep futilely at thin air. The perfect pick is whisked back to Gilchrist, who's poised, stick cocked, for just this chance. He one-times a shot so hard that the puck is by Healy, off the high inside bar of the net and out again, before the goal judge can spot it. The teams play three more minutes without a whistle before the video goal judge confirms what many — including referee Bill McCreary — had missed: Gilchrist's shot was a goal. 2–0 Detroit, on their way to a workman-like 3–2 triumph.

"I forgot what Brian taught me," McCauley says after the game, referring to his junior coach in Ottawa, Brian Kilrea. "He said to do what's natural for me. I was too worried what Yzerman was going to do. I learned something. Now I'm better prepared."

Face-offs — along with setting picks and screening goalies — are part of the "inside" game that went largely unappreciated until the use of videotape prompted coaches and TV analysts to keep notes of who won and lost draws. In the 1960s, author Hugh Hood stood in for a few face-offs with the masterful Beliveau. An awed Hood watched Beliveau's stick flash out "like the motion of a small snake's tongue." The Canadiens captain proceeded to demonstrate all the options he had at every face-off — the point, the net, the right winger — "exactly where he intended, like a billiards champion."

With puck control so important in the new, low-scoring NHL, teams can't afford to give up chances like the one Yzerman and Gilchrist manufactured against McCauley. Special teams and draws in the final minute only magnify the value of having a great face-off man like Yzerman to send over the boards. Doug Jarvis, now coaching in Dallas, was never much of a scorer in the NHL, but he made a living on Scotty Bowman's Montreal teams by winning important face-offs.

Yzerman looks beyond the opposing center for clues about what to do when the puck is dropped. The positioning of other players, what they're saying to each other, the puck-dropping style of the linesman — all come into play. Messier, another fine face-off man, studies the player on the other side of the dot. "Look at his eyes, where his stick is facing, how his body is turned, how he's holding the stick," Messier counsels. "All that should give you some idea what he's going to do with the puck, whether he's going to shoot off the draw [in the offensive zone], pass the puck to one of his defensemen behind him or over to one of his wingers."

A center who can't win a majority of the face-offs in his own zone has to score plenty of goals himself to survive long in the NHL. Taking face-offs was one of the skills Yzerman honed after he got to the NHL. "I was fortunate that I got to play a lot when I was young, early in my career. Most young guys play 25 games or so and practice a lot. They didn't have a lot of good guys here when I arrived, though, so I got to play every night. I was used mostly on the power play and a regular shift.

"I didn't play a lot when we had a lead under Nick Polano or Brad Park or Harry Neale," he remembers. "Then Jacques Demers came in, and my role gradually expanded. I got to kill penalties. The coaches I played for after that wanted you to be good in both ends of the rink, good offensively but reliable defensively."

Giving Yzerman extra responsibilities is consistent with Bowman's philosophy of developing his core players. He's now working on rounding out the skills of Vyacheslav Kozlov, a talented offensive player. "I think any time you give a player an opportunity to kill penalties it makes him a better player," says Bowman. "You've got to play with grit. The odds are against you. You're short-handed. When I started coaching, I noticed that players transform themselves if you give them the chance. That happened with Jacques Lemaire in Montreal. He became a solid defensive player." Under Bowman's direction, it happened with Yzerman in Detroit as well.

A POST-PRACTICE PRESS CONFERENCE in Scotty Bowman's cramped office at Joe Louis Arena. Unlike the players' sumptuous surroundings, Bowman's office resembles a clerk's rather than that of hockey's most successful coach: industrial desk, thinning rug, faux wood paneling. Bowman, in a nylon Red Wings sweat suit and baseball cap, is dissecting the mood of his team for assembled reporters looking for an off-day story — a pleasant task, as the Wings have won seven of their past ten.

Success comes as no surprise to Bowman; he has won more games and more playoff games than any coach in NHL history. Only Toe Blake (with eight) has won more Stanley Cups than Bowman's seven, a discrepancy Bowman hopes to rectify in the spring.

Bowman's press conferences are unhurried and somewhat mechanical. He often answers questions with unrelated answers, shaping the discussion to his muse. The same question can elicit three very different responses — none on the topic. A question about great teams of the past is answered with an analysis of how the Soviets geared up for the Olympics, then how important John Ferguson was to the Canadiens in the sixties. "He has no coach's con about him," Ken Dryden wrote of Bowman. "He does not slap backs, punch arms or grab elbows. He doesn't search eyes, spew out ingratiating blarney, or disarm with faint, enervating praise."

Today the talk is about how to make up for the absence of holdout Sergei Federov, who won't re-sign with Detroit till February, though no one can predict that right now. Bowman gives a careful, non-committal answer about how others, like Kozlov, must step up their game. Notes are scratched into reporters' pads, tape machines silently turn; the transitory nature of sport guarantees the rapid obsolescence of the information he doles out, but stoking the daily beat writers is part of his job description and Bowman knows enough not to fight the process entirely. Feed them and they will go away. It takes a special question to engage his complete attention; then he will give a detailed response, almost always supported by his research.

The press briefing ends. The 64-year-old legend gathers up his charts and his TOI (time on ice) stats from the previous game. "You know," he says to a departing reporter, "this team has fun playing together. That's so important for a team."

"Does Yzerman's leadership have anything to do with that?"

"Yzerman has been very good at captaining the Wings and show-ing that he accepts the Europeans," Bowman replies. "He's been very cordial. If Yzerman wasn't accepting of a guy like Larionov, I could see that things would not go well. But he and Larionov are friends, and their wives see each other." The remark is not some fawning tribute but a statement of fact. It pleases Bowman. As quickly as he makes his point, he's back in his office, shutting the door behind him.

Leadership is a buzzword often heard around winning teams, seldom around losers. It's typically used in conjunction with other clichés, such as "team chemistry" and "a balanced roster." (As Pat Flatley observes, "Team chemistry is a product, not a cause of success. Winning creates the chem-istry. It makes every day a party. The food tastes better, the drinks are colder. When you're losing, everything stinks.") Bowman understands that Yzerman has helped bring Canadians, Americans, and many different Europeans together through his acceptance of them, and that this is no small thing. So do the players themselves. "He provides great leadership on the team," agrees Nicklas Lidstrom, the Red Wings' highly talented Swedish defenseman. "He arranges things on the road. Last time we were in Vancouver, he had us play paint ball. We've done that in a few places."

Yzerman downplays his role in harmonizing the different nationali-ties. "There's a lot of good European players you would want on your team. Who wouldn't want Peter Forsberg? He's one of the top five for-wards in the league. On our team, there's guys like Igor [Larionov] and Slava [Tetisov], they've gone out of their way to fit in and break the stereo-type. They've let everyone know they don't want any special treatment."

His gaze passes over to the stall of Konstantinov, whose locker stands ready even though he will never play again. His teammates still refer to him as if he were taking a long shower. "Guys like Vlady come to play and work hard. They show up for big games and they're a part of the team."

Yzerman gestures around the dressing room. "On our team, if you want to make an issue of something, you can make an issue of it. It's not like we're all going to each other's houses for dinner. But everyone feels comfortable in our dressing room if they come to play and practice hard."

Martin Lapointe contends that what makes Yzerman such an effective leader is his uncompromising work ethic, the intense determination that helped him to evolve from a promising, slender kid to a dynamic NHL scorer to a beautifully rounded two-way player. "It's amazing what a complete turnaround Stevie's had in the public eye the last few years," says Lapointe, who's played for Detroit since 1991. "It's funny because he hasn't been anything different since I've been here. He's always been an inspiration in his own way, not a rah-rah kind of guy. He's a leader by example."

One can see that example working on his teammate Federov, the prodigiously talented but fickle center. When a discouraged, tired Federov would withdraw during the 1996–97 playoffs, he'd see Yzerman and Larionov down the bench with the competitive fire in their eyes, defying him to be his best, allowing him no excuse for quitting, pushing him.

Leadership is a subtle art, for an NHL team is not a democracy. It is a tribe with its chief, its whipping boy, its clown, its shaman. Fans generally have little idea of the real workings of a team; the media are either oblivious or constrained from reporting the details. There have been instances of players taking the wives of teammates (Gary Leeman became involved with Al Iafrate's wife in Toronto; players took sides in the dressing room, and a promising Leaf team was left in tatters), and of teammates becoming involved in business deals that go sour (Geoff Courtnall of St. Louis was on the board of Delgratia, a gold exploration company that went broke in 1998, taking many players' money with it). Isolated by wealth and adulation, driven by fear of failure, players look inward to find acceptance and status from their teammates. That peer acceptance is often the single most important element in a player's attitude to his job. In this, NHL teams are not so far removed from the group of boys shipwrecked on a desert island in *Lord of the Flies*. Like the kids in William Golding's novel, they cannot sustain a democracy of equals for long. They struggle for power and influence within the group; sometimes, a weak or rebellious member is sacrificed to maintain the pecking order.

NHL dressing rooms are inhabited largely by superannuated teenagers and developing personalities, young men who, in the memorable phrase of Dick Beddoes, "reached puberty but forgot to touch second base." Every player wants and needs an identity. On every successful team, someone assumes the role of leader. Though the captain may lead on the ice, it doesn't follow that he will always be the focal point in the dressing room. Someone will be "king," and teammates will buy the same car as he does, buy their clothes at the same store, generally follow his example on everything from stock-market tips to the music played in the dressing room. Only the strong-willed can resist this peer pressure over a long season of travel, practice, and adversity.

Yzerman himself has learned that much of the art of leadership is done quietly, not in fiery rhetoric between periods. "I really think team meetings are overrated," he says, turning down the techno-pop music in the almost deserted dressing room at Joe Louis one day. "I think if you want to make a point to a guy, it's better to do it one on one. Speaking a lot loses its effectiveness. But it is important to have guys in the locker room — and it doesn't have to be the captain — who show some emotion and excitement. The class clown is as important as the guy who comes in and breaks his stick after a bad period. It's good to have that mix of emotion in the locker room."

"There are some things that are common to any sport, whether it's the 1960s, '70s, or '80s: athletes don't want to let each other down," says Dallas coach Ken Hitchcock. "If there is a double standard, and it is okay for a guy to take a couple of nights off, and you still keep playing him, then I think the players on the team get discouraged by that."

Bowman's intuition in controlling and subjugating this dynamic to his own purposes is keen, and Yzerman's example is critical. His sensitive and heartfelt statements on behalf of the team immediately after the limousine accident that almost took Konstantinov's life, and his clever, self-effacing comments about the visit to the White House when the Stanley Cup champions met Bill Clinton, provided eloquent evidence of his role in knitting together a highly diverse group of athletes. ("The police escort from the airport was great," he told David Letterman on "The Late Show." "We all felt like James Bond. Meeting President Clinton was nice, too. I'm Canadian, you know.")

According to Yzerman, Bowman differs from previous coach Jacques Demers in his strategy with a captain. "Every coach is different," he says. "On this team with Scotty, if a young guy isn't playing, it's like, 'You get ready, and you'll play when I tell you to.' You never know for sure. Jacques would let me know a bit more. And explain, so I could pass it on. In the past couple of years, Scotty has called a bunch of us veterans in to talk about a situation. Not really to get our feeling, but to get a message out." For Bowman, Yzerman is a perfect conduit between players and management — level-headed, intelligent, decent, somewhat aloof, wonderfully talented.

Over the years Yzerman has evolved into a quintessential leader in this passionate, ambitious business, but his model is certainly not the only one. The ideal captain can range from the Boy Scout of Syl Apps to the Rowdyman of Doug Harvey. Apps, who led Toronto to three Stanley Cups, was a teetotaling Olympic athlete who never cursed and who interrupted his NHL career to volunteer for service in World War

Two, the paradigm of the clean-living role model. Harvey was a fun-loving, beer-drinking free spirit who also provided fine leadership. Chris Chelios in Chicago fits that description, as did Wayne Cashman in Boston and Mark Messier in Edmonton and New York. All may have been less than saintly off the ice, but they were deadly serious on it.

Yzerman leans more to the Boy Scout prototype, though he may not always get his Clean Language badge. In a game against the Rangers, referee Paul Stewart assessed a penalty against a Red Wing for boarding. Yzerman came to the defense of his teammate, vigorously arguing with the referee. "In my report I wrote that he questioned my ancestry, my sexual preference, and my right to eject him," Stewart told Dick Irvin in the book *Tough Calls*. "So I awarded him the 'whole ball of wax.'" In other words, a minor, a misconduct, and a game misconduct. That outburst was all the more memorable for being the exception. The most penalty minutes Yzerman has ever racked up in a season is 79.

Many of our notions about leadership in sport emanate from the military; Apps's personality profile parallels the romantic notions of what a model officer of the British Imperial Army was supposed to embody at the time of the Great War. Educated, well-rounded, upstanding, and competitive, officers emerged from the British public schools as "gentlemen" — a term often attributed to Yzerman (whose father, unlike the fathers of most hockey stars, is an educated white-collar worker).

The observation that Waterloo was won on the playing fields of Eton resonates to this day. "The French were not beaten by wiser generalship or better tactics or superior patriotism," says the historian John Keegan, "but by the coolness and endurance, the pursuit of excellence and intangible objectives for their own sake which are learnt in game playing." That description rings true for anyone who watched the coolness and perseverance with which Yzerman led the Red Wings to the Stanley Cup.

In our era, the sports figure has inherited the mantle of societal hero from the soldier. Our reverence for the controlled authority figure finds a modern — though less bloody — analogy in the way sports heroes such as Yzerman or Barry Sanders or Michael Jordan are viewed, not just by the public but by teammates and opponents as well. A high standard of performance, steadiness, grace under fire, willingness to sacrifice — such attributes define these players.

"If you watch him closely, he's the same at the start of the game as he is at the end," says Jeff Brown, who grew up playing with Yzerman in the Nepean hockey system. "He plays on an even keel, within himself. Couple that with his leadership abilities and he can do it all." Before becoming a teammate, Fetisov played against Yzerman as a member of the Devils. "It's tough to shut down these kinds of guys," he says. "They never quit. He's not the biggest guy in hockey, but his heart and soul...everybody in this room feels it."

Red Wings athletic therapist John Wharton has admired Yzerman's approach since joining the team in 1991 and recommends Yzerman as a role model for young players. "He has an amazing work ethic," says Wharton. "He never goes more than a week or so without working out, even during the season — bikes, running, sprinting, lifting weights, explosive jumps, the medicine ball… he uses every inch of the gym. He's like a sponge for information on fitness and conditioning, he's got all the best information. And he knows his body so well, he knows what part needs work, which exercises to concentrate on. As stars go, he's very, very low maintenance."

Wharton and Detroit's equipment manager, Paul Boyer, are the first to arrive in the Detroit locker room each day, and the last to leave. They see everything that happens on the team during the course of the season. "I think everybody in the organization looks up to Steve," says Wharton. "Not just what he does on the ice, but morally and ethically too."

That same work ethic has also helped him recover from several injuries, two of them potentially career-ending. Yzerman's first serious injury came in his second NHL season, 1985–86, when he missed Detroit's final 29 games with a broken collar bone. A more serious injury befell him in March 1988, ironically on the night he first reached 50 goals in a season. Minutes after that historic moment, Yzerman crashed into the net against Buffalo; he tore the posterior cruciate ligament in his right knee, one of the major stabilizers in the joint. Rather than have surgery, he opted to rebuild the knee using therapy and his usual near-fanatic exercise regime. His father marveled at how diligently he worked to come back. "Steve built up really big thighs from all the work he did rehabbing his knee," recalls the elder Yzerman. "He'd never want to talk about the injury, just worked like crazy on his own, never complaining." The next season he was back at full strength, amazing the Red Wings medical staff and scoring a career-high 65 goals.

Yzerman's most serious injury occurred in October 1993, and many thought his career was over. Thomas Steen of the Jets caught Yzerman with his head down along the boards and hammered him; Yzerman absorbed the brunt of the blow with his chest. Typically, he stayed down on the ice only a moment, then skated off unaided, despite terrible pain. Steen's check had ruptured both the C5 and C6 cervical discs in Yzerman's back. The herniated discs (located where the neck meets the spine) put pressure on the nerves leading to his right arm and shoulder, leaving him with little power in the area. After missing 26 games, he gamely finished the season and playoffs. But he knew he was in serious trouble; even the slightest bodily contact sent pain shooting into his back.

That summer he and team therapist Wharton flew to all corners of North America for advice on how to treat the injury, searching for a doctor who would give him a favorable diagnosis. One doctor told him to retire; two others urged him to take a year off. But Doctor Robert

Watkins, now at the University of Southern California, said he'd attempt to have Yzerman back within eight months by performing a spinal fusion. Yzerman opted for the surgery.

In a perilous seven-hour procedure in Los Angeles, Watkins cut an incision in Yzerman's throat and, working around the trachea and esophagus, removed the damaged C5 and C6 discs. Then, using an inch and a half of bone taken from Yzerman's pelvis, he fused that bone into Yzerman's spine where the damaged discs had been. While the operation went well, everything depended on how the transplanted bones knitted together. A less than perfect fusion would spell the end of Yzerman's career, perhaps even permanent disability. Yzerman wore a spinal halo screwed into his skull for six weeks while the bones fused. Miraculously, he was back skating after four months, not the expected eight. Wharton believes that the 17-week NHL players' lockout at the start of the next season was a blessing in disguise. Knowing Yzerman's work ethic, says the Wings athletic therapist, he might have tried to play even sooner. Despite the extremely delicate nature of the surgery, Yzerman was back at full strength when the lockout ended, playing his usual shift plus special-teams action, averaging about 26 minutes of ice time a game that season.

These injuries and playing demands might have worn out players even ten years ago, but Yzerman's superb conditioning and Air Detroit stood him in good stead. While other teams fly charter or even commercial flights, the Red Wings travel by their own airplane. This means that they can skate at Joe Louis Arena at eleven in the morning, arrive in, say, Toronto mid-afternoon, play a 7:30 game, and be in their own beds by one the next morning. It's one of the luxuries that owner Mike Ilitch bestows on his team, and Red Wings players feel their success in recent years is no coincidence.

In the old days, a player in New York, for instance, flying out of La Guardia on a commercial flight, added five or six hours to the trip —

plus all the distractions inherent in being among the public. "This is a conversation I had with Luc Robitaille last year," says Pat Flatley, who played in New York. "Some teams are spending $30 million on their payroll but still won't have a plane like the Red Wings do, or a masseur. It's an expense, but relative to what you're paying the team, and in order to keep a $6-million asset on the ice, I think you do it."

"We've had our plane now for about seven years, and our road record has been excellent since we got it," says Yzerman. "Look at Edmonton. They played their first game of the season in San Jose on a Wednesday. Then on Friday, they don't get home until, like, five in the morning before their home opener. It was a long traveling day and they didn't get a chance to skate before they played us. We would have had our choice about when to fly back, and a direct flight." The plane lessens hours traveled, allows for greater comfort, and reduces fatigue, especially late in the season, and especially for players who, like Yzerman, can see the end of their careers.

What is leadership? Consider Yzerman's performance on New Year's Eve 1997 against St. Louis. The Red Wings lead the Blues 4–2 late in the third period and St. Louis coach Joel Quenneville pulls his goalie. The Wings disrupt the Blues' attack and head up ice, Yzerman breaking out with Shanahan and Doug Brown. In the Blues' end, Brown's nifty cross-ice pass finds the tape on Yzerman's stick — the empty net gapes eight feet away — an easy goal. Instead of burying the puck, however, Yzerman slides it to Shanahan, who deposits the goal. Detroit clinches the win, and the C on Yzerman's chest burns a little brighter. It's because of such gestures that, after Yzerman scored career goal number 500, every one of his teammates wanted a photo of himself with the captain.

NAGANO, FEBRUARY 1998. On the list of NHL hockey prototypes, there are the power forwards who make their living at the fringe of the crease, and most of them are here for the Olympics. Yzerman's teammate Brendan Shanahan has earned a place on Canada's team with his power game; John LeClair, the Clydesdale who scores whatever goals Eric Lindros leaves behind in Philadelphia, is here on behalf of the United States; and Jaromir Jagr, whose slippery, skillful, physical presence leads the NHL Penguins, has come to Japan to play for the Czech Republic.

For reasons of size and nastiness, Lindros has become the personification of this power role, even if he also flourishes in the other scoring zones. "There's no one else who's capable of scoring 50 goals and using you as a speed bump, too," said journeyman Shawn Antoski after having his grille work messed up by the Flyers captain. Former NHL goalie John Davidson, now a broadcaster, selected Lindros as one of the five best intimidators in the history of the NHL in his book *Hockey for Dummies*. And former coach Michel Bergeron names Lindros as the one enforcer he'd choose to start an NHL team. Of course, Lindros will also get you 100 points a year, barring injury. Scouts spend decades watching minor hockey without seeing the combination of size, coordination, and meanness packaged in Lindros. He's the prototype modern player.

"Lindros is all power," says Chris Chelios, captain of the U.S. team in Nagano. "With Kariya, you get a stick on him, you can stop him or hook him at least. Lindros, you can't stop him when he's going around you. When you really have to worry with Lindros is when you've got the puck. He has the ability to knock you through the boards and then take the puck and go score. Those other big guys may take you out, but they're not going to do anything with the puck."

Like Lemieux, Lindros has an excellent shot and the puck sense of a smaller man; that allows him to score from outside the perimeter. He doesn't have Lemieux's finesse with the puck, but unlike Lemieux he can intimidate down low, which allows him to collect the "garbage" goals that made Phil Esposito famous. On the edge of the crease, back to the goalie, he is virtually immovable, like Hakeem Olajuwon of the NBA Houston Rockets in the low post. Where Lemieux found it a burden to shrug defensemen off his back, Lindros gives as good as he gets. And behind the net, every defenseman handling the puck imagines him ready to deliver a blow that will send the defenseman reeling.

Like all good scorers, Lindros keeps his hands high on his stick, blade on the ice, ready to redirect a point shot or snap home a rebound. Economy of movement is essential down low; with defensemen on you and a goalie chopping at your ankles, there is little time to take aim, pick a corner, and pose for pictures. Fast hands are everything, and countless hours of snapping shots off the pass have given Lindros the fastest hands of any big man in the NHL. (He has his own opinion of who best shoots off the pass: "Paul Kariya. We played together during the World Championships in 1993, and he was unbelievable.")

Hours of skating — and standing — in heavy traffic have also left Lindros with another legacy he'd rather forget. Because of his linebacker-like hits and willingness to rumble, he's been plagued by injury. Knee and back problems and other maladies have kept him on the sidelines for extended periods and caused hockey people to question his durability. (And that was before March 1998, after the Olympics, when Darius Kasparitis of Pittsburgh caught him with his head down; Lindros suffered a concussion that kept him out for 19 games.)

"His health has been a bit of a problem," says broadcaster Harry Neale. "Otherwise he would be the one player you'd like to have on your team for the next five years." Lindros says that his injury history — plus his brother Brett's premature retirement due to post-concussion syndrome — have made him adapt. "I now do a better job of picking my spots with the physical side of the game," he says. "Just because you're throwing a check doesn't mean that your body isn't absorbing a strong percentage of the aftershock."

Lindros has been named captain of the Canadian team here in Nagano, though he — unlike Gretzky, or Yzerman, or the absent Mark Messier — has not yet shown those qualities of leadership that result in the Stanley Cup. Perhaps these Olympics will be his ticket to greatness. Team Canada GM Bobby Clarke — his boss in Philadelphia — is counting on it with the controversial appointment. Lindros centers a line with Flyers teammate Rod Brind'amour and Shayne Corson of Montreal, and in early wins over Belarus and Sweden, they have shown signs of gelling into a dominant line.

Yzerman, meanwhile, has been playing left wing beside Wayne Gretzky. (Though he's a natural center, Yzerman has occasionally played left wing time under Bowman.) Shanahan has patrolled right wing most of the time, and while Canada is unbeaten so far, there's a feeling that this Dream Line hasn't yet found its stride. The amiable Shanahan in particular is pressing; he has 335 career NHL tallies, but here the goals simply won't go in. His Irish-born mother has sent him a religious medal of the Virgin Mary for good luck that he wears on the lapel of his Team Canada jacket from Roots.

Before the tournament Yzerman had joked of going to the coaches to change linemates if Gretzky didn't pass to him often enough. It's less funny now. Gretzky and Yzerman seem a little apprehensive with each other; on their NHL teams they perform similar roles, generally orchestrating, not finishing, scoring plays. Gretzky — whose goal scoring has dropped precipitously in the past two years — may be passing too much, giving up shots to feed Yzerman and Shanahan. On one rush against Sweden, he passed up an ideal shot to feed Yzerman, who was in too close against Tommy Salo to shift to his forehand.

Gretzky's desire to win Olympic gold — just about the only meaningful prize he hasn't captured in hockey — is palpable, and everyone is rooting for him to push his aging body for this one career-defining moment. "I'm giving him another game," says Yzerman with a wink. Not that Yzerman is having a bad tournament — quite the contrary. He's been typically effective, killing penalties, winning important face-offs. Against the United States in a scoreless game, Canada faces a crucial five-on-three penalty kill for 1:40 in the first period. With the greatest players Canada has produced available to coach Marc Crawford, he taps Yzerman on the shoulder to take the face-off deep in the Canadian end. The Americans throw everything they have against Yzerman, Rob Blake, Ray Bourque, and Patrick Roy. Yzerman slides out to block shots from the point by Chelios and Leetch, sacrificing his body and leading by example. He hurries Brett Hull into shooting wide. The Americans fail to score. That penalty kill turns the game around.

Then, with the score 1 0 Canada in the second period, a vintage Yzerman rush gives Canada an insurance goal. Breaking in off the right wing against 6-foot-4, 225-pound Kevin Hatcher, he employs a favorite move. He starts the puck wide to the outside of Hatcher, then swings it inside to his back hand; Hatcher knows he must shift quickly to his right to prevent the smaller Yzerman from getting around him and having a clear shot on Mike Richter. Yzerman crouches low and pivots around Hatcher's tree-trunk leg. The puck squirts free behind the big defenseman. When Yzerman breaks free, Hatcher has only one option: he pulls Yzerman down. While the two men slide helplessly toward Richter, Yzerman manages to scoop a shot that Richter kicks away. Still sliding, Yzerman topples the American goalie, sending him and Hatcher into the net. Rob Zamuner, following the play alone, buries the gift rebound for a goal engineered by Yzerman.

Referee Bill McCreary hesitates. Yzerman makes a beeline to congratulate Zamuner, as if the goal is beyond dispute. McCreary belatedly signals goal. An incensed Ron Wilson, the U.S. coach, sends his captain Chelios to protest. "McCreary told the teams that he wasn't going to stand for goalie interference only minutes before," says a frustrated Wilson after the game. "What did he call that?" Chelios reminds McCreary of this warning, but is waved away. The goal stands. "My momentum just carried me right into him," Yzerman explains afterward, without a hint of irony.

The win over the United States guarantees Canada a meeting with Kazakhstan, the weakest of the remaining teams, in the quarterfinals. It was a prize worth fighting for. Canada engineers a workmanlike win over the Kazakhs, while the Americans face — and, to their great dismay, fall 4–1 to — Dominik Hasek and the underdog Czechs. So far, so good. Team Canada has kept a low profile since arriving to a tumultuous reception at the Nagano train station, not wanting to create unnecessary distractions. Gretzky, Yzerman, Bourque and Co. are staying at the Athletes Village, five men to a unit — no hotels, no entourages, no haughty dismissal of fellow Olympians who earn the wages of mere mortals. While the American team is reported all over town in the wee small hours, Shanahan and Yzerman have a nightly 11 p.m. date at a dessert bar, where they have ice-cream sundaes before bed.

The understated approach is a tribute to level-headed veterans like Yzerman, Nieuwendyk, and Fleury. Hockey players have always been the pro athletes least affected by fame. The flamboyant basketball star Dennis Rodman stars in a violent action flick; Wayne Gretzky does a guest appearance on "The Young and the Restless." This tradition of normalcy was passed down by Howe and Orr and Hull; now Gretzky and Yzerman pass the common touch on to the Lindros generation. It remains to be seen if the enormous money earned by today's young players will corrupt that decency (Alexei Yashin's donation of $1 million to the National Arts Centre in Ottawa seems a good omen).

Yzerman has emerged from the win over Kazakhstan with a goal, two penalties, and a mean-looking swipe of exposed skin near his left eyebrow — "I was being abused out there," he protests later. The win, combined with the Czechs' shocking upset of the U.S. means that Team Canada has a date with the Czechs in the semifinals. With Patrick Roy playing to perfection so far and the Czechs seemingly dependent on Hasek, it looks as if Canada will prevail. Concern grows, however, with the announcement on the eve of the game that Joe Sakic is out of the tournament with a bad knee. Combined with the earlier loss of Kariya to a concussion, Canada is arguably without its two best offensive threats.

The coaching staff decides to play it cozy against the Czechs, committing only the three forwards to the attack while the defense hangs back, limiting Canada's vulnerability to the counter-attacks that killed the U.S. team. The hope is that the horses — Lindros, Zamuner, Shanahan, Nieuwendyk, Corson — can cause enough commotion in front of Hasek to unnerve him, and that patient, steady pressure on the big ice surface will produce better scoring chances than an all-out attack. The precious few chances the Czechs did generate against the Americans all ended up in the net. Surely they can't be that lucky again — not against Roy.

The Czechs have just 12 NHLers on their team, and only Jagr and Hasek are stars. Few of the others would even make the powerful Canadian squad. But the win over the U.S. team has galvanized them. Quietly, their captain, Vladimir Ruzicka, has united the disparate factions in the Czech dressing room. Some NHL insiders believe that Ruzicka's NHL career was hijacked when Mark Messier, concerned that the Czech's awesome skills might eclipse his role as team leader in Edmonton, ran him out of town. After unproductive stops elsewhere in the NHL, Ruzicka headed back to Europe to play and await the Olympics. This is his chance for vindication.

He and his mates feel destiny's hand on their shoulders. Coming from a nation of just 10 million people, they have nothing to lose as they face unbeaten Canada — which has everything to lose. "We know how lucky we are to have a goalie as special as Dominik," says Jaromir Jagr before the game. "We are such a small country. Who knows when the Czech Republic will have another goalie like him? We have to take advantage of this chance."

An early goal by Canada would be the best antidote for Czech optimism, but Crawford and his assistant coaches, Wayne Cashman and Andy Murray, know that the United States exhausted itself on the big surface by pushing too hard too soon. Tempering its enthusiasm, Canada will opt for a mistake-free start. The death sentence would be to fall one or two goals behind — as the Americans did — then have to play catch-up against the world's greatest goalie.

The Big Hat has been draped in Canadian red and white all week. Gradually the Czech colors — red, white, and blue — have encroached. Today, the Czech fans, with their noisy horns and raucous cheers, are almost even with the Canadians. The Canadian fans, meanwhile, have an uneasy feeling about Hasek that tempers their cheers.

Crawford wants to keep Yzerman with Gretzky, so Trevor Linden, rather than Yzerman, has been selected to center what was Joe Sakic's line. Linden is one of seven centers on the squad, a choice that will be criticized after the tournament. It would be poetic justice if Linden could step up and star; having endured Mike Keenan's dog house in Vancouver, a knee injury, and a trade to the Islanders a week before the Games, he deserves a break.

For the first two periods of the game, it's Patrick Roy who's vindicated. The Canadian goalie has been overshadowed by the ascent of Hasek, but against his nemesis this day he's the one who makes the eloquent statements in the first 40 minutes. Surprisingly, the Czechs have nearly all the good scoring chances in the first part of the game, but Roy is coolly efficient on tricky shots from Jagr, Robert Reichel, and Martin

Rucinsky, keeping the game scoreless.

The Czechs control the pace of the game by slowing down Yzerman, Gretzky, Lindros, and the other Canadian forwards as they come through the neutral zone. They allow Canada's snipers free rein on the margins and absorb big hits from Lindros without noticeable effect. The unheralded Czech defense corps, headed by NHL veterans Petr Svoboda, Richard Smehlik, and Jiri Slegr, talented young Roman Hamrlik, and little-known Jaroslav Spacek, takes advantage of their experience on the big ice surface, steering shooters to bad angles and blocking drives from the point.

After two periods, it's still scoreless. Emotionally, however, the tie is a victory for the Czechs; with their patient, counter-attacking style, they've kept Canada from gaining momentum thus far. With Roy and Hasek appearing invincible, fans are already murmuring about the possibility of a shootout. It's a tantalizing proposition: the two best goalies in the world, head to head, with a trip to the gold-medal game on the line. The underdog Czechs would be content to reduce the game to a duel of penalty shots; for the Canadians, who lost the Olympic gold medal in a shootout with Sweden in 1994, it's a thrill they can live without.

Then halfway through the third period, Jiri Slegr launches a slapshot from the left point. Roy never sees it through a screen; it slips past him on the short side. The Czechs lead 1–0 with barely ten minutes to play. Team Canada is devastated; instead of springing to a whirlwind attack, they listlessly bring the puck up the ice, again and again. For nearly nine minutes, they fail to register even a mediocre chance on Hasek. When Lindros dumps the puck in, the Czech goalie calmly clears it to safety before Corson or Brind'amour can arrive. When Mark Recchi attempts to carry the puck in, it's batted away harmlessly by Svoboda or a backchecking forward. For the first time in the tournament, the larger ice surface seems to puzzle the

Canadians; their defensemen — Chris Pronger, Scott Stevens, Eric Desjardins — always seem to arrive a step too late to keep the puck in the zone. And despite good work on the boards, Yzerman and the other forwards seem unable to work the puck into the hot zones in front of Hasek.

Then, when all seems lost, a miracle. With only 63 seconds left, the puck kicks out in front of Hasek on a rebound. Linden lunges for it. Nearly flat on the ice, he scoops the puck high as he falls; though Hasek has the bottom of the net sealed off, his hands are in no position to stop the high floater. Canada ties the score on its only decent chance in more than ten minutes. There's pandemonium in the stands; along press row, delete buttons erase leads already written.

For the final minute of regulation play and the entire ten-minute overtime, the Canadians storm the Czech end. Where has this inspiration been all game? The Gretzky-Yzerman-Shanahan line menaces Hasek with creative passing, but Hasek keeps them at bay. He robs Linden, Foote, and Nieuwendyk from point-blank range with his lightning feet and hands. The Czechs are simply holding on for a shootout now. For the Canadians, the knowledge that their gold-medal chance could depend on a "skills contest" against Hasek spurs them to even more desperate attacks. The overtime ends with Canada in complete control but the score still tied.

Shootouts rank with torn ligaments and Alan Eagleson on the list of things the NHL can do without. Brought up on the idea that teams play until a goal decides a winner, NHL folk consider the shootout an abomination of the spirit of the game. Hockey is the fusion of many skills, they argue; why should one skill — the art of the breakaway — decide a game? But TV and arena commitments at the Olympics rule out a possibly lengthy overtime. Soccer — which has no love of the format either — has successfully introduced the shootout at the World

Cup and the Olympics. And while the format is a killer for coaches and players and die-hard fans, it appeals to the mass of casual fans who rarely watch hockey between Olympic Games. This shootout, many are saying in the corridors of the Big Hat, would have been unnecessary if Canada had stepped up its play before the final few minutes of the game, committing its defensemen to the attack.

International rules require each team to submit a list of five shooters to go one on one against the goalies. Lindros seems automatic for Canada, but after that? Though Gretzky has never been a breakaway specialist, how can you not give the greatest offensive player in history a chance with so much on the line? And how about skilled veterans like Yzerman? And oh, if only Sakic were here today, the only one of eight players to have beaten Hasek in the breakaway contest at the all-star game in Vancouver a month earlier.

Every one of the splendid players on Canada's bench wants a chance, of course, but no one wants to cost his team the gold either. No matter who is chosen, there will be furious debate if Canada loses. Even so, there is a disbelieving stir when Crawford's list is announced: Theo Fleury, followed by Bourque, Nieuwendyk, Lindros, and Shanahan. No Gretzky, no Yzerman, no Recchi. The Czechs answer with Reichel, Rucinsky, Pavel Patera, Jagr, and Ruzicka. The Czechs win the coin toss and elect to shoot first. The two clubs will alternate until each team has had five shots.

In the Czech goal, Hasek notes that the ice in front of his net is chipped and rutted. The bad ice will make it tough to deke, so he adopts a piece of advice on breakaways given by his one-time coach Vladislav Tretiak. "I'm inclined to think that the experienced goaltender is in a more advantageous position than his opponent," Tretiak wrote. "As soon as the forward crosses the blue line, the goalie comes sharply out of his net, scaring the opponent while at the same time allowing for the protection of a larger portion of the net."

At the Czech bench, Jagr and Reichel have noticed the same thing about the brutal ice. Reichel, first up for the Czechs, vows to shoot on Roy. The rolling rumble of cheers and the insipid music squawking from the scoreboard dim as the Islanders winger picks up the puck at center ice. For a moment, Roy's trademark twitches cease in concentration. Reichel, true to his vow, shoots low to the stick side on Roy, a clean goal. ("I never miss a penalty shot," he'll say after the game. "My strategy is always the same: Go fast and shoot the puck.")

At the other end, Hasek is now primed. Theo Fleury gathers the puck at center; Hasek comes way out to take away the shot, daring the diminutive Calgary center to deke him. As Fleury makes his move, Hasek beats him back to the net and Fleury's shot deflects harmlessly off Hasek's arm.

Next, Roy smothers a backhand by Rucinsky. Then Ray Bourque skates in on Hasek. Bourque knows that the Czech goalie will have the bottom of the net barricaded so he shoots high, but the puck sails over the net. Hasek joyfully dashes to the Czech bench for congratulations.

The next Czech shooter, Pavel Patera, tries the Reichel approach, but Roy catches the shot in his midsection. Then Joe Nieuwendyk allows Hasek to work him off to a bad angle; his weak shot misses the net.

Jaromir Jagr has proven himself the equal of any player in the world in his first real test following Mario Lemieux's retirement. Coming in with his trademark shock of hair flowing behind him, he beats Roy on the stick side, but the puck clangs off the post. It remains 1–0 for the Czechs in the shootout. Canada still can win if they score on their final two chances and Ruzicka misses his shot.

Lindros sees Hasek coming way out to take away the shot. The brawny Canadian captain realizes the only way to score is to beat the goalie back to the net as he retreats. So Lindros tries a speed rush, cutting hard to Hasek's stick side 15 feet from the net. The puck jumps and skips across the rutted ice as Lindros drives to his forehand. Hasek is seemingly beaten, sliding head first on his back toward the post, lunging with his big paddle at the puck. But the ice won't let the puck settle properly, and Lindros's shot hits the outside of the post. Hasek, unsure of what's happened, looks around frantically. When he sees no puck in the net, he scrambles to his feet and again bolts to the Czech bench. The win is within grasp.

Ruzicka misses on the final attempt against Roy. It will all come down to Brendan Shanahan versus Hasek. On the Canadian bench, Gretzky cannot bear to watch. In an agony of tension and disappointment, he walks partway down the runway; he will learn from the crowd's reaction whether Shanahan has scored. His teammates hang their heads or offer silent prayers for one more miracle. The Czech players are now standing, arm in arm, a team united on the precipice of a victory as shocking as the American win over the Soviets at Lake Placid in 1980.

There is a history between the big Detroit sniper and the 32-year-old Czech. In an NHL game Shanahan recently beat Hasek one on one with a move to Hasek's stick side. Despite the uncertainty of the ice, he chooses the same deking strategy again. But he does not approach with the speed of Lindros; this allows Hasek to come out aggressively for the shot yet still back in fast enough to cover the corners. Shanahan is forced off to an impossible angle on Hasek's glove side. His feeble shot is easily blocked by the Czech goalie, who leaps high into the air time after time toward his teammates.

Just like that, it's over. The usually ebullient Shanahan circles the ice, silent and melancholy. Teammates attempt to console him. "I'd like to apologize to the Canadian people for losing," he says later to TV host Don Wittman, trying to blink away tears. His crestfallen face says more about the incalculable burden carried by the Canadian players than any words could. As Chris Chelios said, Canadians feel something is stolen from them when they lose a big hockey game.

Gretzky returns to the Canadian bench and sits for a long time, watching the Czechs celebrate. Slowly he makes his way to center ice to shake hands with the Czech players. "It's devastating," he says after the game. "Words can't describe how bad I feel." Many of his supporters will find words to ask how Crawford could overlook this hockey icon who has always saved his best for the great moments, but Gretzky himself will not publicly second-guess the coaches.

Yzerman, too, stares across the ice for a long while. Later, he will offer no excuses. No, he's not in favor of shootouts, but everyone knew the rules coming in. No, the big ice wasn't a factor. True, we'll never know how we could have done with Kariya and Sakic. And yes, Dominik Hasek is a great goalie.

The next day, a thoroughly dispirited Team Canada loses 3–2 to a Finnish team without Teemu Selanne or its first-string goalie. One Finnish goal by Jari Kurri is scored with Yzerman serving a penalty. The team that seemed destined for Canada's first gold in 46 years leaves Nagano empty-handed. "I know a bronze medal doesn't seem like much today," Yzerman says in the quiet despondency that envelops the team after the Finland game. "We came here for gold. But in a few years, a bronze medal would be something to cherish." There will be more play-offs, Yzerman knows, more NHL games to be won or lost. But he's 33 years old, and he knows there will be no more chances at Olympic gold.

"Now that I'm older," he says later, "I have a more relaxed approach to the game. I do appreciate some of the things that Jagr does, or if someone scores a nice goal. I used to take the game so seriously, but now I can find a lighter side. You play all those games, you can't be super intense all the time. There will be times when you get mad and frustrated. But you've just got to handle it."

IT'S LATE MARCH 1998. The playoff push is on as the NHL's long season winds down. The Red Wings are playing host to Buffalo, and Hasek is still on the roll that led the Czechs to Olympic gold. He's increased his league-leading shutout total to 12 — 10 of them in the previous 42 games. In nine more of those games, he's given up just a single goal, and in 13 others just two goals. His sparkling work has transformed the Sabres, early season patsies, into one of the toughest opponents in the league.

Yzerman, too, has pushed his game to a higher level since the disappointment in Nagano. Canadian teammates such as Lindros, Roy, and Gretzky will never get over the Olympic loss, missing the playoffs or being eliminated in the first round. But Yzerman has used the setback in Japan as a springboard. He has adopted the high-tempo pace at both ends of the rink set by the world's greatest players at the Olympic Games and is sustaining it as he aims for the playoffs. "I'm trying to keep my feet moving and to explode with the puck," he explains. While he will wind up with just 24 goals and 69 points, his lowest NHL totals ever over a full season, 26 of those points will come in the 20 games after returning from Japan. "As you get older, you find it energizing to be finally coming into springtime," he tells the press.

On this warm day in early spring, Yzerman energizes his team. The Red Wings know they have a playoff spot clinched, and that they cannot overtake Dallas for the top spot in the West. It's an invitation to coast, but Yzerman plays with his typical ferocity. On a two-man advantage in the third period, he rips a shot through Hasek's trapper, giving the Red Wings a 2–1 lead. The goal is the 1,400th point of his career and makes him just the 13th player in the NHL's history to hit that plateau. Next, he triggers the play to spring Kris Draper for Detroit's third goal. Finally, killing a penalty, he breaks in two on one against the Dominator. Hasek guesses that Yzerman will pass. Bad guess. Yzerman blasts a shot high on the short side, for his 561st goal of his career, surpassing Guy Lafleur for 12th overall in NHL scoring. Hasek can only shake his head. A power-play goal, a short-handed goal, a couple of records, and a win over the world's best goalie. Not a bad night's work — and a little payback for the Olympics, too. Many players collect bonus money for achieving individual accomplishments, but Yzerman insists on having no personal bonuses in his contract. All his incentives are based on team goals. So even as he savors passing Lafleur on the scoring list this night, he knows that fulfillment will only come later, if he can help win a second consecutive Stanley Cup for the Red Wings.

IT'S THE MIDDLE OF JUNE. Yzerman skates cautiously across the steaming ice of the MCI Center in Washington, D.C., gently gripping the precious cargo in his hands. The fierce mask of concentration, the grinding labor of this endless season have given way to a delighted, gaptoothed grin. A baseball cap has replaced the helmet atop his head, but sweat still beads on his forehead and drips from his growth of playoff beard. As Yzerman glides through the fog at center ice, few of the shirt-sleeved Washington fans can appreciate the emotions stirring in the heart of the Red Wings' captain as he approaches his destination.

Yzerman has received the Stanley Cup from NHL commissioner Gary Bettman before — a year and six days earlier to be precise. But so much has happened since then that the two Cup triumphs might be separated by a decade, not a single year: the bitter disappointment of the Nagano Olympics; the birth of Yzerman's second daughter, Maria, in March; the furor of the Federov holdout; and the return of the man in the wheelchair at center ice.

Anyone who remembers the unrelenting Vladimir Konstantinov of June 1997 is shocked by the figure clad in a Red Wings jacket now sitting in the wheelchair, an unlit victory cigar clutched in his left hand. The effects of the limousine crash are devastating: Konstantinov's face is a mask, his hands claw uncertainly, he cannot speak the words to express his feelings. He gamely holds up two fingers to signify the Red Wings' second straight title. Standing next to him is his friend and mentor, Slava Fetisov. The burly defenseman was in the same crash, yet the 40-year-old Fetisov recovered to skate with the Wings for another season. Konstantinov's career is over; it is now a question of what motor skills he will regain in therapy.

Bettman's performance on the public address system was no tonic for Konstantinov — standing only a few feet away from the wheelchair, Bettman completely ignored the injured Russian, larding congratulations on the owners of the Red Wings and Capitals instead. But Yzerman now administers his own brand of medicine to Konstantinov. Instead of taking the captain's traditional lap around the ice with the Cup, Yzerman delivers it into the hands of his damaged friend. He kneels, speaks softly in his friend's ear, and the two men smile. The suggestion of honoring Konstantinov was Shanahan's, Yzerman explains afterward, a last-second burst of inspiration, but it is consistent with the captain's credo of sharing the spotlight. Chris Osgood, the young goalie who conquered the critics as well as the Capitals, is the second to receive the Cup from Yzerman. "That means the most to me in this entire experience," says Osgood, wiping champagne from his eyes. "Stevie's leadership is why we're here." Explains Joey Kocur, watching from a few feet away, "Steve's the heart and soul of this team."

While Federov and Shanahan had moments of brilliance in the playoffs, the team captain established a punishing standard of intensity in the first round and never relinquished it. Between games in Phoenix, for instance, no one would have criticized the weary Yzerman for sitting by the hotel pool, enjoying the warmth of the Arizona sun. The Coyotes were making him pay a price for every inch of ice he gained. Instead, Yzerman churned away for an hour on an exercise bicycle in the workout room across the lobby on his off-day. He led the Red

Wings through four grueling series against checkers who were sent out for the sole purpose of making him a non-factor. When the annoying Dale Hunter of Washington sought to rattle Yzerman by rubbing his gloves in the captain's face — the proverbial "face wash" — he deflected the rough treatment with a joke. "You just hope they're new gloves," he said with a smile. "Old ones really stink."

Despite nursing sore ribs the entire way (Bowman convinced the world Yzerman's injury was a sore groin), Yzerman reeled off points in seven straight games, every one of them restoring momentum in favor of the Red Wings. In the clinching game against Phoenix in round one, Yzerman notched four points. He matched that figure in the game that eliminated St. Louis in the next round. Against Dallas in round three, he scored at least a point in every one of the games. Then, in the final series against the surprising Capitals, he personally led the Wings back from a 3–1 deficit in game two, scoring a key goal in a 5–4 overtime win that killed the Capitals for good.

In all, he collected 24 points to win the playoff scoring title. But it was not Federov-like dashes or Peter Bondra bullets that won Yzerman the Conn Smythe Trophy as the playoff MVP. As always, it was the subtleties of his craft: in the first three games of the final — when Washington still had hopes of an upset — he won 45 of his 68 face-offs, a staggering 66 percent, against respected opponents such as Adam Oates, Hunter, and Esa Tikkanen. (Over all, he won 61 percent of his face-offs in the playoffs.) His dogged work in both ends, his direction of the power play, and his willingness to take abuse from opponents steadied the young goalie Osgood when it seemed he might crack under the pressure. On a team that also boasts Federov, Larionov, and Kris Draper as centermen, you have to produce at both ends of the rink to win ice time from Scotty Bowman. Yzerman earned every second of the 23 minutes he logged per game.

As he contemplates the Stanley Cup and the Conn Smythe Trophy, Yzerman allows himself a small moment of vindication. Before the playoffs, he put in an offer to purchase Conn Smythe's old summer home in Ontario's cottage country. Now, he's holding the trophy named for the Maple Leafs founder. Who'd have guessed? He tells the press it's an honor to see "Yzerman" engraved next to the greats of the game. After all, he says, "when I came into the league nobody could spell it or even pronounce it." In his voice, you can hear the quiet, iron resolve of a 16-year-old boy who vows that one day everyone in hockey will know his name. Now, at last, they do.

Chris Chelios
DEFENSE EXPERT

Cowboy: *"You don't look like no meaner-than-hell cold-blooded*
damn killer."
Clint Eastwood: *"Maybe I ain't."*

UNFORGIVEN, 1989

IT'S LATE JULY, and the dank, humid air is punctuated by stinging brine. The setting is an arena, the scene the same wherever guys rent ice to play a little pick-up hockey with their pals — here a Blues sweater, there some Mighty Ducks pants, a pair of Sharks socks in the corner. Players flash up and down the ice, executing fancy passes and rink-length dashes, taking advantage of the no-contact rules. Goalies sprawl and lunge for the puck, making improbable saves one moment, then letting easy shots trickle through their pads. It's a game in which everyone can look good. Not that anyone is paying attention to the sweaty heroics. In the gray bank of stands, wives, girlfriends, and children cast an indifferent eye upon the ice, preferring instead to chat with neighbors or play tag under the seats. This scene of banal bliss — at the Ice-O-Plex in Van Nuys, California — plays out every night in arenas all over North America.

Still, a passer-by can't help but remark on the high caliber of play in this beer league. Gee, that tall guy certainly can handle the puck...

83

and who's that fellow with the blue and gold gloves? Sure can move. Reminds me a bit of Joe Murphy. And that defenseman who looks a little like Kevin Costner — the one who skates so upright? — he's a dead ringer for Chris Chelios of the Blackhawks. Wait a minute, it is Chris Chelios! And Joe Murphy. And Chris Simon and Rick Tocchet and Mathieu Schneider and Bob Probert and Alexander Mogilny. Here in southern California, in mid-summer, some of the NHL's biggest stars are playing shinny.

For Chelios — who's spending the off-season at his beach-front home in nearby Malibu — these evening scrimmages serve a dual purpose. On the one hand, they're a throwback to his youth in Chicago, when he played for fun, for the sheer enjoyment of wheeling freely and showing off in front of pals. But there's a serious purpose, too. Chelios is rehabbing the strained knee ligament that plagued him much of the previous season, building strength for the upcoming campaign. While his wife, Tracee, and their four kids catch up with friends in the stands, the veteran defenseman, flashing up and down the steamy ice surface, is doing more than staying in shape. He's battling the invisible clock that's counting down his remarkable career.

The previous season, 1996–97, was both exhilarating and exhausting for Chelios. First, in September, he and Team USA surprised the world — maybe even themselves — by winning the inaugural World Cup (the name was changed from the Canada Cup after founder Alan Eagleson was charged with embezzling funds from the tournament). At first, Chelios had been reluctant to participate. He was still beaten up from the previous season, aching and tired. But fellow Americans pleaded with him to relent. Then, he says, U.S. general manager Lou Lamoriello sweetened the pot by promising him the captaincy. It was too much for a gamer like Chelios; the United States got its man, although Chelios didn't get the captaincy. That went to Brian Leetch.

After two weeks of play in Europe and North America, the tournament came down to Chelios and his American mates versus Gretzky and the Canadians. The Americans lost the first game of the best-of-three final series 4–3 in Philadelphia, but then, led by the spectacular goaltending of Mike Richter, they rallied to stun Canada in the final two games in Montreal. Chelios and the rest of a punishing U.S. defense corps wore down Gretzky and the giants of Canadian hockey. In the final game in Montreal, the Americans blew open a close game in the third period to win 5–2.

"I've been in three or four of these tournaments, and we're used to watching the other guy skating around with the Cup," says Chelios, sitting on the bench at the Ice-O-Plex, waiting for the action to resume. "It was almost as if we couldn't believe we beat them until the last minutes of game three. To come back and win two in a row in Montreal, I wouldn't trade it for anything. At least I could say I'd finally won one."

The World Cup, however, was to prove the high-water mark of Chelios's year. In the regular season, the Blackhawks finished a disappointing fifth in the Central Division, a game below .500. For a team used to competing with Detroit and St. Louis for the top spot, it was a bitter pill. The Hawks were then eliminated in the first round of the playoffs by the defending Stanley Cup champs from Colorado. Though Chelios managed to play 72 games and finish third in team scoring, he was nagged by the knee he perhaps should have been rehabilitating when he played in the World Cup. One acquaintance suggested that the knee would have sidelined 95 percent of players, but Chelios abhors cheap excuses and, reflecting in dismay on the season just past, carefully avoids using the injury as an alibi. "People work hard, nine to five. I skate and play a game I love," he says. "There's a million people who would die to be in that position. People pay to see the game, they want to see you working. That's the way I approach it."

In his Malibu living room the next day, gazing out the picture window at dolphins playing in the Pacific, Chelios looks toward the 1997–98 season and doesn't much like what he sees. "I'm stuck in the dinosaur age," he says. "Bob Goodenow [Eagleson's successor as National Hockey League Players' Association executive director] would kill me for saying it, but I still think this free agency stuff didn't help us at all. Look at Hartsie [Blackhawks coach Craig Hartsburg], he went from being a contender to losing Jeremy Roenick, Ed Belfour, Joe Murphy, and Bernie Nicholls in one year. To a certain extent I'm happy for the guys, but it killed us."

Chelios is still disappointed at the way Roenick — the offensive catalyst of the Hawks — left the team just before the 1996–97 season. A year earlier, in an uncharacteristic fit of generosity, Hawks owner Bill Wirtz had promised Roenick a lifetime contract. Roenick made clear that he was looking for the new contract at once — not at the conclusion of his current deal — and that he wanted it to reflect the NHL trend, not the miserly Chicago pay scale. He announced that he would not risk injury by playing for Team USA at the World Cup, or come back to Chicago, unless he got a new deal. Chicago management played hard ball with their temperamental center, holding him to his existing contract. After sitting out ten regular-season games, he was traded to the Coyotes for three players, including the enigmatic Alexei Zhamnov, who was himself holding out in Phoenix. In short, Chicago sent its problem to the Coyotes in exchange for one of theirs. The Hawks' offense suffered as a result.

"He made a big mistake when he got injured and then wouldn't come back," says Chelios. "He lost a lot of respect from the players for what he did. Was that his agent, was it him? Who knows what he was doing? He was negotiating, I guess. See, I just can't understand the new wave of players. I'm from the dinosaur age."

A loyal employee and ardent Chicagoan, Chelios wants to believe in the Blackhawks' program, but it's hard to ignore facts. Under Wirtz and general manager Bob Pulford, Chicago has been one of the NHL's most conservative teams, a vestige of the cozy days when Wirtz, as NHL chairman of the board, and Eagleson, as executive director of the NHLPA, kept salaries down and players in line. The Blackhawks have been reluctant to accept the dramatic change in hockey economics over the past five years. In the face of escalating contracts around the league, they have refused to concede mega-salaries or to re-negotiate contracts, waiting instead for the market to come back to their level. It never will. For Chicago fans, it's an eerie throwback to 1972, when Wirtz lost Blackhawks legend Bobby Hull to Winnipeg. Wirtz ignored the competing offer to Hull from the World Hockey Association, refusing to see the Jets' million-dollar salary offer as a serious threat. It was serious, of course, and in some respects the franchise has never recovered. Now it was Chelios's turn to watch as Wirtz's stubbornness gutted another talented team of its offensive stars and its fine goalie, Belfour. As the Hawks entered the 1997–98 season, Chelios and Cam Russell were the only vestiges of the team that went to the Stanley Cup final under Mike Keenan in 1992.

This day, however, tanned and fit in shorts and T-shirt, with the Pacific surf pounding below, Chelios has more immediate worries than his team's prospects for the coming season. While his children play noisily one floor below, he talks about what El Niño might do to the concrete pilings that hold up his home. "We've lost a lot of beach already this summer and they say it's going to get worse this winter. They tell us you shouldn't have problems if you got the kind of pilings we do." He gazes out to sea, sipping on soda water, comfortably relaxed in his aerie high above the beach. Chelios turns back from the picture window and points to the mud-brown hills on the opposite side of the house, the ones burned tinder dry by the summer sun. "It's the mud slides off the hills you have to watch out for. Luckily, we're not at the base of any hills."

In this privileged corner of southern California, Tracee Chelios has created a perfect beach house with a bright open kitchen, tastefully appointed furniture, and polished wood throughout the living room. The homes of movie stars and executives dot the surrounding hills. Down the beach an episode of "Baywatch" is being filmed. It seems an unlikely spot for Christos K. Chelios. The son of Greek immigrants and a lifelong hockey fanatic, he grew up watching Bobby Hull and Stan Mikita with his dad, Gus, and his brother, Steve, at the old Chicago Stadium on Madison Street, learning to play the game hard and mean and well. There is no phony tan on this working-class kid from Chicago, no perfect coiffure, no retinue of press agents; all he shares with the Tinsel Town crowd is a generous income from his work.

Ah yes, his work. Because of the way Chelios goes about his work, he's not unanimously liked. But even his detractors concede that he's a master of his craft, a defense expert. Craig Hartsburg, his coach until the summer of 1998 and a good NHL defenseman himself, calls Chelios "simply the best defenseman I've ever seen." Former NHLer Mark Napier, who now coaches junior hockey, says, "He has the kind of puck movement you're born with. You just can't teach how he sees the ice." Former teammate Larry Robinson, now coach of the Kings, points out, "He has a great feel for the game. This is a game of passion. He seems not to have forgotten that." Chelios's agent, Tom Reich, says Chelios embodies everything you want in a team player and an athlete. "He'd throw his body on a grenade for the team," says Reich. "The concept of him playing anywhere else but in his home town of Chicago is impossible for him to contemplate." "He has an old-time mentality," adds former NHL goalie Darren Pang, who now works for ESPN. "It doesn't matter how big or how small the guy is, how tough or how weak the man is with him in the corner; Chris is going to come out with the puck."

Nowhere is this gung-ho mentality more in evidence than when he's killing penalties. Chelios's opportunistic penalty killing allows his team to play an attacking style on the penalty kill. While teams such as Dallas dare opponents to shoot into the forest of legs and sticks they amass in their own zone, Chelios and the Hawks have at times used a system that challenges shooters before they're ready, hoping to force turnovers and create uneven-strength scoring chances. Chelios's surprising mobility, his ability to spring out from a tight defensive cluster to challenge a shooter or scoop up a loose puck without exposing the front of the net, is the key to such a system. Try it with a less mobile defenseman and the result may be disastrous.

Pat Flatley, who played with Chelios at the University of Wisconsin and against him in the NHL, believes he's one of the best ever at killing penalties on defense. "It's funny he doesn't get enough credit for that. He's incredible. He cuts the passing angles off really well in the defensive zone. He anticipates and he's nasty, chopping and hacking. Nobody does it better."

Opponents have described Chelios in less glowing terms. "He's a lousy person," says former Philadelphia star Brian Propp. "He never goes after tough guys. He just goes after guys who don't fight." Pat Burns, now coach of the Bruins, calls Chelios "a junkyard dog who makes a million dollars." (Actually, four million.) Such remarks only motivate Chelios. Like the loner cowboy William Munny whom Clint Eastwood portrays in the movie *Unforgiven*, an unrepentant Chelios dispenses his own brand of justice on hockey's wild frontier, visiting retribution on those who offend the natural law of the NHL.

At times, his adherence to this code has obscured his great talent. There was, for example, the Propp episode in the playoffs of 1989, when

Chelios, playing for the Canadiens, used his elbow to drive Propp's head into the plexiglas at the Forum. An unconscious Propp dropped like a rag doll to the ice. To emphasize the impact, "Hockey Night in Canada" showed the hit repeatedly from various angles. The following game, Chelios was jumped by Flyers goalie Ron Hextall, who tried to pummel him. The press applauded Hextall.

"People don't know the whole story," Chelios says. "My first year, Propp broke two of my fingers. I didn't say anything, and he didn't know he did it. It's the same old thing, what goes around, comes around. I don't want to hurt anybody, but when I hit them, I want them to know they've been hit." When there was talk that Anaheim would retaliate against his teammate Gary Suter for the hit that sidelined Ducks star Paul Kariya for much of the 1997–98 season, Chelios was blunt. "Then we'll go after [Teemu] Selanne," shrugged the Chicago captain, referring to Anaheim's other star.

There have been other incidents: a four-game suspension for scratching an opponent's eyes in 1993–94, another four games that season for resisting a linesman. In March 1998 he was suspended for yapping at referees. During his 14 NHL seasons he has accumulated almost 2,200 penalty minutes, and it's no surprise to hear this self-described "sore loser" cite the Bears ferocious linebacker Dick Butkus as a boyhood inspiration. "If I could score goals like Yzerman and Federov," Chelios says, "I wouldn't have to go after them. But I have to play against them all the time, and so I get in their face. Intimidation works. Unfortunately, that's my role and that's why I do it."

Intimidation does work in hockey, and nobody does it better than Chelios. While some bemoan hockey's in-your-face tradition, inescapable truths doom any player who fails to stand up to harassment. The zoologist Heini Heidiger noticed that animals in conflict had differing reactions depending on their distance from the enemy. Within a certain distance, they would attack; outside that distance, they'd retreat. Heidiger called his theory "critical reaction." A lion tamer, he pointed out, maneuvers his fierce subjects by staying on the margin of the lion's flight-or-attack threshold.

Much the same applies in warfare, where a display of force or noise is often employed at a safe distance to intimidate an opponent. (The pre-game Maori war chant of the New Zealand All Blacks Rugby team harkens back to that tradition.) Only when the ritualized display failed would the attackers violate the "critical" space that precipitated violence. In hockey, with its confined space and its tall glass enclosing play, the path of flight is cut off. Voluntarily or not, the challenged player is thrust into his "attack" space, face to face with players like Chelios in a battle for ice. Should the player try to run, he will not last long in the NHL.

There is a corollary to Heidiger's work that may explain why some players are more aggressive than others. Studies of abnormally violent men show that they consistently misjudge the distance between themselves and their adversary, thereby creating a greater probability of violence. In hockey's ritual show of machismo, with its taunting and shoving, there is plenty to misconstrue. It's here, on the edge of hockey's "critical distance," that Chelios does his best work.

Chelios knows it's virtually impossible to stop great players consistently without intimidation, without bending the rules to discourage them from skating to the hot zones in front of the net. It's widely believed that many skill players — particularly Europeans — can be intimidated if the referees allow it. "Alex Mogilny would get right in my face, but he couldn't stand playing against me," says Chelios. "He hated it. He couldn't stand coming into Montreal. They're not used to that type of player over there. Even skill players here, they're not used to it."

Chelios is all the more effective now that he's mellowed since the days when he amassed 931 penalty minutes in four seasons (between

1990 and 1994). "When he was younger, he was easy to get off his game," recalls Mark Napier. "I remember one game in Buffalo when I played for the Sabres, I goaded him into two penalties just by giving him a little bump behind the net. On one, he elbowed me in the neck. On the other, he whacked me with his stick."

Chelios picks his spots more carefully now. And he's less likely to abuse officials. "I leave the refs alone now," he says. "I think after this many years, I've developed some respect for them, and I think they have for me. I think I get more breaks than I used to. Six or seven years ago, it was automatic that if you were out of a game, you'd go after someone. I just figured if you don't do anything else during a game, then get even. You don't want to cheat the fans, you have to make it look like you're doing something out there. And that's where I picked up most of my penalty minutes."

Not that Chelios plays favorites. If you're wearing an opposition uniform, you're fair game. Flatley remembers his first encounter with Chelios in the NHL, when they'd both left the Badgers and had made the big time on different teams. "I was skating behind the net, and he stuck me in the back of the leg and chopped my ankles off," laughs Flatley. "That's Chelly just letting me know he's there." Conversely, if you're wearing a Hawks uniform, he'll go to the wall for you, the ultimate team player.

Critics who dwell on the nasty side of Chelios sometimes fail to appreciate the rest of the abundant package he brings to the ice. In 1995–96, at 34 — an age when many of his peers are already gone from the game — he became the first defenseman to lead the Blackhawks in scoring when he notched 72 points. Through the 1997–98 season he's scored 156 regular-season career goals and added 606 assists in 1,001 games. His low, accurate point shot — one of the best in the league — and uncanny anticipation have helped bolster the offensive stats of teammates from Stephane Richer, Mats Naslund, and Bobby Smith to Jeremy Roenick, Steve Larmer, and Tony Amonte. These gifts may not be the first thing people recall after he retires, but they're what will ultimately propel him into the Hockey Hall of Fame.

"CLOSE UP THE CENTER, MAKE THE GUY PASS. Be ready to get back as soon as the pass is made, but if you can make him pass to the wings maybe it'll be a bad pass, maybe our backcheckers will get it, maybe it'll put somebody offside — and even if none of those happens, it's better to have a winger with the puck, coming in from a bad angle, than having a guy coming right down the center." That description of how to play defense, from the book *Boy on Defence*, is as accurate a job description today as it was when Scott Young wrote it in the early 1950s. Deny the center of the ice, feed the puck to the boards and the corner, then wait — and hope — till the backcheckers arrive.

"It takes a little brains," Chelios says of the position. "Not like forward, where you can get away with scoring and don't have to play defense or too tough in your own zone. With defense, you have to be thinking." Former NHL defenseman Harold Snepsts summed up his view of the position when asked why he didn't wear a helmet: "Don't worry, Doc," he replied, "if anything happened I could always come back as a forward."

Chelios himself started out as a forward; it wasn't until he played junior in Moose Jaw that he dropped back to defense. After a year in Saskatchewan — "I just went crazy, running everywhere" — he accepted a scholarship from "Badger" Bob Johnson, the renowned coach and teacher at the University of Wisconsin. "I learned everything [about playing defense] in college," he says. His fine play attracted the scouts' attention, and he was selected by the Canadiens, 40TH overall in 1981. He remained in college and was part of the Wisconsin team that won the 1983 NCAA hockey title. Next came a trip to the 1984 Olympics at Sarajevo with a Team USA that hoped to repeat the 1980 "Miracle on Ice" at Lake Placid. The young Americans fell short this time, ending up seventh.

Only then, after Sarajevo, did Chelios finally report to Montreal. "Playing for the Canadiens is like getting a Harvard law degree," he says. "Montreal players know what it's like to win." He was not an overnight sensation. Playing with savvy veterans Larry Robinson, Rick Green, and Craig Ludwig, he needed five seasons to master the yin and yang of the blue line. Ken Linseman, a former opponent, recalls that Chelios was "very green in his rookie year, and a lot of people took runs at him. Then the veterans like Robinson and Green toughened him up, showed him what to do." Pretty soon, the college boy was the one handing out lessons in hockey intimidation. "He definitely had the talent," remembers Robinson. "The only question was whether he would last. He played the game as if there was no tomorrow."

In particular, Chelios had to learn to channel his aggressive play and his high-pressure, "pinching" style, his knack of forcing the action. Too many gambles at the blue line trying to keep the puck in the offensive zone left him caught up the ice. And too much time in the penalty box detracted from his on-ice play. Only after his fifth year — at the age of 27 — did he finally win league-wide recognition: the Norris Trophy as the NHL's best defenseman and a place on the first all-star team. In all, he's won the Norris three times and been runner-up once in the past nine years. He's been a first team all-star four times and a second team all-star twice. He ranks with Raymond Bourque (who has won the Norris five times) as the top defenseman of the 1990s, and he's arguably the best American ever to play the game. "Who's better?" asks Hartsburg. "He's a great player and a superstar."

What has enabled him to excel? How does Chelios go about the game? Simple, he says, is always best. "When you mature as a defense-

man you find out that it's simpler if you keep the game simple. Bob
Gainey taught me in Montreal about not taking reckless chances.
Gainey would make the simple pass and get the puck out of the zone.
We'd be up 6–2, and I'd be trying to go end to end to get the big goal.
But there was no need for it. Or else I'd get the puck, get across the blue
line, then make the pass. Now I move the puck as soon as I get it, then
join in the rush a little later. Same as when the other team just dumps
the puck in and goes for a change, then you have time to look around.
It comes with maturity."

Defense is generally considered the toughest skating position to
master. Forwards sometimes develop into elite players in their second
or third year in the NHL on native skill alone, but defensemen who
achieve the delicate balance between defend and attack without spending at least five years in the league, as Chelios did before blossoming,
are virtually unheard of. Gifted offensive players like Brian Leetch and
Nicklas Lidstrom struggle for years to find a defensive game to complement their scoring skills; likewise, defensive stalwarts such as Adam
Foote and Scott Stevens must master the offensive push of the puck to
complete their package of skills. Some players — Phil Housley, Al
Iafrate — never quite round out their games and remain one-dimen-
sional. There are no short cuts to a complete game on defense.

"It's not so much what to do, as when to do it," explains former
NHL defenseman Dave Farrish, who now coaches Springfield, the
Coyotes' AHL farm team. "I try to teach our players to have the confidence to stand up to the forwards at the blue line. To be aggressive and
force the play if they can — the way Chelios does. But the instinct for
the right moment to make your move can only come from experience."

The NHL is full of serviceable defensemen who took a decade or
more to learn the tricks of the trade. Bob Boughner, Luke Richardson,
Todd Gill, Jeff Beukeboom, Joe Reekie, Drake Berehowsky — all strug-

gled before finally developing into reliable starters. And because there's no substitute for experience, veteran defensemen often hang on longer than forwards do. Chelios, Kevin Lowe, Larry Murphy, Jamie Macoun, Craig Muni, Kjell Samuelsson, and Marty McSorley were among the many defenseman 35 and older who took a regular shift in 1997–98.

Not that the subtle skills of defense are widely acknowledged. On the ice, of course, defensemen represent one-third of the players at any time, but in the Hockey Hall of Fame just 47 defensemen can be found among the 210 players inducted, 22 percent of the total. Most of them had gaudy scoring numbers, too. To win the Norris Trophy, you'd better score if you want respect: In the past 15 years, only Rod Langway has carried off the award by emphasizing great efficiency in his own zone. The rest are the glory boys of the blue line, Leetch and Coffey and Chelios and Bourque, defensemen who put up 65 or 70 points a year.

The indignity continues at the pay window, with scorers getting the best salaries. In 1997–98, center Sergei Federov made a staggering $26 million, including bonus; Joe Sakic made $17 million, with his bonus; unheralded Chris Gratton made $10 million including bonus; Lindros made $7.5 million, Gretzky $6.5, Pavel Bure $5.5 million, and Yzerman $5.08 million. Among goaltenders, Dominik Hasek made $7 million, followed by Patrick Roy ($4.4 million), Martin Brodeur ($4 million), and Mike Richter ($3.9 million). The best-paid defensemen in 1997–98 were Chelios and Scott Stevens, at $4 million.

In part, people blame Bourque for depressing defensemen's salaries. Even when he was the top defenseman in the league, Bourque was paid like a journeyman by Harry Sinden in Boston. When Bourque took the Bruins to arbitration, asking $5 million a year, Sinden said simply, "No defenseman gets that kind of money." The arbitrator agreed. Bourque's 1997–98 salary of $3.25 million was below market for a player of his caliber.

Chelios, too, has been underpaid, for reasons that have their roots in his years with the Canadiens. His tenure with Montreal — which started so promisingly — ended bitterly. Though he was named Montreal co-captain with Guy Carbonneau and won a Stanley Cup ring, he was vilified for off-ice incidents that included urinating in public. "It's just unfortunate Mr. Corey [Canadiens' president Ronald Corey] had it in for me," he says now. "The thing I don't understand is that they talk about me being undisciplined. Hey, I never got suspended for missing a curfew. I never got a drunk-driving charge. Carbo [Guy Carbonneau], he got drunk driving, he got suspended for missing curfew. And I got traded."

Chelios had a reputation for playing hard on and off the ice, but believes the reputation was blown out of proportion. "If I was in a bar and had a beer, the next day it was reported as 20 beers. Or I'd be reported in two or three different bars after a loss when I was home instead. I think in Montreal, it wasn't being American, it was being English. I took a beating before I ever got to the team. It just got too personal. You don't want to go through that. I'm not a bad person, I know that. But the media perceives you the way they want to. I could handle it because I loved playing there, but I've got kids. . ."

The trade from Montreal to Chicago — he was swapped for an aging Denis Savard in 1990 in one of the most lopsided trades ever — also led to an acrimonious split with his agent, Don Meehan, a dispute that ended in legal wrangling. Chelios remains bitter about Meehan, a close friend and business associate of Serge Savard, the Canadiens' GM who traded Chelios. In his lawsuit, Chelios alleged that Meehan — one of the most powerful agents in hockey — had bungled his contract with the Habs, costing him money in deferred payments, and had forced him into quickly signing a new, below-market deal with Chicago to recoup those losses. In his statement of defense, Meehan denied these allegations. The suit was settled out of court.

Chelios will not discuss the split — "It's in the past" — but he was one of many Meehan clients who had their money invested in high-risk mortgages and joint-venture holdings in Toronto real estate, most without prospectus or proper reporting. Meehan and his business partner, Jerry Ublansky, took shares in many of the same investments; transferred titles on properties without proper authorization from players; neglected to report on failed mortgage deals for months, sometimes years; and invested players' money in second, third, and fourth mortgages they themselves were organizing, while failing to offer safer investment vehicles. Many of the high-risk mortgages collapsed along with the Toronto real estate market in the early 1990s. It took a warning from the Law Society of Upper Canada in 1991 to force reporting of the failures to investors. Ublansky has already received a nine-month suspension from the Law Society of Upper Canada for his role in these and other investments involving hockey players.

In one typical joint venture, Meehan placed $1.937 million from players (Chelios put up $25,000), their families, NHL management figures, and other investors — more than 80 in all — into an industrial building in downtown Toronto, just as the market crashed. There was no prospectus; no partnership agreement; no notice that the partners were assuming a $725,000 mortgage on the property; no hint that monies were being taken out of the joint venture and invested in other unreported mortgages; no explanation of why Meehan's company, Newport Sports, had obtained 9.5 shares of the venture with no capital outlay; and no explanation of where the shares disappeared two years later when they stopped appearing in financial records.

If the joint venture raised $1.937 million but the assumed mortgage knocked $725,000 off the price, where did that $725,000 go? And what about the $285,000 discrepancy between the real purchase price of

$1.937 million and the reported price to investors of $2.275 million? When CBC TV began an investigation of Meehan's financial doings in 1994, the Mississauga-based agent hurriedly sent out letters offering investors their principal back — in effect, returning their money having borrowed it interest-free for up to seven years. Many investors, embarrassed at having lost money, quietly accepted the offer and moved on. Meehan's latest scheme is putting clients' money into racehorses in which he has an interest.

Meehan — like Alan Eagleson — also made a handsome living representing players and NHL management figures at the same time. (For a time, he represented referees as well.) Concerned about Meehan's friendships with NHL management types, one well-known player who left Meehan still refuses to talk about the reasons he dismissed the agent. When the NHLPA finally brought in rules forbidding an agent from representing both players and management at the same time, Meehan simply handed off his management clients (such as Brian Sutter and Jacques Demers) to Toronto lawyer Harry Radomski, a longtime and close business associate, who has represented Meehan in legal matters.

Information about Meehan's activities was made public in 1994, but the cozy hockey establishment continues to embrace one of its own rather than investigate the validity of the allegations. Though the Law Society of Upper Canada is believed to have been investigating Meehan since 1994, there is no estimate of when — or even if — it will report.

After his nasty split with Meehan, and the turmoil of leaving Montreal, Chelios thrived in his home town. As a kid who had learned to play the game in Evergreen Park and at Mt. Carmel High School, the 16-year-old Chelios had been broken-hearted when his family moved from Chicago to San Diego to pursue a restaurant business opportunity. But he never lost touch with his roots on the circular journey from Chicago to southern California to Moose Jaw to Madison, Wisconsin (where he met his wife), and then to the U.S. Olympic team before he signed with the Canadiens and was then dispatched back home.

In familiar surroundings, without the Montreal media bashing, his career blossomed anew. He won his second Norris Trophy and another post on the first-all star team. The Hawks made it to the 1992 Stanley Cup finals, only to lose to Mario Lemieux and the Penguins. Then, in 1994, came the Gary Bettman statements during the owners' lockout of the players. With negotiations getting nowhere and tempers short on both sides, Chelios made plans to play in Switzerland. To reporters he mused aloud that the NHL commissioner might be well advised to look out for the safety of his wife and kids. Some irate player might mistake collective bargaining for a hockey game, he suggested, and take matters into his own hands.

Chelios sincerely regrets the remarks; he acknowledges they were ill-timed and poorly articulated. But he contends he wasn't referring to himself when he talked of an avenging player. Still, a firestorm erupted and Chelios was obliged to apologize personally to Bettman. He lost endorsement income and was fined for the remarks. Ever since that episode, he says, he's been nagged by the controversy, "a bear with a thorn in his paw." Today, he hopes he has restored his reputation by keeping his mouth shut and by his charitable work on behalf of "Cheli's Children," his Chicago charity for underprivileged kids.

"SUMMER IS THE ONLY TIME TO MAKE GAINS IN FITNESS," says the Maple Leafs' head athletic therapist Chris Broadhurst. "During the regular season, you're just trying to maintain the fitness you've built up. Players can't afford to be out of shape at any point in the season. It used to be ten years ago we had three or four really good athletes on each team — you know, great cardiovascular endurance, great flexibility, strength. Now, with players using personal trainers and strength coaches, every team has 18 to 20 good athletes."

No one is more aware of this change than Chelios, whose conditioning and durability have helped him stay on top. And so he submits his battered body to a fanatical summer regimen with his personal trainer, T. R. Goodman, in Malibu. Defensemen have a shorter career expectancy than other position players, on average two years less. The churn on blue-liners through injury and abuse has led to a wholesale bulking up at the position; today, Chelios, though six feet and 190 pounds, is considered small at his position. He must build his body when he gets the chance. His summer holidays consist of working at his hockey school in Chicago, a few short weeks at the family cottage in Wisconsin, then back home to Malibu and the conditioning regimen. Training camp is no longer for getting in shape; it's the first day of the new season, and god help anyone who isn't ready for it.

"I took a month off after the playoffs because I was injured," he says after another draining workout. "Now I'm 100 per cent. I can play with the knee the way it is. I do an hour of weights, then I'm on the bike for an hour. We're in the gym four hours total a day." He works out five days a week — this day he was joined by Dan Kordic of the Flyers — as well as playing in those pick-up games at the Ice-O-Plex. Some players work out fewer days with longer circuits.

Chelios has averaged at least 30 minutes of ice time a game throughout his career, and so needs the aerobic endurance of a marathoner. He also works short, intense bursts into his training to simulate the exertion demanded by 60-to-90-second shifts (a far cry from the two- or three-minute shifts players logged 40 years ago). This anaerobic training involves pushing the heart and lungs to the point where they cannot supply the muscles with oxygen; this in turn triggers the alactic energy system, in which stored energy is used to feed the muscles. By combining aerobic and anaerobic training, Chelios postpones the moment at which stored reserves must be used to feed the muscles, thus speeding up his recovery time between shifts and between games.

Strength is the other area of dramatic improvement among NHL players. They build compact bulk to sustain them through eight or nine months of rugged play, adding strength in the legs and abdomen especially and providing more cushion on the bones to soften checks on the boards. Goodman uses weights to isolate and develop distinct muscle groups in Chelios's body, sometimes working a separate muscle group each day till the entire body has been toned. Chelios's workouts include both free weights and machines such as Nautilus and Cybex.

The Canadiens defenseman Emile "Butch" Bouchard was one of the earliest adherents of pumping iron, in the early 1940s (he was actually pumping railroad ties mounted with iron plates in the shed of his father's home). In this fashion he bulked himself up 20 pounds to a "gigantic" 6-foot-2 and 205 pounds. According to the conventional wisdom of the day, however, and for years afterwards, weight training was thought to create stiff, inflexible muscles and to slow players down. Thus did many a player avoid the off-season weight room that is now almost compulsory.

Indeed, early weight-lifting experiments did produce muscles that were so taut they often tore. Players like Ron Harris, a journeyman NHLer in the 1960s, built themselves into awesome specimens but spent an inordinate amount of time on the injured list with muscle pulls. Nowadays, trainers look to achieve tone and strength, but not unwieldy bulk. Another innovation that prevents the "Charles Atlas look" is extensive stretching. The muscle groups built up by weight training need to be supple as well as strong; flexibility is enhanced through regular 10-to-15-minute sessions of stretching.

Use of steroids and other artificial growth stimulants has been widely rumored, but thus far the NHL's (virtually non-existent) drug policy has detected no offenders. "We've seen players in the last two years put on weight using Creatine [a legal substance used for bulking up, sold through health-food stores]," says Broadhurst. "What we've found is that though their weight is up, their fitness is down. It's not functional weight they're putting on, and we have to get them to shed that weight before they can really add strength. We've found it takes 12 to 18 months for a player to really adjust to any extra weight." Creatine has also been blamed by some baseball trainers for dehydrating athletes and leading to muscle pulls and strains, but there is no clinical proof.

Because running is stressful on the joints and the back, the exercise bike has become the machine of choice for building cardiovascular endurance and ridding the muscles of lactic acid. In NHL dressing rooms these days, it's not uncommon to see half a dozen players churning away on bikes or stretching on the floor — after a game. Nor is it unusual to see players who've had only a few shifts doing full-scale workouts. Virtually all the players have washboard-flat bodies, and the days of finding a Guy Lafleur or a Denis Savard enjoying a post-game cigarette are long gone.

Improved training techniques — many developed in the 1950s but only employed seriously in hockey the past decade — have transformed the players' fitness levels. So has the technology that allows players to monitor, for example, the work load in a single muscle, revealing when it has shut down and transferred the work to neighboring muscles. The skill and vigilance of club trainers and therapists is another huge asset to the modern player. In the past, trainers were usually former players, rink rats, or hangers-on who laundered equipment, sharpened skates, and occasionally filled in as back-up goalies in practice. Today, trainers and therapists such as Broadhurst with the

Maple Leafs, John Wharton with the Red Wings, and Peter Friesen of the Carolina Hurricanes are the products of intensive schooling and training in health and therapy, employing everything from shiatsu to acupuncture in their daily regimen.

Strength coaches and masseurs have also become invaluable to NHL teams eager to keep their high-priced players on the ice. Some players receive up to an hour of deep, total-body massage on off-days, and 15 to 20 minutes on game days. (Some NHL clubs still cut corners by not employing either or both positions.) Personal trainers like T.R. Goodman have become integral to keeping veterans like Chelios competing at the highest level. Chelios acknowledges Goodman's contribution at every opportunity and gave him a motorcycle as a way of saying thanks. "I don't care if a guy's 6-foot-10, he's not going to catch me. Nobody's going to be in better shape than I am. I've got my trainer. That's the edge I have."

Though Chelios is a big-boned man, solidly compact and rugged, he looks slight compared to the current crop of 6-foot-4, 220-pound bruisers. "He's not a big guy by any means in today's NHL," points out Darren Pang. "He has to get by with anticipation and smarts."

According to those who've played with and against him, his greatest asset is the phenomenal strength in his legs and abdomen. It gives him a platform that allows him to push larger players out of the way. One opponent calls Chelios "almost impossible to knock off his feet — and if you do succeed, he'll get a piece of your ankle on the way down." Ray Bourque, his main rival as the best defenseman of the past decade, has the same incredible strength in his hips and legs to help him gain enormous leverage — he's an inch shorter than Chelios, at 5-foot-11, but weighs 20 pounds more, and has thighs like cedar stumps.

Chelios, Leetch, and Coffey have survived as lighter players through speed, guile, and superb offensive skills, but sheer size has become the yardstick by which the modern defenseman is measured. Players are dramatically bigger than they were in the years of the Original Six. In 1971–72 the average player was 5-foot-11, 184.2 pounds. In 1997–98, the average was 6-foot-1, 200.2 pounds, a difference of two inches and more than 15 pounds. "It's not hockey out there anymore," says an annoyed Bobby Hull. "There's no room for the little man. It's just a bunch of big kookaloos running around. They're like a bunch of robots."

Hull, Gordie Howe, Bobby Orr, Guy Lafleur, Stan Mikita, Marcel Dionne, and Wayne Gretzky are all six feet or shorter. At 175 pounds, Pierre Pilote won the Norris Trophy three times with the Blackhawks in the 1960s. Hall of Fame defenseman Leo Boivin was a hard-rock defenseman, though he stood just 5-foot-7, and another Hall of Famer, Tim Horton, was considered an NHL strong man at 5-foot-10 and 180 pounds. His teammates on the Toronto blue line during their Stanley Cup years in the 1960s — Bob Baun and Carl Brewer — were about the same size. Elmer Vasko was nicknamed "Moose" because, at 6-foot 2, 205 pounds, he was the biggest player in the league.

Most of today's top scorers — Eric Lindros, John LeClair, Jaromir Jagr, Ron Francis, Josef Stumpel, Keith Tkaczuk, Mike Modano, Peter Bondra, Alexi Yashin, Jason Allison, Mats Sundin — are 6-foot-2 or taller. Defensemen have to be big enough to deny the front of the net to these linebacker-sized scorers; hence the crop of huge young rearguards such as Chris Pronger (6-foot-4), Derian Hatcher (6-foot-5), Peter Popovic (6-foot-6), Hal Gill (6-foot-6), Mike Wilson (6-foot-6), Enrico Ciccone (6-foot-5), Chris McAllister (6-foot-7), Michal Sykora (6-foot-5), Kyle McLaren (6-foot-4), and Francois Leroux (6-foot-6). On the horizon towers Zdeno Chara (6-foot-8) of the Islanders.

Another top prospect is the 6-foot-4, 190-pound defenseman taken by Carolina in the first round of the 1997 draft. Nikos Tselios is the younger, taller cousin of Chris Chelios (Chris's father changed the spelling of the family name). Tselios no doubt gets his height from a grandfather who was seven feet tall; the rest of the Chelios clan is considerably shorter. Besides being a big cousin, he's a big fan. "I think I most admire Chris's smartness on the ice, the way he plays the game all-around," says Tselios, who's been a student and an instructor at Chelios's hockey school in Chicago. "He's gritty, and he thinks team first."

"It's all size these days," Chelios agrees. "My cousin's a good example, he's going to be a late bloomer. He's got to learn, but I think he'll make it. I think he can be like Pronger. I told him when he goes to the Hurricanes' camp, don't pick out the wrong guy — like Stu Grimson. Keep it simple, but do something to get noticed as a defenseman." Players in the Ontario Hockey League certainly noticed him, once the family tie became known. "Yeah," smiles Tselios, "they don't like who I am."

The NHL's obsession with size is particularly evident on defense. In the 1997 draft — led by 6-foot-4 center Joe Thornton — no defenseman taken in the first round was under 6-foot-1. The top draft pick of 1996 was 6-foot-3 defenseman Chris Phillips, taken by Ottawa, and the top pick in 1995 was the defenseman Bryan Berard, who barely qualifies as a big man at 6-foot-1.

"In my book, the minimum size these days for a defenseman is 6-foot-1, 6-foot-2, 200 pounds, even more," says Gilles Lupien, an agent and former Canadiens defenseman who stands 6-foot-5. "Even worse, now the goalies have to be 6-foot-1 and taller. When I look at a player, he has to come to an eight on a scale of one to ten. When he's 5-foot-9 or 5-foot-10, I give him a six. That means on the toughness scale he has to score nine or ten to get to eight in total. The small players have to give more than everybody else, because they have the problem of height."

Ask John Ferguson whether he'd draft a defenseman under six feet for his San Jose Sharks and he replies without hesitation: "Absolutely not. Let me give you an example. St. Louis used Chris Pronger against

Detroit in their playoff series in 1997. When one of the Blues' other defensemen went down, they had to bring in Chris McAlpine, who's only six foot. Really, a guy that size in the NHL right now cannot keep people away from the front of the net. The Blues were overwhelmed."

THE HUMAN MALE is one of only a hundred or so species, out of the millions on earth, to exhibit "arena behavior" — the ritual defense and protection of turf against other males. Other animals that engage in this behavior range from the African kop to the sage grouse. Zoologists believe that arena behavior speeds up the evolutionary process and contributes to socialization. The zoologist Helmut Buechner observed that (a) the territorial proprietor almost always wins; (b) the psychological advantage of the proprietor reduces the incidence and severity of actual fighting; and (c) antagonism is confined to the arena — elsewhere relations between males are amicable.

In many ways, uniformed men playing hockey — with its impersonal violence, home-ice advantage, and enclosed space — mimic the animal world. Males fight for territory, not for females; when players talk of bonding among teammates, it is the shared experience of territory conquered and a net held against attackers that is being celebrated.

Size, of course, is key in controlling territory — whether a sheet of ice or a breeding ground. There have always been big men in the NHL; players like Dit Clapper and Babe Pratt were 6-foot-2 and more than 200 pounds when they played back in the 1930s. But size was only a happy coincidence; until the legalizing of the forward pass, players used speed and deception to overcome defensemen on the less-cluttered ice surface. Clever back passing and one-on-one skills were needed more than brute strength to get close to the opposition net.

Even the advent of the forward pass and "head-manning" the puck compelled teams to control only the limited zone of 30 or 35 feet around the net from which players could score using the wrist shot or a passing play. It didn't take a lot of size to accomplish the task in such a limited space. Outside this scoring hot zone, players could skate largely unchallenged, because they were a marginal threat to score from so far out. One only has to witness modern women's hockey — which typically lacks big shooters — to see how this style of play shapes a game.

It was the popularization of the slapshot and the improvements in sticks that largely opened up scoring chances to a much wider area in front of the net and necessitated bigger players who could push scorers to bad angles. Long-range shots off sticks with banana-curved blades created an enlarged scoring area, an advantage for scorers who had only recently been overcome by improved goalie equipment and training.

The traditional role of the big enforcer — to instill fear — is distinct from the modern uses of size to clog up the playing surface and deny skating room. While the two strategies have evolved concurrently, they are not the same thing. The enforcer's role is intimidation, but the big man's role is obstruction in center ice or knocking defensemen off the puck in the corners. In short, controlling the space on the ice.

An improved understanding of scoring plays and their genesis also mandated bigger players. While fans had watched the Bert Olmsteads and Wayne Cashmans and Yvon Lamberts digging along the end boards for years, and seen Gretzky setting up behind the net again and again to initiate scoring chances, few realized how important their work was. Then, in 1988, research showed that over 60 percent of all scoring plays start behind the net, in the narrow corridor between the boards and the goal line. Control of this zone is therefore paramount. Teams needed bigger, stronger players to win the corner battles and clear snipers from the hot zones.

Today, the speed and size of players — their ability to obstruct in the neutral and defensive zones — have created a traffic jam on the ice.

"When I first started ten years ago, there was one fast player on each team," says James Patrick of the Flames. "Now there are six or seven guys you have to be aware of." NHL coaches can flood the center-ice zone or create an impregnable wall, effectively denying them Lloyd Percival's hot zones by disrupting play before it reaches the offensive zone. Territory has shrunk in a game where territoriality has always meant control in the enclosed, claustrophobic space of a rink. "That's usually your biggest problem, trying to get it into the other team's end," says Steve Yzerman of Detroit. "Getting it in is half the battle. A majority of teams now line three or four guys up across the blue line."

Better athletes armed with a game plan that includes trapping, or keeping a third forward up near the blue line in the offensive zone, are stifling NHL offenses. This emphasis on size and defense has been accelerated by the unwillingness of coaches to play riskier styles that could get them fired. "Uncertainty over their jobs leads coaches to conservatism," says Oilers president and general manager Glen Sather. "Coaches need to be secure, so they play for ties, not going all out for wins." Certainly, the statistics reflect the decline in scoring. From a high of 8.3 goals per game in 1982 the two-team average dipped to a modern-day low of 5.8 in 1997. As well as player size, expansion, improved goalie equipment, and the rapid turnover of coaches have all conspired to produce this return to 1950s scoring levels. The drag on scoring has many people in the game recommending changes to the rules. And it has many offensive stars muttering.

"The games suck, " Brett Hull told reporters in St. Louis early in 1998. "I wouldn't pay to watch them. It's boring. The whole style of the game is terrible. There's no flow to the game at all. There's so much hooking and holding. You impede the progress of players getting the puck, skating with the puck, and creating plays. Every team's doing it. When a guy like Mario [Lemieux] leaves the game and tells you why he's leaving and you don't address it… that's stupid." (After a chat with NHL officials, Hull disavowed his remarks.)

Indeed, says Lemieux's agent Tom Reich, the obstruction and lack of skating room did contribute to Lemieux's decision to retire. "They were gang tackling him in the slot. With Mario it took two guys to stop him. There's a long-standing difference of opinion at the heart of these problems in the NHL. I think Gary Bettman should extend the protection he gave goalies to the puck carriers."

Detroit coach Scotty Bowman believes the defensive focus is cyclical, but was among those who suggested that, in the current rinks, the goal lines should be moved several feet farther from the end boards, and the blue lines closer together. "You talk to veteran players and they feel a lot of obstruction and interference in the offensive zone," says Bowman, long a proponent of speed over size. "I'd like to see more room in the attacking zone. I don't think we need three zones and six lines. You don't get all ten players in the neutral zone, but many times they're all in the other zones of the rink. I think it would open the game up to remove the red line."

Bowman had other suggestions, such as two referees to help eliminate the rules interpretation that goes on now. ("The referees are consulting the linesmen so much these days, it's almost like you've got two refs already," notes Sather. "It's rare to see him make a call and not have a conference with the linesmen.") Others insist more referees will slow the game down; with one watch you always know the time, with two you're never sure. But in basketball, where there are three officials, the referee closest to a play always has the pressure of knowing his colleague may call a foul and show him up for not having called it himself. Peer pressure dictates that he apply the letter, not the spirit, of the law. As Roy MacGregor pointed out in *Road Games*, the real problems arise when infractions are not called. Players take the law into their own hands and, as the Flyers of the 1970s proved, the hockey inmates do a poor job running the asylum.

No sooner were Bowman's ideas out of his mouth in the fall of 1997 than a special NHL committee struck to deal with the dearth of scoring recommended moving all the lines two feet closer to center ice for pre-season games in 1998, thereby creating more room behind the nets and in the offensive zone. The committee — headed by Sather and Bob Gainey of Dallas — also proposed adding a second referee for 20 percent of the games and shrinking the goalie crease — all changes later approved by the Board of Governors for the 1998–99 season.

The league also revived its waning war on obstruction fouls after the Olympic break in 1998, vowing that this time the NHL was determined to end the clutching and grabbing that made neutral-zone play so deadly. Fans and players who'd heard that line before rolled their eyes and waited to see how long the resolve would last (until the late rounds of playoffs, as it turned out). With the calling of borderline fouls in the neutral zone back in vogue, most coaches responded by switching to more forechecking, breaking up plays in the offensive zone instead of at center ice. Some teams, such as Chicago and Edmonton, had been doing that all along.

Of course, the simplest solution was missed during construction of the 16 new NHL arenas built in the past decade or now in the works; all have an ice surface of 200 by 85 feet instead of the larger international surface with its roomy area behind the nets and extra width for stickhandling. (The international ice size is approximately three stick lengths wider than its NHL counterpart.) Apparently the lure of two or three extra rows of high-priced seats proved too much for NHL owners to resist. "The way the game has progressed, it's almost too fast for the ice surface," says James Patrick. "Maybe the rink — the ice — should be a little bit bigger."

Hockey purists who pined for the larger ice surface had their arguments buttressed by the faster, more creative game engendered by the large ice surface at the Nagano Olympics. Some NHL die-hards dismissed the games as too wide open, but fans watching the exciting, untrammelled play of Pavel Bure and Jaromir Jagr and Teemu Selanne were not fooled.

Most teams today try to beat the neutral-zone trap, or the wall of defenders across the blue line, by dumping the puck in and chasing it down in the corners, hoping to create a turnover with a big hit — and waking up their dozing fans. Defensemen the size of Chelios repeatedly get rocked by forwards the size of Chris Gratton, Keith Primeau, and Eric Lindros; often the defensemen have their backs to the play and are working against boards and glass with little give. Surviving this punishment for an entire season requires a big, strong body. "You don't have much time to turn and look," says Detroit's Larry Murphy. "It's the exception rather than the rule: you're facing the boards, and you've got to get rid of the puck or face being knocked off it. The best way to get it out is to play it off the glass."

The installation of so-called seamless plexiglas in many arenas, with its taller wrap-around surface, has helped defensemen move the puck out of their own zone, but the rules makers punished defensemen when they rescinded the "tag-up" rule on offsides. Defensemen used to be able to shoot the puck into the defending zone while their forwards were still offside, so long as the forwards returned to the blue line to "tag up" and put themselves back onside. The original rules, back in effect, force defensemen to wait until all their mates have cleared the zone before shooting the puck in. "That's a real tough rule for defensemen," says Chelios, "because you're handling the puck longer in the neutral zone and taking some big hits out there."

Another reason for the popularity of size in today's NHL is that it's incontrovertible. A scout can sleep easy at night knowing that other variables — skating, shooting, passing, scoring touch — may be altered by injury or stress, but the 6-foot-2 young man you see playing junior will be 6-foot-2 on draft day. You can cover yourself against second-guessing when it comes to size, a factor not to be underestimated in the annual scouting ratings.

Smaller players are also marked down on draft-day lists because of concerns about their stamina. The feeling is that the small player has trouble enduring the long, taxing NHL season. "A small guy usually starts the season well," points out Lupien, "but around Christmas, he'll start to fade a bit. It's because he's always going against guys 6-foot-2, 220 pounds, and it's tough going in front of the net."

There are exceptions, of course. Theoren Fleury of the Flames is just 5-foot-6 and 160 pounds, but has made a fine career in Calgary through sheer skill and nastiness. Lupien himself has a client, Donald Audette, at 5-foot-8 and 180 pounds, who has lusted with Buffalo on his scoring touch. And 5-foot-9, 170-pound Igor Larionov has long thrived in the NHL, most recently with the Red Wings, because he may be the best passer this side of Wayne Gretzky. But these mites are getting fewer in the NHL.

Former NHL star Anders Hedberg is in no rush to declare the average-size player extinct, however, even on defense. Now director of player personnel for the Maple Leafs, he came up with most of the best prospects that maligned organization selected when he was a European scout. "Size cannot be the only determining factor in a defensemen," he says. "The top-scoring defenseman are not that big. I was with the Rangers when Craig Patrick received a lot of criticism because we drafted a 5-foot-11, 172-pound defenseman out of Haven's Farm, Connecticut. They said it's impossible, he can't play. But when you look today at Brian Leetch's puck-handling skills, you realize size has no bearing.

"If you're just looking for a regular player to play for a number of years and be reliable," Hedberg continues, "then you go for the guy who's 6-foot-2, over 200 pounds. But not if you want a guy to make the last play on defense to win a game for you."

In Montreal to play the Habs at the Molson Centre in the fall of 1997, the Blackhawks are off to a brutal start. After losing their first seven games, they now sit at 2–9, having lost to Dallas and to a weak Carolina squad in the past week. Newspaper reports have Chelios playing poorly, and on this night, back in his first NHL home, he appears out of sync, as do all the Hawks. He knows that the Molson Centre is not the best place to find your game. "When I played for Montreal," he says, "we used to get every break in the world from the refs. Everybody knows that. It's still the same."

The Hawks start out as if intent on running their record to 2–10. The Habs' Stephane Richer and Vladimir Malakhov score on Chris Terreri in the first 3:48 of the game, both on rebounds the Hawks' defense fails to clear. But then Chelios rallies his team, rocking Habs near the net and keying several breakouts with crisp, pinpoint passes. The Hawks shut out Montreal from that point on, as the captain works his mojo.

In the second period, Valeri Bure, the brother of the Canucks star Pavel, gets a little too close for comfort in the slot on the power play, and Chelios gives him a lumber sandwich to clear space for his goalie. The predictable mêlée ensues with threats of recrimination and violence from Shayne Corson of the Habs. The threats are quickly forgotten, but Chelios has distracted the Canadiens, a young, talented team that needs to remain focused.

Emboldened, the Hawks rally for two goals in the third period, the second by Sergei Krivokrasov with just 2:24 left in the game. Suddenly they have the momentum, and a sure loss now looks like no worse than a tie — quite acceptable on the road in Montreal. Chicago presses for the go-ahead goal. First Tony Amonte, then Greg Johnson, and finally Chelios himself have great scoring chances, but luck and Andy Moog stymie them.

No one on the Chicago bench can believe what happens next. With little over a minute remaining, a modest wrist shot from the point by Montreal defenseman Craig Rivet floats toward the Chicago goal. The blade of Martin Rucinsky's stick shoots out, tipping the puck past a startled Terreri. 3–2 Montreal. While Chelios and the Hawks are still absorbing that blow, Vincent Damphousse backhands another one past Terreri. No win, no tie, no luck — the Hawks lose 4–2.

In the dressing room afterwards Chelios is perplexed and frustrated. "I wish I could figure this team out," he says, shaking his head. "We have to just work our way out of it. We can't quit." These are the clichés spawned by losing, Chelios knows, but he also knows it's too early in the season to send up the white flag in front of your teammates.

A few weeks later, when the Hawks come to Maple Leaf Gardens, they still look nothing like a playoff team. Though riding a six-game unbeaten streak, they're only 7–10–1, which won't get it done in the competitive Western Conference. The team's offense is non-existent — just 34 goals, third worst in the NHL — and the power play is 6 for 97, worst in the league. Chelios himself has only seven assists, no goals, a plus-minus of -7, and a growing cadre of sportswriters who are adding the adjective "aging" to their descriptions of the captain, and wondering aloud whether he's "losing a step."

Toronto, even lower in the standings, is a good place for Chelios and company to get happy. But after only three minutes of the first period the Leafs take the lead on a goal by defenseman Jason Smith — just the fourth time all season the Leafs have scored first. A Chicago power-play goal from Bob Probert ends a 0–17 streak with the man advantage and evens the score; then Greg Johnson pops one to send the Hawks to the dressing room up 2–1. A backhand goal by Frederic Modin of the Leafs early in the second period ties it at 2–2, but Chicago remains in control of the game against the young, jittery Leafs. Chelios and the other Hawk defensemen are pinching at the Toronto blue line, creating turnovers and panicking the inexperienced Leaf forwards.

When Toronto goes on the power play, Chelios, killing the penalty, tries to relive his impetuous youth. He leads a counter-attack across the Leafs' blue line, trailed closely by Jeff Shantz. As he crosses the line, Chelios veers to the center of the rink, creating an isolation play. Both Leaf defensemen go with Chelios as he skates parallel to the blue line, leaving an open lane for a drop pass to the trailing Shantz — except that Shantz has peeled away, leaving the puck sitting there like a lost wallet.

Chelios's momentum carries him toward the Toronto net; he's caught up ice on a transition. Igor Korolev grabs the unattended puck, and before Chelios can recover, the Leafs' counter-attack ends with Korolev scoring the go-ahead goal. 3–2 Leafs; worse, it's a crushing swing in momentum. Chicago fails to score on a five-minute butt-ending major to Toronto's Kris King in the third. Then two late goals on Terreri have Toronto celebrating just its second home win of the year, 5-2.

In the cramped visitors' dressing room at Maple Leaf Gardens, Chelios speaks in a pained monotone and dresses quickly. "I have to make a better decision. I probably shouldn't have done that." Shantz was equally at fault for his indecision, but Chelios knows he unnecessarily complicated the game, just as Bob Gainey taught him not to do.

Craig Hartsburg is more blunt when he speaks to reporters. "When it's 2–2 on the road, just get the puck in deep," he mutters. He refers to Chelios's mistake as a "bone-headed play." The league records it as another loss, and a visitor to the dressing room senses that there will be more abject nights during one of the twilight seasons in a distinguished defenseman's career.

Is BOBBY ORR DEAD? One of hockey's sacred notions is that Orr revolutionized the role of defense in the NHL. Certainly, no one has ever played the position as he did between 1966 and 1978. He made offensive plays no defenseman had ever dreamed of. In his 12 injury-plagued NHL seasons, he not only posted the best points-per-game average of any defenseman, he has the fourth-best average of any player in NHL history.

Orr is the only defenseman to register more than 100 assists in a single season. He did it six times. He amassed 270 goals in just 657 games: had his knees held up, or had today's arthroscopic surgery been available to him, his numbers might be higher by half again. "He was two steps ahead of anyone," recalls Brad Park, himself a Hall of Fame defenseman. "Then, after his knee injuries, he was one step ahead."

By the age of 30, the player many consider the best ever was finished. Playing hurt is one of the NHL's most revered badges of honor, and Orr was not about to pull himself out of the game because of pain. Said someone familiar with his medical chart in those years, "You wouldn't send a racehorse back out there as quickly as his doctors and agent allowed Bobby to get back to playing."

Before Orr, only one defenseman had ever scored 20 goals in a season (Flash Hollett in 1945–46). Some defensemen, notably Doug Harvey, had led counter-attacks out of their own zone. Harvey was the catalyst for the Canadiens' "fire-wagon" hockey, and by 1960 the Habs had boosted scoring in the NHL by almost a full goal a game. Harvey initiated the rush by clearing his zone, then head-manning the puck to a streaking forward like Dickie Moore, Bernie Geoffrion, or Jean Beliveau. But the most goals Harvey ever scored in a season was nine, and in his top season he had just 50 points. Despite his example, most coaches still asked their defensemen to stay back, punish forwards with body checks, and dump the puck out of harm's way.

Orr was a one-man fire wagon, clearing his own defensive zone and carrying the puck the length of the ice, often finishing the play himself or setting up Phil Esposito in the slot. He also had a deadly shot from the point on the power play. Orr exceeded the 20-goal plateau seven straight years, four times scoring 30 or more goals and once tallying an incredible 46 goals. His chief rival as a defenseman in those years, Park, topped out at 25 goals in a season.

The wonderful speed and dexterity that made Orr an offensive dynamo also allowed him to rule his defensive end. Partnered with Dallas Smith, he could miss a scoring opportunity at one end of the rink and motor back to his own end in time to foil counter-attacks. It was fashionable to deride Orr's defensive-zone play in his youth, but his eight consecutive Norris Trophies were a testament not only to his offensive genius but to his hard hitting, his leadership, and his toughness around the net. And, yes, Orr was a mean (if infrequent) fighter as well. "When he was on the ice," marveled teammate Don Awrey, "he had the puck 50 percent of the time, and he was always on the ice. He absolutely controlled games."

When Orr retired from the Blackhawks in 1978, gimpy and discouraged, it was widely accepted that he'd left behind more than his impressive statistics. He had freed up other defensemen to involve themselves in the rush, creating uneven-strength breaks as their teams counter-attacked. He was the antidote to the European teams' five-man attacks that once confounded NHL players. In the years after Orr's arrival in the NHL, scoring did zoom to unprecedented heights as defensemen took to the offense. The league average in Harvey's prime was five and a half goals a game; by the year Orr quit, it was seven. Ten years after he quit, the average was almost eight. Teams sometimes hit double figures in a game — as many goals as a successful team of the 1950s, or the late 1990s might garner in a week.

Defensemen such as Park, Denis Potvin, Guy Lapointe, and Paul Coffey made the 20-goal barrier as antiquated as the rover position. When Coffey scored 48 for Edmonton in 1985–86, it was widely agreed that the game was forever changed and that Orr had been the architect of this fundamental shift. Today, however, that legacy seems shattered by the neutral-zone trap, the left-wing lock, and an army of large, aggressive defensive specialists. Defensemen are once again on a leash. Coaches seem unwilling to commit defensemen to the attack, and the NHL has been reduced to a succession of uneven rushes — three attackers on four defenders, even two on four, as coaches keep a forward hanging back at the blue line to shut down counter-attacks. The result has been a drop of more than a goal per game from the NHL average since the start of the decade; a tedious, fitful style of play; and open season on outnumbered puck carriers who are being held, hacked, slashed, and boarded onto the injured list.

Even more distressing for fans of Canadian hockey, today's young offensive defensemen are not being produced in this country, but in Europe and the American colleges and high schools. Too many games, too many parents pushing their kids toward pro careers, and too much emphasis on winning in minor hockey are stunting the development of the next Orr. While more than 60 percent of the players in the NHL in 1995–96 were Canadian born, just five of the top fifteen scoring defensemen were Canadian, and none was under age 30. Again in 1996–97, just five of the top fifteen scoring defensemen were Canadian; of those, only Darryl Sydor and Eric Desjardins were under age 32. Six of the top dozen scoring defenseman in 1997–98 were Canadian born, but only Scott Niedermayer and Rob Blake were younger than 32.

At the Nagano Olympics, Canada had little choice but to take the 37-year-old Bourque, the 34-year-old Al MacInnis, and the 33-year-old Scott Stevens. The next generation of productive Canadian defensemen has become a lost generation, waiting for someone to break out. Niedermayer seemed to be fulfilling his promise in 1997–98, but Bobby Clarke and Team Canada left him at home for the Olympics. There are fine Canadian defensemen, of course; defensively gifted rearguards like Adam Foote and Sylvain Lefebvre and Chris Pronger are highly sought after by rival general managers. But they don't sell seats, and they don't invite comparisons to Bobby Orr. The gifted young scorers on defense these days are players such as Leetch and Bryan Berard of the United States, Nicklas Lidstrom of Sweden, Sandis Ozolinsh, Sergei Zubov, and Oleg Tverdosky of Russia, Roman Hamrlick of the Czech Republic, and Janne Ninimaa of Finland.

Is national origin the most important variable in the creation of skilled defensemen these days? Or is it simply training methods? "College players practice all year," Chelios points out. "They know the game better. Junior players just come out and play. In Moose Jaw, for instance, I just would take the puck and go. There was no time to work on the game. I mean, a lot of these high-scoring defensemen come out of college. I learned everything about playing defense in college with Bob Johnson. Wisconsin's also got a great goalie coach — Curtis Joseph came through there. Then there's Grant Stamberg at Maine. Paul Kariya and Keith Carney came out of there, and those guys know what they're doing."

Former NHL defenseman Pat Stapleton, who developed a national training program after his retirement, compares the growth of a player to the growth of a bamboo tree. You plant a bamboo seed, you water it and fertilize it, for one year, two years, three. Nothing comes out of the ground until the fifth year. Then the sprout breaks through and grows 90 feet in six months. Did the bamboo grow 90 feet in six months,

Stapleton asks, or did it take five years and six months?

"There's a reason why Canadian defensemen's scoring skills are stifled," says Tom Laidlaw, a former NHL defenseman who's now an agent for players such as Bryan Berard. "I hope coaches don't take this the wrong way, but I think it's because the players are asked to play such a team game. Part of hockey is the team game, and those are great things to teach a guy — but not the only things. If you've got a player with the potential to be a great offensive player and all you do is ask him to bang the puck off the boards every time he gets it, then he's not going to develop those skills. The trap and the defensive style really restrict the things that a lot of defensemen can do.

"Thinking back to Bobby Orr, all his coaches wanted him to do was to stay back and play that strict game. But he had that fire inside of him and he wanted to go with it. Bryan Berard — I'm not saying he's Orr — but he's the same way. We have the battles that coaches want him to stay back, and I have to say, 'No, you're Bryan Berard and what makes you a player is, you go. You take chances. Sometimes you get burned for taking those chances, but you also make some great plays in trying.'

"You have to realize that if a team wants to get the most out of a Bryan Berard, they have to let him develop into the player he wants to be. Herb Brooks was one of my coaches when I played with the Rangers, and we had a great Finnish defenseman named Reijo Ruotsalainen. Herb had a great saying. He said, 'Asking Reijo Ruotsalainen to play like Tom Laidlaw would be like asking Picasso to paint your garage.'"

Former San Jose coach George Kingston knows this dilemma from the coach's perspective. "When we had Sandis Ozolinsh with the Sharks, he probably cost us 20 games with his mistakes," recalls Kingston. "Now, do I sit him down and try to win games, or do I let him learn on the job? Our management said they wanted to go pro-development.

Then they changed their mind, and I was fired." Now Ozolinsh is a star, but with Colorado.

The results-now approach is backing up into amateur ranks as well. Junior coaches want to demonstrate that they can coach the "pro" style; minor hockey coaches zealously absorb this philosophy at seminars and summer camps, seeking to build powerhouse teams that will attract more top talent; and junior hockey owners, who don't want a losing team, choose coaches who'll be friendlier to the bottom line than to player development. No one is willing to play a risky style that stresses development over winning. With never-ending seasons of 100 games or more, minor hockey in Canada is defining itself through the job specs of the NHL rather than improving the sport and its individual young participants.

"The coaches at the minor level are turning the kids into robots," agrees Mark Napier, who coaches the St. Mike's junior team in Toronto. "They force the kids into a system too early, and they never learn to improvise. It's especially tough to get the older kids out of that mold. I tell them to be creative, improvise, but they still go up and down the wings in straight lines or simply dump the puck out of the zone along the glass."

Another disincentive to skills development comes inadvertently from the increased demands of both the 18-year-old NHL draft and the World Junior Championships. When one superior skill can make a teenaged player into a first-round choice with a million-dollar contract, some teams, parents, and agents insist on polishing that one skill instead of going through the time-consuming process of building a well-rounded game. The goal is to produce the best pro prospects rather than the best players a decade down the line.

The prime stage for these draft-eligible players to show their mettle has become the World Junior Championships at Christmas. Scouts, general managers, and agents now flock to this annual event to preview the best draft-eligible players from around the world. Unless kids play — and play well — at this tournament, they can be downgraded in the draft and lose millions as a result. Playing the "pro" style — physical, intimidating, chippy — rather than the skilled style dictated by the larger ice surface, is often the easiest way to get noticed.

Canadian Hockey's infatuation with winning the World Junior Tournament has produced another disincentive for skills development. European teams tend to be less organized, less game-smart, at this formative stage, and Canada has learned that a disciplined team system can win the junior title. It's worked well lately — Canada has won five of the past six titles — but asking 18-year-olds to ape professionals by playing a rigid, trapping system is like asking a young concert pianist to play with one hand to reduce the chance of wrong notes. As George Kingston points out, this is the stage at which kids are supposed to make mistakes.

Perhaps those most affected by this rush to pro readiness are defensemen. With the dump-and-chase style giving them less time to make a play, young defensemen learn simply to get the puck out of their zone as quickly as possible. "They are not getting enough time with the puck on their sticks in games, or in practices, either," says Mark Howe, now coaching with Detroit. "Watch a practice today, and the kids never have the puck on their sticks. They're always doing skating drills without the puck. You've got to have them learning the feel of the puck on their stick while moving and turning on the ice." Former NHL defenseman Garth Butcher sees the same thing in the minor players he coaches in British Columbia. "We've got to give kids the confidence of feeling the puck on their stick, not simply banging it up the boards or glass and out of the zone."

Swedish center Peter Forsberg of Colorado adds his voice to the chorus: "We handle the puck much more [in Europe] than they do over here," he points out. "Here, they dump it in and the players are more aggressive on the forecheck. There, they hang back and handle the puck. And we probably practice in a different way. Over here, you go hard for 15 seconds. Over there, you take it easy and try to handle the puck. The pace is not as fast as it is over here."

Glen Sather sees the results of this development system on his own team. "You take our captain Kelly Buchberger. He works his ass off, he's a great skater and tough as nails. He's got a ton of heart. He's played most of his career chasing the puck. Then he gets it and turns it over. His puck skills have never been developed. These guys coming up today never learn to handle the puck."

George Kingston, who coaches the German national team, has spent almost his entire life studying the game. He offers a revealing statistic that speaks to the problem of why Canadian defensemen are falling behind their European counterparts. "According to a Swedish study, the most dominant player on the ice — usually the center — is in contact with the puck for just 47 seconds a game," he says. "The most dominant player! The least contact is made by the defensemen and the right winger, about five to ten seconds.

"Now, take those numbers and extrapolate them to a minor or junior player who's playing nothing but games. What kind of puck-handling experience is he going to develop touching the puck five to ten seconds a game? How will he develop the skill to take and give a pass or shoot the puck? You can only develop that in practice, and we've seen that while in Europe the proportion of practices to games is sometimes as high as five to one, the proportion in Canada is almost exactly reversed. We've studied it and we believe that about two practices to one game is the right proportion for developing young players' skills. Otherwise you get LCD hockey — lowest common denominator hockey."

At one time, young players learned the skills of stickhandling and "ragging" the puck by playing shinny or pick-up hockey on local rinks. But the tradition of pond hockey, where everyone from Frank Malone to Bobby Orr polished his unique skills through endless hours of play, is rapidly dying off. Urbanization has dried up many ponds and sloughs, and the demands of games, tournaments, and practices leaves little time for idle games after school or on weekends.

Make no mistake: hockey has never had more talented athletes than it has in this decade. The players' conditioning and mental approach outstrip anything that has come before. Many of the sins in minor hockey are sins of commission, not omission, by people who mean well. The problems are all fixable if the will and the money are directed properly. Bob Nicholson, the president of Canadian Hockey, believes he and his colleagues simply have to sell the message properly. "We need spokesmen like Lindros or Gretzky to sell that learning hockey skills can be fun," he says. "We have to play fewer games, maybe divide the ice in half so there's less wasted time for the younger kids. Most of all, make it fun again."

In short, Canadian hockey needs to break with a past that has shaped — and sometimes shackled — the game. The weight of that history, as Ken Dryden pointed out in *The Game*, can suffocate the changes necessary to rejuvenate the game. While Don Cherry and the game's traditionalists embrace the old-time ethos — no visors, lots of fighting, smaller rinks — they ought to remember what happened in Britain. The British invented soccer — much as Canadians invented hockey — but when the South Americans and continental Europeans showed better ways of developing and playing the game, the British could not cast off cherished maxims about tactics and strategy that had evolved into gospel. As a result, teams from the British Isles have been relegated to also-ran status since winning the World Cup in 1966. It's the students in Brazil and Argentina and France and Italy who are teaching the master these days.

Ajax, the Dutch soccer powerhouse, has a development scheme with some noteworthy applications for hockey. Prospects in the Ajax system play no more than a handful of games a year until they reach their teens. Instead, young players are fed a steady diet of skills development — often in other sports as well — and play on half a field, to develop the feel of touching the ball necessary to become adept at scoring and creating offense. Nor are they dispatched hundreds of miles away from home to complete their apprenticeships in the game.

Learning from soccer is not a new idea; Father David Bauer used it with Canada's national team back in the 1960s. Bauer's teams would practice once a week without sticks, moving the puck only with their feet. It will take many things for Canada to regain its preeminence in hockey. Most of all it will take open eyes and ears, which seem to be in short supply at the top levels of the game these days.

CHRIS CHELIOS LEANS AGAINST THE WALL at GM Place in Vancouver. It's January 1998, and he's a member of Team North America as the NHL tries to spice up its moribund all-star format by having the league's best from this continent play the best from the rest of the world (read Europe). The Saturday morning workout is over for the North Americans, and Chelios is preparing to run the gamut of reporters on media morning. He's freshly showered, his hair still damp, his beard a stubble (he can seemingly affect this look if he goes much more than an hour without shaving). His expensively tailored jacket hangs lankly off him. Up close, the latticework of facial scars betrays his age and his profession. From a distance, though, with his boyish self-confidence and self-deprecating smile, he looks not unlike a high school senior waiting for the dance.

Chelios probably does feel like dancing these days. Following their dreadful 0–7 start, the Hawks have rebounded and now sit seventh in the Western Conference, a game under .500. After a "vocal" team meeting on December 17 — many players didn't like Hartsburg's defensive system; Chelios and others argued for more offensive freedom — the club began to roll. The Hawks scoring has finally awakened, with Amonte and Zhamnov producing at full throttle of late. Since Christmas, Chicago is averaging more than a goal a game more than it did in the first half of the season. Goals against, meanwhile, have dropped from 2.42 to 2.14. While no one is touting the Hawks for anything monumental in the playoffs, the recent surge has given Chelios new hope. "Wait till we get Brett Hull," he jokes of the St. Louis sniper who's soon to become a free agent. (Indeed, Hull will come close to signing with the Hawks before signing with the Dallas Stars.) "We've changed around the whole system since the start of the season."

What Hartsburg and the Hawks have done is indeed impressive. With a mobile defensive corps, Hartsburg has his defensemen pinching, trying to keep the puck in the offensive zone, while he sends two forwards in deep on the forecheck, forcing the play in a modified version of Scotty Bowman's left-wing lock. In Hartsburg's system, however, the center, not the left wing, hangs back, waiting to pick up turnovers to key the transition game. As the Hawks' improved record seems to indicate, you can play a sound defensive system without lapsing into hockey narcolepsy, also known as the trap.

There's a fresh wound on Chelios's face, stitches neatly sewn into his chin. Otherwise he's has been healthy of late. His ice time had dropped to 25 minutes or so a game, but he's back over 30 minutes some nights and showing no ill effects. His knee feels strong. All the work with T.R. Goodman is paying dividends.

"I'm not talking to Lindros," Chelios jokes, casting a mock menacing glance in the direction of the Flyers captain, whom he'll play alongside at the all-star game but will then confront at the Nagano Olympics. "I'm staying right out of his way."

Next day, during the game itself, he looks like the Chelios of the Ice-O-Plex, using the unwritten no-contact rules to play like Brian Leetch. Except for a gentle shove on Bobby Holik, Chelios is unusually docile. He racks up three assists, jumping up into the rush, reveling in this hockey version of the busman's holiday, as North America wins 8–7. (The only loser this rainy day in Vancouver is "Canada's own" Bryan Adams, who muffs the words to "O Canada.") On his team's third goal, Chelios pinches in at the point, intercepting a clearing pass; his shot is deflected home by Lindros. Chelios laughs delightedly, aware of the irony of setting up a goal by someone who'll be an Olympian enemy in a month's time.

Leetch, also dazzling in the freewheeling format of the all-star game, will likely inherit Chelios's mantle as the top American defenseman in the NHL and may surpass Chelios as the best player of all time from the United States. In some ways the two men are polar opposites on the ice, illustrating the contrasting demands of playing defense in the NHL. Despite racking up impressive point totals most of his career, Chelios builds his game from the defensive zone out. It's a game built on menace and movement. Leetch has gained his pre-eminence while battling critics who say he's a one-way player.

The most gifted offensive defenseman since Coffey, Leetch has won the Norris Trophy twice in the past six years while earning all-star status four times. His creativity in bringing the puck up ice is unparalleled and keyed the Rangers' Stanley Cup win in 1994. For his performance that spring he — not Mark Messier or Mike Richter — was awarded the Conn Smythe Trophy as the top performer in the playoffs.

"Leetch is clearly the best defenseman in the league," asserts Harry Neale. "He may well be the best skater in the NHL other than the goaltenders. He's phenomenal, he can play half the game, too. Sure, he's not perfect defensively, but he's improved a lot. Plus he's got that great imagination that guys like Gretzky and Lemieux and Kariya have."

"When you have an outstanding player," says Ottawa coach Jacques Martin, "quite often it's their ability to see the ice, their ability to be ahead of the play, to anticipate things that the ordinary players don't pick up. Brian has been outstanding because of his ability to jump into the rush, to be a threat and then recover. At the same time, he's improved his defensive skill tremendously. He can play against the opposition's best forwards and do a good job."

Michel Bergeron says that all Leetch needed was a little time to learn the defensive aspect of the NHL game. It's the luxury that his abundant scoring granted him where another player might have been demoted or traded. "They used to say that Guy Lafleur can play like Bob Gainey," notes Bergeron, "but Bob Gainey cannot play like Guy Lafleur."

As the 1997–98 season proved, however, Leetch cannot play like himself and Mark Messier at the same time. Leetch thrived when Messier was his teammate with the Rangers, but with Messier playing in Vancouver in 1997–98, Leetch had a miserable year. His 50 points were the lowest in any full NHL season he's played, and his -36 was the league's worst plus-minus statistic. His poor season helps explain why the Rangers missed the playoffs.

Leetch is candid about his shortcomings and his subpar performance in 1997–98. "I'm so used to seeing all the game from the back, with everyone in front of me, that when I get along the boards in the offensive zone, I have difficulty finding where the net is," he explains. "I have a tendency to throw the puck out blindly or to bury my head in the corner and not make the play to the open guy. I'm much better at moving the puck ahead of me and then coming in from behind the play."

And while Chelios can turn an attacking forward away using his strength or his stick, Leetch must be more conscious of preventing forwards from getting a step as they break to the goal. Unlike Chelios, he won't use a two-hander to impede a player's progress. "I'm not the strongest player, so positioning is important for me, to be ready regardless of the guy's offensive skills. A player might not have the moves, but if he gets a step on me, he can get inside and get to the net. So it's important to stay in front of the player and in front of the net. I can recover quickly, but I have to keep position."

Positioning is critically important on defense. All defensemen know that the quickest way to get caught out of position is to watch the puck, not the man as he skates toward you. Every coach from atom to pro preaches watching the logo on the forward's chest, not his feet or the puck, to determine where he'll go. Chelios describes his technique for playing an oncoming forward as "not allowing the gap to develop between the forward and me. That happens when I get tired."

Darren Pang believes the subtleties of positioning are what make Chelios special, particularly in front of the net. "He's always thinking out there: don't get tied up with the forward, don't screen the goalie, stay to the proper side of the forward. Watch him work Eric Lindros, a guy who's four inches taller and 50 pounds heavier. As the puck comes to his side, he'll get the stick between his legs, turn Lindros's body away from the net that way. Then, when it goes the other way, he's keeping contact, but this time just pushing off with the hand, never getting on the wrong side of Lindros so the big guy can spin and get a clean shot, never screening his goalie. That's experience, that's what comes from knowing his job."

Of course, the top forwards know about the "gap" and have developed ways to counter a clinging defenseman. Gretzky is a master of the art. Instead of speeding up as he crosses the blue line, Gretzky often slows down and moves toward the boards, trying to create gaps in the defensive coverage by drawing the defensemen to him. Done properly, this technique opens up seams for his wingers to skate to. "If I go to him and get three or four feet from him, he'll just pass the puck and then skate," explains Washington rearguard Mark Tinordi. "It's hard to hit him. His style makes him a difficult target."

The other key for a defenseman who, like Leetch or Chelios, frequently gets into the rush is a reliable partner to complement his skills. Chelios's partners in Chicago — Gary Suter, Eric Weinrich, Keith Carney — are experienced at the transition and switching game necessary when playing alongside their very active captain. Leetch's defense partner for much of the past six years has been Jeff Beukeboom, and they've learned to anticipate each other's moves. "Jeff's a big guy who separates the man from the puck," says Leetch, "so I can pick it up and start the play the other way. He tries to make the easy play and if it's not there, he just gets it out of the zone. That way I can be anticipating a pass getting through and jumping up the other side. I know that he's not going to make some crazy pass up the middle where I'll be caught out of position."

While Chelios, Leetch, and Bourque are acknowledged as the best all-round defensemen in the NHL over the past decade, Al MacInnis of St. Louis undoubtedly has the best shot off the point. He's won the hardest shot competition at the all-star game four times, and his 98-mile-an-hour blasts on the power play are feared by teammates, opposing defensemen, and goalies alike. What makes the shot doubly effective is not just its speed, but the low trajectory that allows for tip-ins and deflections. MacInnis usually keeps his shot less than a foot off the ice. He developed his shot by firing against the family barn in Nova Scotia. Now, the 6-foot-2, 200-pound MacInnis maximizes his torque by keeping his hands high and relatively close together up the stick, creating a larger arc on the swing. He also employs a fairly upright stick — a number six lie — with a bit of a "wedge" to give his shots more lift. Like many defensemen, he also uses a longer stick than normal, which maximizes the whip and the arc.

Before metal shafts, the advent of the curved blade was the major change in sticks. For almost 75 years, stick blades were straight, but then an accident changed the course of hockey history. Stan Mikita, who shares credit for inventing the curved blade with Andy Bathgate, says that one day he broke a blade in practice. In frustration, he took a shot using the oddly shaped blade. To his amazement, the puck reacted differently. He tried again; same result. Mikita began bending his stick blades by soaking them in water or using a blowtorch, producing banana-like bends and golf club-like lofts. Shooters like Mikita and Bobby Hull were gaining 10 to 20 miles per hour on their shots, pucks were dipping and diving, goalies were ducking, and the NHL was forced to write rules to restrict curves to less than an inch and a half. Today, the curved blade is so widespread that Doug Gilmour's virtually straight blade looks like a museum piece.

About half of all NHL players today use aluminum or fiber-composite shafts on their sticks, but MacInnis and Chelios both prefer wood. "When you're taking a lot of slapshots off the point like I do," notes Chelios, "the aluminum stick is good for two or three shots then it's bent. I don't want to deal with a feeling like that. Once you get used to something you don't want to change." Chelios has another reason for using wood: it leaves behind a more memorable souvenir. "I used to use Titan sticks. They were a heavy stick that wouldn't break easily, and if you slashed someone they felt it. I can't use that heavy a stick anymore."

Like many players, Chelios is touchy about his sticks. "I don't like anybody coming up and testing the whip. Ludsie [Craig Ludwig] used to do that in Montreal. That bugs me, because it loses its strength." He's less fussy about his skates. "If they're comfortable, I don't care how sharp they are. I just don't want a bad edge. If I have a nick in the edge, I know it. It seems that between the rinks, with all the travel, somehow there's always nicks in them." While the average NHLer goes through three or four pair of skates a year, at about $400 a pair, Chelios prefers more "experienced" footwear. "I've been with CCM skates since I was ten. As long as they're comfortable, I can wear the same pair all year."

If Chelios is finicky about his sticks, his ex-teammate Jeremy Roenick is downright fanatical. The Phoenix star won't let anyone else touch his sticks. He also won't allow someone else's stick to touch his. "If someone even accidentally touches my stick, I'll throw it out or give it away. If I'm sitting in the next stall and a guy's stick is in my stall — or falls into my stall — I'll ask him to remove it. I won't touch it."

Donald Audette of the Sabres is similarly sensitive. "Let me tell you, nobody touches my sticks except me. This is a very big thing with me. My sticks are like my eyes, so to speak." Former Red Wing, Oiler, and Lightning sniper Petr Klima used to break his stick after every goal: "I only have one goal in each stick," he explained. (Not everyone is entranced by the mystical properties of hockey sticks. When Muhammad Ali was presented with an autographed stick by the Edmonton Oilers, the Greatest said to the Great Gretzky: "I like your company/ and I like your style/ but this gift is so cheap/ I hope you don't come back for a while.")

Different players look for different characteristics in their sticks. Former Toronto captain Rick Vaive named his stick "Big Bertha" because it weighed 1.5 pounds, about a third more than the average. The heavy stick gave him a particularly heavy, hard shot. Gilmour, a former Leaf captain himself who's now with the Blackhawks, prefers an almost straight blade to give him more consistency on the backhand. Wayne Gretzky uses a stick with a very shallow lie. Most players use a lie between five and seven; Gretzky has gone as low as a four. He also uses a very short stick, perhaps the shortest for a man his height in the NHL. Like Theo Fleury and Wendel Clark, who also prefer unusually short sticks, Gretzky believes it aids his puckhandling ability and his quickness getting off a shot. At the other end of the spectrum, Toronto defenseman Jason Smith and Colorado rearguard Sylvain Lefebvre both use sticks that are as much as six inches longer than the norm, to help them tip the puck off forwards' sticks and clear errant pucks from in front of the net.

The director of Global Team Sales for Bauer supplies 22 percent of the sticks in the NHL. The preferred lie, he says, generally relates to skating style — the more upright the skater, the higher the lie. Chelios, who skates as tall as Clint Eastwood in the saddle, needs a more upright lie, while Gretzky's lower lie suits his hunched-over style.

He says that some players move to a metal stick to get a better feel when they grip it. "You can have a smaller circumference in the handle of the stick but still maintain a high level of stiffness. The load off the stick is a little different than that of wood. But you have players like Chelios who prefer the natural feel of a wood stick, the spring that it has." Manufacturers are trying to emulate the smaller circumference of metal sticks in wood sticks by adding fiberglass and resins to the core of the shaft, making it lighter while retaining stiffness. Defensemen like MacInnis like a stiff shaft for the power it gives their shots. Players who work closer to the net sometimes like a whippier stick to allow them to get off quick shots.

Golf club technology is creeping into hockey as well. The "bubble shaft" popularized in golf is also used in balancing hockey sticks. Brett Hull, as mentioned, uses the Easton model with the bubble shaft. And the new compounds featuring aluminum, Kevlar, or titanium are creeping into stick shafts. These sticks have the advantage of using blades that fit into the shaft, allowing for easy replacement and considerable savings.

Athletic therapist Broadhurst of the Leafs has seen many players who went to metal sticks switching back. "They're saying that the composite sticks are great for performance things like shooting, but aren't made durable enough. They find the metal sticks are breaking easier. Basically hockey stick technology is ten years behind where golf is in terms of development and refining which elements work best. They'll catch up again, I think."

THE NAME CARDS ARE NEATLY ARRANGED on the long table at the Main Press Conference Salon in Nagano, Japan. From left to right, the cards read: Lou Lamoriello — Ron Wilson — Keith Tkaczuk — Brian Leetch — Chris Chelios. The reporters and technicians stir restlessly, anxious to get on with the press conference, speculating about the placement of the cards. Tkaczuk is in the middle — does that mean the bruising Coyotes center will captain Team USA here at the 1998 Olympics? How does Leetch, captain of the victorious World Cup team of 1996, feel about that? And what about Chelios? After being passed over in 1996, and with this as his final shot at an Olympics, will he be happy to see Tkaczuk with the captaincy? Suddenly a young Japanese man in the tell-tale gray jacket of the Olympic Organizing Committee takes the stage and hurriedly transposes two name cards. Now Chelios is in the middle with Tkaczuk off to the right. So Chelios is captain after all.

A murmur is still running through the assembled media types, many of whom anticipate a USA-Canada final for the gold medal, when the Americans spill onto the stage. Chelios casually assumes the middle seat, slinging his Team USA jacket over the back of his chair, sipping from the bottle of water placed before him and taking in the media people, many of whom he knows from the NHL. Working this room — as well as the Team USA dressing room — will be part of his job over the next ten days.

He's joined at the table by Leetch of the Rangers, Team USA coach
Ron Wilson (the victorious American coach at the 1996 World Cup, now
on loan from his job as coach of the Capitals), Tkaczuk of the Coytoes,
and the dour Lamoriello, general manager of the New Jersey Devils and
major domo of the U.S. team here in Japan. Already there are rumblings
of discontent about Lamoriello, a noted hard ass. Players say he forced Bill
Guerin to sign an inferior new contract with the Devils as a condition of
being selected to the Olympic squad, then traded him to Edmonton as
punishment for holding out. Smaller grievances about the pre-Olympic
meetings at the January all-star game in Vancouver also fester.

Behind the front-table guests sit Guerin, Mike Modano, Brett
Hull, and the other American players, garbed in their Team USA jeans
and turtlenecks. For most, it's the first time they've worn team uniforms since junior hockey, even if these uniforms are casual. They
slump into their chairs, sipping mineral water, plainly weary from the
12- or 14-hour plane and train voyage that has brought them to
Nagano. Already it's clear that the time difference between Japan and
eastern North America may be the toughest opposition the six NHL-
dominated teams, especially Canada and the United States, will face
in this short tournament.

Earlier in the day, Chelios and Leetch had been taken aside by
Lamoriello and Wilson as they got off the team bus; that's when Chelios
learned he was to be captain of this first group of NHL stars ever to
compete for the United States at an Olympic Games. "He's a great com-
petitor," Lamoriello tells the media. "He'll do anything to win. That's
something you don't teach. It's born within a player."

Then it's Chelios's turn to speak. With a good performance here, he
knows, he can help his team to win the one hockey prize not even Wayne
Gretzky can claim, Olympic gold. "I'm honored to be the captain," he
says. "This could" — he corrects himself — "this will be my last

Olympics, and that has something to do with how I feel as well." He recalls hearing Team USA winning Olympic gold at Lake Placid in 1980, while he himself was playing in Saskatchewan. He was the only American player on the Moose Jaw club, silently cheering as he watched his Canadian teammates suffer another Olympic disappointment. He also recalls the letdown of leaving the Sarajevo Olympics without a medal.

"I've never been on a team with so much talent before," he says after the formal press conference, glancing around at the other players doing one-on-one interviews. It's a powerful squad, all right: Hull, Chelios's old pal Roenick, Modano, and the powerful John LeClair to supply offense; Mike Richter, the hero of 1996, and John Vanbiesbrouck to tend goal; Leetch, the hulking Hatcher brothers, and Chelios' Chicago partner and friend Gary Suter to help out on defense.

Suter's presence in Nagano is the story du jour for Canadian reporters. Suter's crosscheck of Paul Kariya has knocked the Mighty Ducks star out of the Anaheim line-up and, as it turns out, out of the Olympics as well. The crosscheck — a blow to the face — is the sort of pointless violence that hockey indulges far too often (and the sort Chelios has been occasionally accused of exacting — though he has never caused such a serious injury). And Suter is a repeat offender, having seriously hurt Gretzky by checking him face-first into the boards during the 1991 Canada Cup; Gretzky ended up missing half a season with a bad back. For the Kariya hit, the NHL suspended Suter for just four games; with evidence now emerging that Kariya's head injury might be career threatening, the punishment looks lame in retrospect. Still, NHL vice-president Brian Burke — who assessed the suspension — refuses to increase the penalty, hinting vaguely at problems with the NHLPA and the American Civil Liberties Union.

Though Suter is under suspension by the NHL, he's allowed to participate in Nagano. NHL suspensions don't apply at the Olympics, and

Canadian journalists want to know why. Discombobulated NHL officials offer two responses. Burke says it would be unfeasible and unworkable to try to coordinate NHL punishments with the sometimes arcane workings of the International Ice Hockey Federation. Shortly thereafter, the perpetually chipper NHL commissioner, Gary Bettman, tells the press that such all-encompassing suspensions are a good idea that needs some study. Huh?

Chelios has no such ambivalence. "Gary Suter's a friend of mine, and he would never deliberately go out of his way to injure another player," he says indignantly. No one challenges the assertion, although one reporter does relay the news that Roenick is telling reporters across the room that the Suter incident will no doubt ratchet up the resentment between Canada and the United States when they meet in five days. "I won't comment on anything J.R. says," he says through gritted teeth.

Of more concern to Chelios is how his team will adapt to the larger ice surface. "I think it hurts the defensemen, because the goalies won't be able to handle the puck so much. It's got to help the Europeans," he says presciently. "They like to freewheel, set up their plays. They'll do a lot of forechecking, make the defense handle the puck a lot. It's going to be a disadvantage for Canada and the U.S. "

With that he takes a final sip of water and heads off to the Big Hat Arena, site of men's hockey, for a taste of that big ice. His father, Gus, has come to Japan, a solid, swarthy man in his sixties. He's staying in a nearby hotel, his omnipresent fishing cap along for good luck. And while Chris's wife, Tracee, and two of their children have also come to Japan, Chelios stays in the Olympic village while they stay in the swanky ski resort town of Karuizawa, two hours outside Nagano. This is not a foreign vacation; it's a business trip. He'll talk to the family after the medals have been handed out.

The Americans have just three days to prepare for their first game, three days to rediscover the magic that carried them to the 1996 World Cup. Chelios will be paired with Suter on the blue line. It's a good symbiosis; Suter knows the captain's habit of making forays into the offensive zone, and any vengeful Canadians who go after Suter will also have to deal with Chelios. Ron Wilson has said that the Americans will use the round-robin games at the start of the tournament as a warmup, a time to gel, but in this format time will prove tighter than anyone realizes.

Team USA's first game matches them against the defending gold medalists from Sweden, and though these early games only determine the quarterfinal pairings, rather than eliminating some teams, the Americans need a good start. After Sweden, they'll play Belarus, and then, to conclude the round robin, the Canadians. They certainly don't want to lose two of those three games and get stuck facing someone like Dominik Hasek and the Czech Republic in the sudden-death quarterfinals.

Canada and the United States are the media favorites, but hockey people know that Sweden has an equally good chance of winning the gold. Unlike the Czechs and the Finns, who scoured the NHL for anyone with the proper passport, Sweden has the depth to have left behind capable NHLers such as Frederic Modin, Peter Popovic, and Anders Eriksson. Led by the formidable Mats Sundin and Peter Forsberg on offense, anchored by the splendid Nicklas Lidstrom and Ulf Samuelsson on defense, they represent a nice balance between experience and youth. If goalie Tommy Salo — a notoriously streaky player — gets hot, the Swedes could conceivably repeat their triumph in Albertville in 1994, before NHLers were freed up to play at the Olympics. As Team Canada assistant coach Wayne Cashman points out, the Swedes and the other Europeans will be comfortable on the familiar-sized ice surface. This won't be a Canada Cup played in a bandbox surface suited to North Americans. The Swedes' considerable NHL experience also means that they won't be easily intimidated by the physical game of Chelios, LeClair, and Tkaczuk, a game Forsberg and Samuelsson can emulate should the occasion arise.

After a week of watching not-ready-for-prime-time teams such as Italy, France, and the home-town Japanese vying for qualifier spots, hockey fans at Big Hat are anxious to see the real thing. Despite its name, Big Hat is a beanie by NHL standards — only about 10,000 can squeeze in around the pampered IOC potentates, whose seats are the only ones in the stadium with backs. For this game, Big Hat is festooned with every conceivable variation on the Swedish and American flags. There are Vikings painted blue and gold, entire rows swathed in USA paraphernalia, and whole static sections of Japanese who don't quite know what to make of either group.

If it's great hockey they want, they get it from the opening face-off. In the first minute, Chelios rings a shot off the post behind Salo. With Old Glory waving in every corner of Big Hat, John LeClair and the American forwards overwhelm the Swedes, who get their only spark from Sundin, the Leafs captain, who neatly dekes Chelios with a gorgeous shift and shimmy, only to be stopped by Mike Richter. Then, 11 minutes into the game, Chelios traps a clearing attempt from the Swedish defense at the right point. He fires quickly through a screen set by Roenick. Salo doesn't sees the puck till it's too late. The low shot beats him on the short side, and the Americans seem on their way.

Late in the first, however, Forsberg rallies the Swedes with a play that justifies his ranking among the top half dozen players in the world. He carries the puck deep in the U.S. zone, heading behind the U.S. net with Kevin Hatcher in hot pursuit. Richter sees Forsberg disappear from view over his right shoulder and deftly slides to the left post to prevent Forsberg from completing the wraparound. When Forsberg sees Richter commit, he reverses his hand, flicking a quick back pass to a trailing Daniel Alfredsson. Ottawa's 1997 Calder Trophy winner, ten feet behind Forsberg, has a narrow but makeable shooting angle on Richter's vacated right side. Too late, Richter tries to move back. Forsberg circles the net in time to see Alfredsson pop home the Swedes' first goal. "No one on the bench expected Peter to make that pass," Tomas Sandstrom will say after the game. Clearly, neither did Richter.

The teams exchange goals, and the score stands at 2–2 by the middle of the second. Fans expecting the best of hockey are not disappointed by the crisp passing and swirling offensive schemes — in particular from the Swedes — or by the clean, heavy hitting on the big ice surface. First Calle Johansson of Sweden and then Mathieu Schneider of the United States lay punishing hits on opposing forwards. The players are pushing themselves to a new level, matching skill for skill in what many call the best game they've seen in years.

Forsberg breaks the tie at the end of the second period. After fighting off Schneider and then Modano behind the net, he slides the puck off a defender's skate to Alfredsson. Once again, the deft winger buries the puck behind Richter. It's 3–2 Sweden, and Forsberg's father, Kent, who coaches the Swedish team, allows himself a quiet smile at his son's wizardry.

The Americans storm Salo at the other end of the rink, but the Islanders goalie is on his game, robbing Hull with a blocker save with 12 minutes to play. It remains only for Sundin to undress the American defense with three minutes left, capping a great rush with a backhand shot high in the net behind Richter. The game ends with Chelios drawing a penalty for a gratuitous elbow to the head of Patrik Kjellberg as time expires. A message, but who for? The Swedes, or his own distracted teammates?

The 4–2 opening-game loss brings with it an inescapable sense that the Americans may be in dire trouble; confused and disjointed on the bigger surface, they expended too much energy early in the contest and were barely hanging on at game's end. Too often, they threw the puck into the center of the ice — coughing it up to the Swedes' defense — in an attempt to create an up-tempo style. Pushing the adrenalin higher has backfired, as Sweden coolly counter-attacked again and again while the U.S. forwards were caught up-ice.

The dismal impression is reinforced the next day in the Americans' game against Belarus, the soft touch in their division. Once again, Chelios opens the scoring for the Americans, but they can't put distance between themselves and the Belarussians, who have just three nondescript NHL players in their line-up. It takes late goals from Hull and Adam Deadmarsh to subdue the team whose green-and-orange uniforms make them look more like Beck Taxi cabs in Toronto than hockey players.

Chelios is on the ice for both opposition goals in the 5–2 win, and after the game he vents his frustration at the wayward course of the aspiring gold medalists. "The trailers following the play are killing us on this big ice surface. We're getting too much separation between our defense and forwards. We can't let them get into the slots, the forwards have to pick them up. Nobody talks about these guys, but they were good. They counter-attacked strong every time we made a mistake — four on one, they were gone like rockets. We can't be dumping the puck into the middle of the ice, they'll eat us up with the counter-attacks. We've got to keep it on the boards, play our game. Lucky we play Canada next — at least we know what kind of game to expect with them."

Before the Canada game, however, the American team takes a public relations hit and another blow to team morale. Chelios, Hull, and Roenick are among the American players spotted in a Nagano bar at 6 a.m. following the Belarus game. When reporters quiz U.S. coach Ron Wilson about the questionable training methods, he distractedly says, "Where do these stories come from? Just who is it that supposedly saw these players out so late anyhow?" From the scrum surrounding Wilson, hands pop up here and there, sheepish reporters themselves just returned from a late-night revel. Wilson suddenly appreciates the lawyer's cliché about never asking a question to which you don't know the answer.

Was the late-night session irresponsible behavior, or something more laudable? Team USA obviously had a few kinks to iron out after their first two games; unfortunately for the Americans, a small city jammed with reporters, Olympic and NHL officials, and star-struck fans is a tough place to let your hair down in private. A win over Canada will put out the media firestorm, Chelios knows, but Patrick Roy has a point to prove at these Olympics. Left off Canada's 1996 World Cup team, the veteran goalie wishes to make a statement concerning the identity of the world's best goalie. Dominik Hasek is being widely celebrated as that goaltender, and Roy wants to make his case.

He does so, eloquently, at the expense of the Americans. With the game scoreless late in the first period, the United States has a two-man advantage for almost two minutes. Chelios and his teammates repeatedly feed Hull, who has five open shots at Roy. Two hit the Colorado goaltender, three miss the net. Another flurry of shots — including two blasts from the point by Chelios — are neatly turned aside by Roy. Then Rob Zamuner steps out of the penalty box and converts a masterpiece of passing — Sakic to Gretzky to Zamuner — with Richter out of position. Thus buoyed, Canada adds two goals by Keith Primeau and one from Sakic to stretch the lead to 4–0 before Hull finally scores a late, meaningless goal in the third period to break Roy's shutout.

Roy has plainly savaged the Americans' confidence with his stalwart game, turning aside 30 shots. Making matters worse, Chelios forgets the ritual pre-game exchange of flags with Canada's captain Lindros, and Roenick adds to the bad-boy American image by skating off the ice without shaking hands with the Canadian players — an Olympic tradition. For the Americans, these Olympics are turning into an all-round public relations disaster.

Coach Wilson, however, prefers to see the Gatorade bottle half-full. After the game he emphasizes the many good chances his team generated and says that maybe Roy's reputation forced his shooters to be too fine, aiming for corners when a good, hard shot at the five hole might have done the job. "That sometimes happens with a great goalie like Patrick," says Wilson, struggling to remain upbeat. Between the lines, he's perhaps also saying that his goalie, Richter, is not having the same effect on opposing shooters. While occasionally spectacular, Richter has allowed too many borderline goals for such a high-caliber tournament.

By losing to Canada, the United States has indeed drawn the poison pill known as the Dominator in the quarterfinals. Hasek has been seemingly unbeatable, both in North America and here in Japan, and his baffling style — one reporter compared him to a juggler on roller skates — will be a formidable challenge. "I wouldn't say we're panicking," Chelios says carefully before the Czech game, "but now there's a sense of urgency."

Part of the challenge for the Americans — and the rest of the NHL stars here — is getting acclimatized in Nagano, establishing pre-game rituals, getting proper nutrition and sleep, arriving at the right time at the rink. The internal engines of NHL players are fuelled by these rituals, and each nation has sought to replicate them here in Japan. Because the team is housed together, five players to a unit, at the Olympic Village in Imasi, and bussed en masse to events and receptions, there's a certain control of preparation. But as Chelios's late-night beer-and-bull session illustrated, it's not total control.

"You have to remember that some of these guys were having trouble sleeping, adjusting to 14-, 15-, and 16-hour time differences," says Darren Pang, who knows the vagaries of NHL travel as a goalie and a broadcaster. "Their eating habits were all thrown off. It was a way for them to unwind a bit."

Back home, Chelios's own pre-game schedule of eating and sleeping has evolved. "When I was in Montreal, I'd go to the rink with Lafleur and have a hamburger or a hot dog three hours before a game. Now I'm more disciplined. The toughest part for me is an afternoon game; it's tough to eat spaghetti at eight in the morning. I like to eat around noon for a night game. Then I take a nap for an hour or two, although that doesn't matter so much. I just nap because my roommate on the road does. I never used to, but when you have a roommate, you can't watch TV or walk around so there's nothing else to do."

Pre-game nutrition is a crucial element to preparing athletes during the season or a big tournament, says Broadhurst, one of the physical therapists with Team Canada in Nagano. "We try to load them up on carbohydrates, give them fuel to compete. Bodies wear down during a season. We're simply trying to do maintenance on what the player built up during the summer. So we try to get them 3,000 to 5,000 calories a day.

"It's also important to get them to replace the lost energy after a game. Some of these guys will lose up to six pounds of water weight. They don't want to eat so soon after a game, but we try to help them rebuild their energy levels. Unfortunately, a lot of players get used to the large calorie intake during their careers and have real trouble keeping the weight off after they retire."

The Japanese cuisine — with its noodles and fish — was familiar and appetizing for many players and there was a great deal of western food in Nagano. Still, Team USA and the other clubs brought foods from home to help ease the transition. Clubs even brought familiar snack food (Oreo cookies, granola bars, potato chips) to help diminish the culture gap. Nothing, however, was going to ease the burden of having to defeat Hasek and the Czechs, then likely Russia, and then maybe Roy and Canada, if the Americans intended to leave Nagano with the gold.

Two important psychological factors weighed on the Americans as they prepared for Hasek and Jaromir Jagr. First, the Czech Republic was a confident team, having shut out Finland and routed Kazakhstan. (Their only loss had come when Russia scored twice in 30 seconds in the third for a 2–1 win.) Worse for the United States, the Czechs were suddenly a team with a cause, thanks to Ulf Samuelsson's passport. The Swedes had completed their half of the round robin at 2–1, and in the quarterfinals were slated to meet Finland. Russia had won the right to face lowly Belarus, the boys in the taxi suits, by going unbeaten in their three games. Then a Swedish journalist discovered that Samuelsson had taken out U.S. citizenship to make it easier to travel with his NHL club. Under Swedish law, that meant he had revoked his Swedish citizenship.

Sweden had used an ineligible player to win its two games. The rules of the IIHF are unequivocal: Samuelsson must be suspended and Sweden's wins defaulted. This cheered the Czechs, because it meant they, not the Russians, would draw Belarus, while the Russians suddenly inherited a peck of trouble in Sweden. Naturally the Russians were incensed: their reward for coming first was a meeting with the defending gold medalists? Even Wayne Gretzky was miffed that Samuelsson had given up two weeks' holidays to play for patriotism, only to have the whole episode screwed up by a bunch of bureaucrats. "He's a Swede, everybody knows he's a Swede, and he should be allowed to finish the tournament playing for Sweden as far as I'm concerned," said Gretzky, urging Gary Bettman, Bob Goodenow, and the entire NHL corps to back Samuelsson.

At this point, president Rene Fasel and the other good burghers of IIHF decided to ignore their own rules and do some creative thinking. They declared Samuelsson out of the tournament, but the Swedes' two wins were upheld. They told Gretzky they appreciated his contribution, but would he please stick to playing hockey. And they told the Czechs to get ready for the Americans, like it or lump it. Czech coach Ivan Hlinka decided to lump it, filing an appeal with the independent arbitration board less than 24 hours before the quarterfinals. Arguments were made, TV programmers were vexed, while journalists were amused by the mess. After much head scratching, the arbitrators decided that Russia shouldn't be punished for something Sweden had done, the Czechs would still have to face the Americans, and could we now get on with the tournament, please? The Czechs felt that everyone from the IOC to the IIHF to the NHL was out to get them; Chelios and the Americans thus inherited a buzz saw in their quarterfinal sudden-death game.

The Czechs began their march to destiny playing moody, indifferent hockey, needing sensational stops by Hasek to keep them in the game. The Americans threw wave after wave at the Buffalo netminder. He absorbed a point-blank blast from Hull off the shoulder; he outguessed the Americans on a two on one, sliding across to stuff Suter's goal-mouth conversion of Adam Deadmarsh's pass with his pads; he robbed Pat Lafontaine in close not once but twice.

The Americans finally dented the Czechs' seemingly impregnable defense late in the first, when Modano converted a lovely feed from Amonte, beating Hasek with a chip shot in the only place he is said to be vulnerable: up high. The period ended 1–0 U.S., and with Jaromir Jagr limping off after a crunching check, many felt it was only a matter of time before Hasek gave way and the Americans filled the net.

Between periods, while the Americans composed themselves and talked strategy, Vladimir Ruzicka stood up in the Czech dressing room to deliver a brief sermon. Dom was killing himself for us, Ruzicka pointed out to his mates. Sure we don't have the NHL stars the other teams do, but we can't go out the way we did at the World Cup (the

Czechs didn't even qualify for the final round in 1996). We're still in this game, and if we play like a team, with Dom performing his magic, we can win it!

With that, the Czechs were reborn, a turnabout that stunned the Americans, the Olympic hockey tournament, and the many reporters who'd never known Ruzicka to raise his voice except to tell a coach he wasn't backchecking and that was final. With Hasek continuing his inspired play in the second — batting, blocking, and swiping away 14 shots — Jagr took over the game at the other end. First he set up Ruzicka for the tying goal with a clever pass and then, just 58 seconds later, he put the Czechs ahead for good, snapping a quick shot through Suter that fooled Richter on the stick side. Rucinsky then put the Czechs ahead 3–1 with three and half minutes left in the second period. Outside the rink, in the TV trucks, CBS executives were passing around the cyanide. This was a ratings Armageddon in the making.

If Chelios and the Americans were discouraged, they didn't show it in the third, as the Czechs fell into a defensive shell around Hasek. For 20 minutes, the U.S. shooters tried faking him, drilling him, running him over. At one point, LeClair crashed through the crease, his stick smacking Hasek square in the face; the collision left Hasek temporarily dazed on his knees, his goal stick lying 20 feet away. He bounced back up. On another chance, Chelios, who has one of the hardest shots in the NHL, unloaded with all he had from the top of the circle. His shot ripped off the shoulder of the 160-pound goalie, knocking him down like a ten pin. The puck stayed out, and Hasek bounced right back up. When Derian Hatcher was left with a clear lane to the net he put all his 225 pounds into a drive, but Hasek flicked out an arm to deflect the puck away.

In all, the Americans directed 15 shots at Hasek in the third period, 39 on the game. Ron Wilson estimated they'd out-chanced the Czechs

25–11. But the final score read Czech Republic 4, USA 1. The nightmare scenario for the Americans had come true. They had met the Dominator and been dominated. The vaunted U.S. team, on whom CBS had placed high hopes for large audiences back home, ended up with just one lousy win, no medals, and a sixth-place finish to chew on till Salt Lake City in 2002.

After the game, hair slick from the shower, somewhat dazed, Chelios tried to make sense of the experience as he sat glumly in the Main Press Centre, surrounded by reporters. It was hard to figure. Sure, the ice surface was larger than back home, but a team with eight non-NHL players, a team no one had included among the favorites, was headed to the semifinals while the greatest team of American players ever assembled was headed home. "We tried like Ron said to use the preliminary games to build up for these games. Maybe we should've gotten going sooner. We knew we could end up facing Dominik, and still… it's our own fault.

"We need to change our attitude in America," Chelios continued. "When the Canadians lost to us at the World Cup, it was like we stole something from them. It's their game and we stole it from them, that's the way they feel. We have to get that way. Fans in America are good fans, they'll cheer for you if you put out the effort. But the Canadian guys know that the fans up there won't accept losing. I know, I've seen it…."

So who're you rooting for now, Chelios was asked. From most players you'd get a political answer. Not Chelios. "I've got lots of friends on Canada. I'm going to be rooting for Canada to take it. I'd like to see them win."

With that, the despondent captain walked off into the cold night air of Nagano to meet his family. Was it just a reporter's imagination, or was he walking with a barely detectable limp?

THERE WOULD BE NO RESCUE from this taxing season when Chelios returned to the States. When the NHL schedule resumed, the Blackhawks won just eight of their final 26 games. The Edmonton Oilers and San Jose Sharks vaulted past Chicago to capture playoff spots; the Hawks missed the post-season for the first time since Chelios's arrival — for the first time since 1969, in fact — and coach Hartsburg paid the price with his job. He refrained from publicly musing about where he might have finished with Belfour, Roenick, Joe Murphy, and Nicholls in the line-up.

Chelios ended the year with only three goals — his lowest single-season mark ever — and 42 points. In all, it was his most disappointing season since coming to Chicago, perhaps his most disappointing ever. When the Norris Trophy finalists were announced, his name was nowhere to be found. Rob Blake, Nicklas Lidstrom, and Chris Pronger were the finalists, with Blake picking up the award. It was a concrete reminder for Chelios and MacInnis and Bourque that a new generation of defensemen has risen to prominence, that their own best days are now behind them.

What made the Hawks career from awful to promising and back to awful again in the course of a single season? Hockey teams are inspired by coaches and motivators, but they are propelled by the collective will of the team members. Establishing this collective will and guiding it to a positive result is often what good teams do to transform themselves into championship teams. "Put a group of males together," writes sociologist Lionel Tiger in his book *Men in Groups*, "and once some dominance order is established, the group will either split into competing coalition units or seek some exterior object for collective 'masterful' action."

The masterful action usually implies some shared risk or responsibility among the members and enhances their sense of collective destiny. In an extreme example, Japanese kamikaze pilots were sent off in threes on their grim missions in World War Two, strapped into their seats, each equipped with a pistol to shoot any member of the crew who had second thoughts about incinerating himself for the Emperor. Less dramatically, the bonding group may be fans of a sports team who travel to games with their favorite club, carousing and occasionally brawling in support of their heroes. It may be friends who like to hunt or golf together, fellow employees, or, in the case of Chelios and his teammates, members of a highly paid trade association. What they share is a common interest and an assumed acceptance of the group's goals. How to achieve those goals and share the risks on the way is sometimes a mystery. Such mysteries help explain why even the single-mindedness of Chris Chelios was unable to push the Blackhawks to a higher level.

No other captain in the NHL nurtures the traditional sense of team — the boys' club concept — more than Chelios. He's as old-fashioned as the 20-year-old shoulder pads he's worn since junior hockey. Friends and former teammates describe his loyalty to team as absolute. He talks fondly of arriving early at the rink to cultivate the atmosphere of team, a habit he picked up when playing with the Guy Lafleur-led Canadiens. In Chicago, he says, "I used to get there early, but just looking at Steve Larmer, how miserable he was all the time, I quit going early. Now I stay late. I just love hanging out by the rink."

The negative press surrounding Team USA in Nagano and how it was handled within the team epitomize Chelios's style of leadership. The late-night bonding session over beers with Hull and others reflects his encouragement of the fraternal nature of team sports described by Lionel Tiger. Tossing back beers and talking till dawn hardly qualifies as news in hockey, of course, unless someone drives home on the wrong side of the highway. The Leaf teams of the 1960s that won four Stanley Cups regularly adjourned to George's Spaghetti House in Toronto to commiserate about their dictatorial coach Punch Imlach and share a few laughs. Ken Dryden noted the therapeutic benefits of hoisting a few beers on the great Canadiens' teams of the 1970s. "When things go wrong, someone, usually Lapointe, decides it's time that we should have a meeting to make everything right again. It never takes long, a little beer and beer-talk and our problems disappear...."

The idea of teams spending hours and hours of leisure time together has become as quaint as pond hockey. Much of team travel has now been reduced to same-day flights and brief bus trips on the eastern seaboard. The influx of new cultures and languages has also driven a wedge into the notion that "the team that sins together, wins together." In hammering out problems over Kirin beer, Chelios hoped to restore that sense of shared experience. Unfortunately, the problems of the U.S. team on the ice and the culture gap in Japan conspired to make his effort seem irresponsible.

Perhaps even more damaging to the Americans was the media fire storm after members of his team caused several thousands dollars' damage to their rooms in the Olympic village after losing to the Czechs. The mischief was minor in comparison to other stunts pulled by players over the years, but the breaking of furniture and spraying of fire extinguishers provided a perfect opportunity for the media to portray highly paid athletes as insensitive and boorish. Adding to the image problem was the failure of the culprits to come forward. The U.S. Olympic Committee huffily announced that if the offending players were not revealed, all players on the U.S. team would be barred from the 2002 Olympics. The media joined in, demanding to know the names of the players who had "insulted" their Japanese hosts.

It would have been easy for Chelios, as captain, to expose the responsible parties and clear himself. Anyone who's ever played with him knows it's the last thing he'd ever do. Team loyalty prevented him. For weeks the pressure mounted on him and his teammates to come clean and offer up the guilty. Instead, Chelios sent a cheque for the damages to the Nagano organizers, along with a letter of apology on behalf of the team. No fingers were pointed, no names mentioned. The USOC was not placated, nor were the Japanese organizers, and the media criticized the effort as insufficient.

No matter. Chelios had proven himself loyal to the one concept he places above all others — the team. And when the summer workouts become too taxing, the injuries too slow to heal, the new season too hard to get motivated for, he'll make the decision about his future with the team in mind. The code that took Chris Chelios to the pinnacle of the game is the code that will dictate when to leave it behind.

Glen Sather
MASTER
BUILDER

Before I built a wall I'd ask to know
What I was walling in or walling out,
And to whom I was like to give offense.

ROBERT FROST, "MENDING WALL"

THEY SAY IT'S A TRUE STORY, and even if it isn't, it's too good not to tell. Pugnacious junior Link Gaetz of Spokane showed up at the 1988 amateur draft sporting two black eyes. To everyone in attendance at the Montreal Forum that day, the burly defenseman looked the essence of hockey toughness — to everyone except Glen Sather, that is. Asked to appraise the young prospect, the Edmonton Oilers president, general manager, and, at the time, coach — took one look at the battered Gaetz and said, "I'll take the guy who gave him the black eyes."

Shrewd, swift, sardonic — the anecdote sums up Glen Sather. For more than 20 years now, his knack of seeing beyond the obvious, of assessing talent, of trading shrewdly, of thinking creatively, and of motivating players, has earned him a reputation as one of the most astute hockey men the NHL has seen. Challenging the conventional wisdom while building an Edmonton juggernaut in the 1980s may turn out to be his enduring legacy, but his more recent feat of putting together competitive Oilers teams year after year in trying circumstances is, to some hockey people, even more impressive. "He's a tough cookie, but unquestionably one of the shrewdest GMs and coaches ever," says Tom Reich, the diminutive Pittsburgh-based agent. "He's as hard as the bark on an old tree. The only chance to do business with him is to earn his respect. Otherwise you have no chance. What he's done fielding an up-and-coming team in a small market like Edmonton is his best work. He deserves to be in the Hall of Fame." His secret, says another agent, is his ability to canvass a variety of people around hockey. "He'll know what a GM is saying to people around him, whether a player's taking heat from management, probably what the guy had for breakfast. He finds things out before anyone else."

June 21, 1997. Another summer, another draft. Sather surveys the scene inside a stifling Pittsburgh Arena. This is the house Mario Lemieux made famous after being selected first overall by the Penguins in 1984, and Sather is hoping against hope that he can steal the next Lemieux with the Oilers' first pick, fourteenth overall. It's a long shot, he knows, but then great players have dropped this far in the draft before — the Oilers, for example, plucked both Mark Messier and Glenn Anderson deeper in the 1979 draft. Lately, though, Sather's luck with first-round picks hasn't been great. Of the Oilers' first rounders going back to 1982, only Ryan Smith and Jason Arnott still skate with the team in 1997.

As always, Sather is dressed casually but impeccably. With his Armani glasses, Hugo Boss jacket, and Gucci loafers, he — not Don Cherry — is hockey's sartorial man. There is a feel of the poker player about him, the gambler with cards up his sleeve as he stands next to the boards, watching the controlled chaos of draft day. "On the Islanders," recalls Pat Flatley, "we didn't like him, because he won all the time, and he carried winning very well. He had a bit of a swagger. But that's good, that's leadership."

From the Edmonton table just inside the blue line, Sather studies the row upon row of young hockey talent, agents, parents, hangers-on, girlfriends. "You know the biggest change in hockey?" he says. "There's 300 kids here, 600 parents, and 900 hangers-on. They've all got entourages. In the old days, you might have a half dozen guys show up for the draft. That's the biggest change." The trademark deadpan look and the faint flicker that crosses his lips suggest that Sather does not consider this progress.

To his right sits the great defenseman Bobby Orr, now an agent. It's tough to tell what excites Orr's clients more: the prospect of an NHL career or having the illustrious Orr as their agent and pal. At the moment, 18-year-old Joe Thornton is being celebrated as the first draft pick overall this year, chosen by Orr's old club, the Boston Bruins. He's a 6-foot-4 center with a shock of curly blond hair that makes him look like Huck Finn. All the scouts say he can't miss being a star, but as he watches Thornton do his "photo op," Sather knows that "can't miss" players sometimes do. "These guys think that because they've been drafted in the first round, they're a sure thing. None of these guys are a sure thing. A lot of them get better after they get traded once. It's a dose of reality."

To the novice, the entry draft is an exciting spectacle, a hotbed of rumor and newfound riches. Sather, however, knows the drill. With the weary air of a waiter who's been stiffed for a tip once too often, he can see the heartbreaks and disappointments that lie ahead for his young team and his financially strapped owner, and for many of these eager young players and their families. Sather waves to agent Mike Gillis seated nearby with his charges. "The most important thing I ask a kid in the interviews," he says, "is 'Who's your agent?' Some agents' goal isn't to get this guy on a team that's built around his style, but to get the most money under any conditions. Some of these guys never develop past the junior draft. Look at how many guys are back in the draft again [because they didn't sign when they were first drafted], and you'll see that it's truer today than before."

The draft has been an annual ritual for the native of High River, Alberta, since he became the Oilers' coach in 1977. Edmonton was then a World Hockey Association team, and Sather a journeyman wise guy trying to extend his career in the town where he'd played junior. After one modest campaign as a player, Sather was given an ultimatum by Oilers general manager Bep Guidolin: Go behind the bench or go home. Sather was already a successful businessman with hockey schools in Alberta and British Columbia, and some well-chosen real estate holdings. Hockey was not his only option, and coaching a pro team is an invitation to heartbreak. But he hadn't won a Stanley Cup during his 10 NHL seasons with Boston, Pittsburgh, New York Rangers, St. Louis, Montreal, and Minnesota. The game was in his blood and ah, the chase! Sather took over as coach and in 1980 added the position of general manager. His name and the Oilers' have been synonymous ever since.

In nearly 20 years of drafting players, Sather has gone from an embarrassment of Oiler riches to a hockey thrift shop — courtesy of the changing economics of the NHL and the declining fortunes of his boss, Peter Pocklington, the team's principal owner, who has lost control of the team after 22 years. But if Sather has any regret, it's not for himself but for the game and for the business of hockey, which he sees skidding out of control. "The draft was supposed to put a ceiling on salaries, but now almost every kid in the first round is getting the maximum — in U.S. dollars. I mean, look at a kid like Boyd Deveraux [Sather's first pick in 1996]. He's a good, hard-working guy. The investment in him costs the team $950,000 a year. But he's not good enough yet to take a regular shift, and he's too good to play junior. You get teams like us that aren't at the top of the revenue stream that get good draft picks like Deveraux who aren't ready to play. You have to wait for these players, and it lessens your chances of going out and signing a free agent. Add in the exchange on U.S. dollars....It ties our hands."

Chicago's selection — the thirteenth of the draft — booms across the public address system. "Chicago selects Daniel Cleary of the Belleville Bulls of the Ontario Hockey League," announces Bob Murray, the new GM of the Blackhawks. The disheveled Cleary shambles up to the massive stage at the end of the arena floor, dons a Chicago sweater and cap, and grins till his face hurts while Murray pumps his hand for the cameras.

Then it's time for the Oilers to make their selection. Sather and his staff huddle in earnest conversation. Most of the difficult work has already been done. Sather, his scouting director Barry Fraser, and their staff have long since decided on priorities and ranked prospects. It should be as simple as selecting the top name still eligible on their predetermined list. But often, a team's draft table becomes a pitched battle of wills as opposing opinions are fervently aired. Sather listens carefully to others' views, but everyone at the Oilers' table knows the final call will be entirely his.

Sather may have justification to resent Pocklington for severely hampering his ability to wheel and deal as he once did, but he also knows he has a modicum of job security that most of his colleagues don't. In the hockey business that is priceless. It has allowed him to take risks on the talent unearthed by the rumpled, bespectacled Fraser and the Oilers' small army of contacts, scouts, and bird dogs. Over the years, they have drafted an entire wing of the Hockey Hall of Fame. Messier, Paul Coffey, Jari Kurri, Anderson, Kevin Lowe, Grant Fuhr — none was a consensus can't-miss prospect, but in Edmonton they all blossomed.

Sather hopes eventually to add Michel Riesen's name to that list. The skinny 18-year-old forward from Biel of the Swiss league is the

Oilers' first pick, Fraser announces to the crowd, fourteenth overall in the draft. Riesen is the first Swiss ever taken in the first round, which is about all the public knows about him. Fraser, however, has seen him play a couple of dozen times, and Sather has learned to trust his chief scout. On the four occasions Sather went to see Grant Fuhr play as a junior in Victoria back in 1981, the young goalie looked anything but NHL material. Sather asked Fraser, "Are you sure you know what you're talking about?" Fraser said, "This kid's going to the Hall of Fame some day." Sather trusted Fraser's evaluation, and Fuhr made them both look like geniuses. He will indeed join Wayne Gretzky and the other great Oilers in the Hall of Fame one day.

In the media area half an hour later, Sather fields questions. Someone asks whether there isn't a downside to drafting a European player first overall. What about the second-guessing if he doesn't adapt to North American life? "Hey, there's a downside to drafting a guy 6-foot-4, 220 pounds, like Jason Bonsignoire [Edmonton's top choice in 1994] who doesn't work out," replies Sather, who's seen Riesen play only once, at the World Junior Championships. "Riesen's a guy who can have a huge upside. Rather than some big guy who can't skate, this guy's got talent, ability, lots of things going for him. He's got skill like Jari Kurri, but Jari used to back off. This guy's not afraid to be physical."

Kurri was an especially astute heist by Sather and Fraser. While everyone acknowledged the skills of the young Finnish player, only the Oilers believed they could persuade him to bypass the Olympics and start his NHL career right away. Other teams figured to wait until the middle rounds of the 1980 draft to select such an apparently long-term prospect; Edmonton scooped him up in the third round, based on inside knowledge gleaned from Fraser's scouting. Kurri, of course, became Gretzky's favorite winger and, eventually, the greatest European scorer in NHL history.

Still, drafting 18-year-old players, as the NHL clubs are doing today, is capricious at best. For every Joe Thornton or Patrick Marleau (the second pick overall in 1997) who peaks at the right time and is chosen in the first round, there is a Jeff Farkas of Boston College. Farkas, a sure first-rounder a year earlier, was rated twenty-fifth by the NHL's Central Scouting Bureau heading into the 1997 draft but will sink to the third round and be taken by the Maple Leafs as the fifty-seventh selection. Some will consider even that a reach for an undersized finesse player. "Typical of the Leafs," sniffed one agent. "They still think they got a steal. The guy was dropping in the draft, because he's plateaued. The secret is to get a guy who's rising in the draft."

Like Michel Riesen, perhaps? "Let's see what happens when he plays against guys who are 20 or 25 pounds heavier," Sather says tersely. Much as he likes Riesen, he knows the odds: none of the 12 young men he selected for the Oilers in 1990 — from Scott Allison through Keijo Sailynoja to Sami Nuutinen — is still in the NHL. Indeed, the team that drafted most successfully that season, New Jersey, picked seven current NHLers, and on this day only three remain with the Devils. Jaromir Jagr was the best player taken that summer, and four teams passed on him. Eighteen clubs thought better of Keith Tkaczuk, nineteen of Martin Brodeur. Doug Weight, now the heart of Sather's team in Edmonton, heard 33 other names called before the New York Rangers selected him.

Why the high error rate? Most hockey people will tell you that projecting 18-year-old players is like projecting great wine in the vineyard — difficult at best. So many things can go wrong between the vine and the bottle. Teenage hockey players can so easily fall by the wayside and never find their way to the NHL. The Gretzkys and Orrs — teenagers who star immediately — are freaks who defy hockey's natural law.

Not that the NHL did such a wonderful job when it was assessing 20-year-olds. Scanning the lengthy list of players drafted who never made it to the big time has the same numbing effect as reading lists of war dead on a cenotaph. From first picks overall, such as Greg Joly (1975) and Doug Wickenheiser (1980), down to tenth-round selections, the churn has been incredible. Sometimes injuries halted promising careers, sometimes players were drafted into chaotic conditions, sometimes the pressure was too much. And for many clubs, drafting involved equal measures of guesswork and wishful thinking. While football and basketball moved to skill testing and audition workouts for scouts, hockey continued to rely only on the visible evidence of game conditions.

"I never spoke to one scout when I was a junior," recalls former Bruins star Rick Middleton, selected in the first round by New York in 1973. "I used to see them in the stands, but they never talked to us. I heard I might be drafted by someone, but we had no idea." When the young men didn't immediately meet the expectations of their teams, they were often discarded. Middleton himself was traded by the Rangers to Boston after just two seasons. Luckily for the Bruins, he blossomed into a great player in their uniform. The best intelligence of the day simply wasn't very intelligent.

Take the 1975 draft. Despite having won the Stanley Cup, the Philadelphia Flyers had obtained the first pick from Washington. They used it to draft Mel Bridgman, who went on to have a decent career as a checking center. While several players from that draft — Ralph Klassen, Rick Lapointe, Pierre Mondou, Tim Young, Bob Sauve — had respectable careers as role players, not one from either the first or second round ever became an all-star, won an NHL trophy, or led the league in any statistical category. Many — second pick Barry Dean, seventh pick Greg Vaydik, eighth choice Richard Mulhern, ninth selection Robin Sadler, thirteenth pick Gord Laxton — disappeared without a trace. Of the top 36 selections, 16 can be considered outright failures, 14 had borderline careers, and 6 were average players. None developed into star material. While it may be the worst draft ever, those results were not that extraordinary.

The 1977 draft was perhaps more typical. It had a few gems and yet Mike Bossy (15), one of the NHL's all-time greatest scorers, almost slid out of the first round. Barry Beck (2), Doug Wilson (6), Mark Napier (10), Ron Duguay (13), John Tonelli (33), and Rod Langway (36) all had good to excellent careers. But the first choice, Dale McCourt, flamed out after a fast start, and nearly half the players selected in the first two rounds — names like Jean Savard, Jeff Bandura, Bob Gladney, and Dave Parro — were never heard from again. In some cases injuries cut them down; others were victimized by inept organizations; many of them simply couldn't make the grade. And this all happened when NHL teams had two extra years to scout the talent.

If you don't think those two extra years are important, consider what happened to Guy Lafleur and Lanny McDonald. Both were highly touted — Lafleur was the top pick overall for Montreal in 1971, McDonald the Leafs' first choice (fourth overall) in 1973 — but both looked like flops until they were 23 years old. It took that long for maturity and confidence to knit with their considerable talents. Both went on to enjoy Hall of Fame careers. "I think too often expectations get out of hand," says Senators coach Jacques Martin. "When you look at a player 21 or 22 years old, I like to compare him with a 21- or 22-year-old in university with no responsibility. The young hockey player with the big salary, it's not his fault he's making that kind of money. He's just beginning. He won't get into your plan until he's 25 or 26."

Their teams were willing to give Lafleur and McDonald three years to develop; today they would need five years to reach 23 and their maturity as men and players. As Sather points out, no one gets five years to prove himself anymore, especially if he signs a multimillion-dollar deal, like Alexandre Daigle in Ottawa (since traded to the Flyers) or Thornton with the Bruins. "You can't afford it. You don't know whether he'll turn it around, and so you get pushed into an early deal."

When the NHL was forced to draft 18-year-olds in 1979 under threat of anti-trust action in the United States (as if the draft itself was not already a breach of anti-trust laws), the task of projecting talent became even more difficult. And when the artificial ceiling on salaries maintained by Alan Eagleson's house union dissolved in the late 1980s, the cost of signing that embryonic talent pushed the stakes even higher. Did these new pressures encourage NHL clubs to become more serious and scientific about selecting talent? For many clubs, it would appear not.

Beyond the obvious half dozen prospects each year, the crash-and-burn quotient remained high as many teams scrimped on scouting, employing ex-heroes, cousins, and cronies to assess talent. Traveling in packs to see junior games, scouts tended to reinforce each other's views, which often led to unanimity of opinion. A dissenting opinion was a risky proposition for an employee with little job security — especially when it proved wrong. Better to point to the other positive opinions from rival scouts when your "hot prospect" turns cold.

"Before, you drafted on skill and waited to see if the kid could make the team," recalls Bruins assistant general manager Mike O'Connell. "Now all our scouts meet the individual. It's kind of intimidating for a kid, almost like a police interrogation. But it's something that's very important."

The New York Islanders were highly successful during this era primarily because their general manager, Bill Torrey, and his scouting staff were miles ahead of most of the opposition. (Torrey disciples such as Jimmy Devellano and Neil Smith became successful GMs elsewhere.) Other teams used up draft choices like so many tissues; the Islanders seemed never to miss with their top picks. Denis Potvin, Clark Gillies, Bryan Trottier, Billy Harris, Mike Bossy, John Tonelli, Brent and Duane Sutter, Lorne Henning, Tomas Jonsson, Dave Lewis, Kelly Hrudey — all were taken in the first two rounds between 1972 and 1980. Bob Nystrom and Ken Morrow, middle-round picks, were instrumental in the Islanders' four straight Stanley Cups from 1980 to 1983. Information from Torrey's pro scouts enabled him to make deals that brought in Butch Goring, Dave Langevin, and Bob Bourne, all valuable contributors to the Islanders dynasty.

No detail was too small. In 1973, Torrey traded for Potvin's brother Jean, not so much for his modest talent as his ability to help his younger brother Denis adapt to the NHL. "Had Torrey been General Custer at the Little Big Horn," said the younger Potvin years later, "not only would he have won the battle, he'd have traded for the two best Indians as well."

If the Isles were the zenith of NHL organizations, the Toronto Maple Leafs of this era were perhaps the nadir. Employing former Leaf players such as Dick Duff, Johnny Bower, and Floyd Smith as talent spotters, the Leafs under Harold Ballard managed the near-impossible task of drafting in the top ten virtually every year without improving their club. When they did hit on someone useful — such as Vincent Damphousse, Russ Courtnall, or Luke Richardson — they traded him before he hit his prime. Despite signing the first truly successful European player, Borje Salming, Toronto stuck close to home thereafter, shunning the many skilled Europeans who were transforming the game in favor of local talent.

Typical of their drafting, Toronto in 1977 used both their first-round picks on Marlboro juniors who played in the same building as the Leafs — all based on the recommendation of former Leaf captain George Armstrong, then the Marlies coach. In selecting John Anderson and Trevor Johansen — average players — the Leafs missed Bossy, John Tonelli, and Rod Langway. In 1989, with three first-round picks,

Toronto raided another nearby franchise — Belleville of the OHL — for all three players, hoping perhaps that having covered the field they were sure to come up with one winner. None of those picks (Scott Thornton, Rob Pearson, and Steve Bancroft) remained with the team for long, and only Thornton still holds down an NHL job.

Toronto was not the only franchise to draft foolishly, of course. The mighty Canadiens have squandered more first-round picks than any NHL team since the draft began. From the "twin towers" of Ray Martiniuk and Chuck Arnason in the early 1970s to Danny Geoffrion and Doug Wickenheiser in the early 1980s, to Alfie Turcotte, Jose Charbonneau, Eric Charron, Lindsay Vallis, and Brent Bilodeau in more recent times, the Habs have proven that playing in their storied uniform guarantees nothing. Unlike the Leafs, however, the Canadiens stockpiled choices, allowing for failure, and they did better in the middle to lower rounds of the draft. With eight Stanley Cups between 1971 and 1993, Montreal showed that the first round of the draft, while important, isn't the only route to winning.

To understand how important a good draft — particularly in the middle rounds — can be, look no farther than Detroit in 1989. Sensing the increasing importance of European players, the Red Wings hit a mother lode. Mike Sillinger and Bob Boughner, Detroit's first and second picks that year, are middling players, but Detroit scored big with Nicklas Lidstrom (3), Sergei Federov (4), and Vladimir Konstantinov (12). The next season the Wings picked up Viacheslav Kozlov with their second pick. Those draft choices built the foundation of Detroit's Cup-winning teams of the 1990s. Many other teams took a couple more years to realize what was happening in Europe. By then, many of the best prospects were gone to the Red Wings.

Once looked upon as an equitable means of distributing talent and a way of lowering signing bonuses, the draft has been an abject failure at both. No one knows this better than Sather, who paid for and developed stars in Edmonton only to lose them at the peak of their careers when salaries soared. At its best, the draft is an amusing media sideshow, grist for callers to talk shows, and a boon for the people who sell the callow players their first good suit. At its worst, it is a disincentive for competition, a blatant restraint of trade, and a textbook example of driving up demand (and salaries) by restricting the supply of talent. Which is to say there's not much merit left in drafting more than a single round of 18-year-olds each year. That would identify all the prospects ready to play above junior, while allowing the rest to develop at their own pace. Having so many undrafted players available would depress salaries, a boon for the financially taxed owners. The NBA is reducing its draft to one round for precisely this reason.

Those who support the draft argue that it prevents the rich teams from cornering all the top talent, controls costs, and helps weak teams by giving them first crack at the top prospects, thus ensuring competitive balance. Those who oppose it ask whether fans in Edmonton, Calgary, or Ottawa really believe their stars will not eventually end up with the Rangers, Flyers, or Red Wings. After today's draft, each NHL team can access only one-twenty-sixth — its protected share — of the world's available hockey talent to solve its personnel problems. Scarcity drives up price (witness, for example, Chris Gratton's $10-million signing bonus from Philadelphia after he had scored just 67 goals in four years with Tampa). Under the old system, weak teams had the same chance as anyone else of signing the next great star. After all, the Bruins were the worst NHL organization in the 1960s, before the draft was instituted, yet they somehow discovered and signed Bobby Orr. Finally, the draft allows teams to go cheap on scouting, rewards managerial ineptitude, and enshrines a lack of competitive balance.

From the player's point of view, being treated like a chattel tends to destroy loyalty to a team and promote a mercenary attitude. It also flies in the face of every concept of freedom held dear in North America. "I was a free agent when I negotiated every contract I had as a pro," recalls Ulf Nilsson, who played alongside Bobby Hull in Winnipeg in addition to serving a stint with the Rangers. "And I had more loyalty and desire to play for those teams as a result. I believe that everything wrong in pro hockey today starts with the draft."

Eliminating the draft would ensure the long-term financial viability of junior and European hockey by letting a team that develops the next Mario Lemieux or Teemu Selanne to get market value by selling that player's contract to the highest NHL bidder. It would lower the price of middle- and lower-ranked talent. It would reduce the pressure on juniors to be ready at age 18, allowing for longer development time and the refinement of hockey skills. And it would force the hacks and cronies out of the sport by rewarding people who really know how to scout talent, and how to manage and administer a pro sports franchise. People like Glen Sather.

IN HIS 1982 BOOK *The Game of Our Lives,* Peter Gzowski summed up Sather as well as anyone can in a paragraph. "Competition throbs through everything he does. On airplanes he plays liar's poker for the price of a head set; in restaurants he turns the negotiations over who will pay the bill into a complex game of guessing numbers, for which he holds the pencil and explains the rules. Minor matters of office administration he sometimes settles on the racquetball court. Even in casual conversation, he seeks the edge, keeping his partner off balance with a barrage of light-hearted insults and cackling with delight when he scores a point. Like most competitive men, he enjoys the contest almost as much as the victory. He prides himself on being scrupulous but tough."

Like all tough guys, Sather rarely inspires indifference. His trademark blond hair is tinged silver now, and he still sports a "dueling" scar on his lip, courtesy of teammate Johnny McKenzie's stick following through on a shot. When raised to anger or excitement, he flushes, hence the nickname "Tomato" — as in "Tomato Face" — a name Harry Sinden stuck on him during Sather's playing days. ("Slats" — the more common nickname — came from his teammates in Oklahoma City, a Bruins farm club.) Behind the wire-rimmed glasses the blue eyes still flash at the prospect of a deal, still bore through a foolish reporter. There is nothing quite so piercing in this world as the pregnant pauses Sather inserts in his delivery when dismissing a foe or a vapid TV interviewer.

Though he lives and breathes hockey, Sather's life is not circumscribed by a rink. He has made — and sometimes lost — plenty of money in real estate; he currently owns the Tatanga Ridge condo development in Banff, where he lives in the home once occupied by the man who designed the Banff Springs Hotel. Despite the financial demise of his boss Pocklington, he's financially comfortable, having pocketed an estimated $5 million from the sale of the Oilers in 1998. He's an outdoorsman, a hunter and angler who studies the wildlife near his home and on frequent fishing trips to the Arctic with the likes of ex-president George Bush. With his wife, he went to Kenya for a photographic shoot just days after the 1981 playoffs. He's also a legendary prankster. When he traded Jeff Norton to Tampa Bay for the unknown Drew Bannister, he introduced a visiting accountant as Bannister. The local media types bought the act hook, line, and sinker.

As a player, Sather was nothing special. He scored 80 goals in 658 regular season games, and one more in 72 playoff games. His true value is more accurately reflected in the 810 penalty minutes he picked up along the way. He was a grinder, a mucker, an agitator with a razor-sharp wit and a penchant for the good things in life. "He was always first class," recalls Bruins teammate Fred Stanfield. "Usually on some-one else's money." And he was a nasty bit of business come playoff time. "A tough, arrogant kid who really worked hard in practice and never gave an inch to anybody," recalls former Pittsburgh teammate Les Binkley. "He was clever as hell. He knew the game inside out."

His business savvy was evident all along. He made the Red Wings pay for his university education in the off-season as a condition of sign-ing with them. Before the days of fat contracts, he laid the groundwork for his future through careful investments and financial planning. Success at the bank and success on the ice were sometimes thought to be mutually incompatible in the recidivist climate of pro hockey, but after Guidolin hired him, Sather proved his managerial worth faster than you can say "Wayne Gretzky."

In 1978, when he first set eyes on the then-17-year-old flash from Brantford, Sather claims he mistook Gretzky for the stick boy with the Indianapolis Racers of the WHA. Then the game started. Gretzky went around one of the Oiler defensemen "like he was a lamp-post" to score. The skinny kid scored again 39 seconds later, and Sather knew he had to have him. "I ask myself where my coaching career would be if I'd been wrong about Gretzky," he recalled years later. "But I was sure I was right. He had that sparkle in his eyes where others have glass."

When Indianapolis ran into financial problems, Gretzky's services were purchased from the Racers by Edmonton owner Pocklington; despite vigorous protests from other clubs, the Oilers then protected Gretzky when they joined the NHL. In this fashion the Great One escaped being subjected to the NHL draft, and Sather made an instant reputation in this hockey version of white-collar crime. Nurtured by the Oilers, Gretzky, of course, became the greatest offensive player ever in the NHL, an intuitive scoring machine as hard to check as he was to stop. "Hitting Gretzky," marveled Sather, "is like trying hit confetti."

But Gretzky alone didn't guarantee a championship. As Flyers fans can attest these days, Stanley Cups are not won merely by big-name players. Sather knew he had a chance to build a dynasty around Gretzky, but who should play alongside the precocious young center? What style should the team employ? In retrospect, it seems natural, even inevitable, that Sather would have adopted the European game of passing, switching sides, and using attacking defensemen to complement Gretzky's genius. But in the late 1970s, NHL hockey was emerging from the Philadelphia Flyers' reign of terror. In this climate of "goon" warfare, the conventional wisdom said you had to grind and intimidate and fight to win. Sather's notion of playing fast and loose seemed risky indeed.

Some believe that Sather's love of the offensive arts goes back to his days as a role player on the Lafleur-led Canadiens' team of 1974 ("Those Montreal teams trapped, too," he points out). He himself dates his conversion to a trip he made to Finland and Sweden with the Oilers in 1978–79. Having been impressed in the WHA with the skills of Europeans such as Anders Hedberg and Ulf Nilsson, Sather had his suspicions confirmed watching peewees play in Turku, Finland. "It was the movement, the skills, the push of the puck that excited me," he remembers. "Those little kids had the right idea." He never forgot the dazzling attacks, the switching sides, the inclusion of the defense in the attack. When delivered of Gretzky, he simply loosed the whirlwind on the opposition. Europeans, and those who played like them, were welcomed in Edmonton. "I think [European players] like it here," Sather says, "because they know I enjoy watching them, that I appreciate their skills and won't stifle them."

Sather recalls how difficult it was in the early days to get Gretzky some open ice to work his magic. In every city, a star such as Darryl Sittler or Gil Perreault would be assigned to blanket him. Sather would have Gretzky come to the team bench through one door; then, when his shadow left the ice, hurry down to the other door and jump back on the ice. Sather needed players to draw attention away from Gretzky, players who were fast, and who could think with the imaginative Gretzky.

In the early days, Gretzky was scoring 50 or 55 goals a year with wingers such as Blair MacDonald and Dave Semenko. While both had career seasons playing with the Great One — MacDonald had 46 goals and 94 points beside Gretzky in 1979–80 — Sather knew his superstar was still not reaching his full potential. After experimenting with numerous other wingers, Sather settled on Kurri as the right winger. In his first game with Gretzky, Kurri scored three goals, and the two remained prolific linemates until Gretzky's trade to Los Angeles eight years later. On the left wing, Sather and John Muckler, the Oilers co-coach at the time, used a succession of hard-working players — Semenko, Raimo Summanen, Esa Tikkanen, Mike Krushelnyski — to dig in the corners and keep the opposition from taking liberties.

But even great offensive teams must be built from the net out, and Sather put his stamp on this position as well. Most coaches would have been content to stand pat with Andy Moog, the talented young goalie drafted by Sather in 1980 who starred in the Oilers' stunning upset of the Canadiens in the 1981 playoffs. Moog clearly had a long NHL career ahead. But he was not the virtuoso Sather wanted, the goalie who could be left alone while his defensemen zoomed up to join the attack. Sather used his first-round pick in 1981 on the 5-foot-9 Fuhr, mere weeks after Moog's triumph against Montreal. While the two goaltenders alternated for much of the next six seasons, it was the acrobatic Fuhr who played the meaningful playoff games. Moog eventually forced an end to the partnership, demanding a trade, despite having picked up three Stanley Cup rings in Edmonton.

The same year he drafted Moog, Sather found the architect of his gang attacks in the smooth-skating defenseman Paul Coffey. At the time, in 1980, Coffey was a shy young junior defenseman, hungry for even a taste of the NHL. "I'll never forget, Sather was wearing cowboy boots and staring me down," Coffey told journalist Jim Fischer. "Finally he said, 'I hear you're a hotshot junior. Do you think you can play for our team?' Meanwhile I'm thinking to myself, 'Geez, I don't know.' Before I could say anything, Sather says, 'Maybe if you're still around in the draft, we'll pick ya.'"

Sure enough, when the Capitals selected defenseman Darren Veitch just ahead of them in the first round, the Oilers took Coffey from the Kitchener Rangers. Under Sather's and Muckler's tutelage, he became the ideal rushing defenseman to key the fast-break offense for the great Oilers teams, a beautiful skater and passer who went on to become the top-scoring defenseman of all time. Veitch, meanwhile, played ten unspectacular seasons for three clubs without getting to a Stanley Cup semifinal.

Coffey's job was to lead the offense — and the power play — up ice, the booster rocket who launched the Gretzky payload into the opposing end. In his early days, however, Coffey seemed to lose his confidence playing alongside veteran Pat Price. Sather traded the voluble Price for Garry Lariviere, a less vocal defense partner and a better match for the shy Coffey. Kevin Lowe, from Lachute, Quebec, became the other stay-at-home bedrock defenseman. Charley Huddy, Steve Smith, and Randy Gregg filled supporting roles on the blue line.

Sather also understood that it wasn't enough to gather all the scoring on one line. Messier — who'd also been an underage player in the WHA — became the second-line center behind Gretzky. He and Glenn Anderson took to Sather's blitzing offence and formed the basis of such a potent second line that opponents couldn't afford to key on

Gretzky. A dominant physical presence and a free spirit, Messier had his first 50-goal season within three years of being drafted by Sather. He also possessed something Gretzky didn't: an intimidating mean streak that bought him space from checkers around the NHL. When Gretzky left Edmonton in 1988, Messier effortlessly moved into the role of team leader.

Sather, of course, had several undeniable advantages in implementing his scheme. First, he had the greatest offensive weapon ever to play the game. He was also fortunate not to have had a massive media pack breathing down his neck, ready to pounce on every mistake, as he would have had in Montreal or Toronto or New York. Many of the media people who did follow the team in Edmonton were so charmed by Sather that they tended to give him the benefit of the doubt. And he was sufficiently young and "with it" to relate to his youthful charges, like Messier, of whom he once observed, "Sometimes you'd see Mark on the ice and you'd think his mind was at Newport Beach watching the waves come in."

"Sather understood how to get the best from each player," recalls Mark Napier, who played on the 1985 Cup-winning team. "He knew that you didn't yell at Coffey in front of everybody, you had to take him aside." When Sather picked up provocateur supreme Ken Linseman, he put a clause in Linseman's contract that reduced Linseman's salary if he exceeded a set number of penalty minutes. "I was probably the first guy in NHL history with that kind of clause in my deal," laughs Linseman today. Linseman indeed went over his limit, but in the flush of winning the Stanley Cup in 1984, Sather let him keep his money.

That's not to say that Sather was a sensitive, touchy-feely, new-age guy. Messier remembers the day he went to the wrong airport in Edmonton for a team flight. He phoned Sather to say he'd be late. Sather said fine, he'd leave a ticket for Messier at the counter, but the team was going on ahead. Only when Messier arrived at the right airport did he discover that the ticket was for Wichita, Kansas, where the Oilers' Houston farm team was playing. The trip to purgatory lasted nine days.

"Slats didn't care what happened off the ice, that was your business," recalls Coffey. "But when you came to the rink at 10:30 in the morning, you had better be ready to practice. And when you came to the rink at night, you had better be ready to play. Slats made sure that everyone felt a part of the team, whether it was Wayne or a fourth liner. Our leaders and top players all worked hard. That made it contagious."

Coffey himself learned about Sather's implacable side when the two tangled in 1987. Coffey felt he wasn't getting the respect — or the money — he deserved after helping the team to three Stanley Cups in seven years. Many organizations might have caved in at the prospect of losing such a brilliant player, but Sather stood his ground, holding Coffey to his contract. The impasse became personal and affected the whole team; Coffey missed the first six weeks of the 1987–88 season and was finally dealt to Pittsburgh. The Penguins initially said they wouldn't renegotiate either, but after a week or so they gave Coffey a new deal. Seeing Coffey sit out, force a trade, and then get his money back — and more — galls Sather to this day. "We have nobody to blame but ourselves," he told journalist Jim Matheson. "So many poor business practices. And does spending the money guarantee you're going to win the Stanley Cup? Last time I looked, only one team wins."

As Coffey discovered, Sather does what needs doing, whether farming out a young prospect, firing a friend, or trading a player he's developed. In 1980, he tried to replace himself as coach with his old playing buddy Bryan "Bugsy" Watson. The experiment failed, and after just 18 games Sather was forced to sack him. He called it perhaps the toughest thing he'd ever have to do, though he probably qualified that remark the day he was forced to trade Gretzky to Los Angeles. Pocklington had been convinced that Gretzky was a depreciating asset — a car, not a star — and that he had to get value for his investment before it disappeared. Just months after Gretzky's wedding had been the social event of the century in Edmonton, Sather reluctantly sent the Great One to Los Angeles in exchange for several mediocre ones. Later he was obliged to trade the rest of his stars — Fuhr, Messier, Anderson, Lowe, Kurri — because of Pocklington's worsening financial situation. In the end, only Sather himself remained from the glory days.

"I don't enjoy trading a player," he says. "When I was coaching and managing it was probably a little tougher, because you have a personal relationship with them. But if you don't make a trade to help your team, then you're not doing your job to put the best product on the ice — and the best job to help the rest of the players do their job."

When the stalwarts of those great Oilers team moved on, Sather showed his smarts by patching the holes inventively. Some of these trades have achieved mythic proportions too. Typical of his larceny was a 1989 deal in which he turned the ashes of the controversial Gretzky trade into another Stanley Cup. Sather was stuck with the slick but uninspired Jimmy Carson, a product of the Gretzky deal. "You can have all the talent in the world, but if the pumper's not there, it doesn't matter" was how Sather summed up Carson's heart. He shipped Carson to his home town of Detroit in exchange for feisty youngsters Adam Graves and Joe Murphy, who quickly combined with Martin Gelinas (another player from the Gretzky deal) to form a potent Kid Line.

"We thought if we put them on the same line it would get rid of some peer pressure," Oilers coach John Muckler noted later. "We wouldn't have won the Stanley Cup without that line." (Carson played three seasons in Detroit without reaching the Stanley Cup semifinals before being traded again.)

If that trade was classic Sather, so is his reaction when congratulated for his dealing. "I don't pat myself on the goddamn back, say I'm so smart every good deal I make," he bristles. "Every day in this business is an adventure, a challenge. You can't sit back and think about those things. I think about what we have to do tomorrow."

All the more necessary now than ever before. Managing NHL teams has grown considerably more complicated since the days when a loyal hockey man — who might have been challenged by running a convenience store — was given free rein. Despite the increasing complexity of finances and of scouting half the globe, some owners still entrust their businesses to "hockey" people, not business people. A typical example was Baz Bastien, who performed the general manager duties in Pittsburgh from 1977 to 1983, a period in which the Pens twice missed the playoffs and never advanced past the first round. Bastien, a goalie, had lost an eye in a hockey accident. He went into management in Detroit before moving to Pittsburgh.

Greg Millen played goal for Bastien in Pittsburgh and remembers Bastien's trade coup. He snared minor-league winger Rod Schutt from Montreal for virtually nothing; problem was, Bastien thought he'd picked up all-star winger Steve Shutt. When Schutt arrived in Pittsburgh, Bastien gleefully told the dressing room of snickering players how tickled he was to have Steve Shutt join the Penguins. "They didn't spell their names the same," recalls Millen, "and for sure, they didn't play hockey the same."

Another Pittsburgh general manager, former goalie Tony Esposito, was only marginally more adept than Bastien. He got the managerial post, many believed, mainly through his friendship with Alan Eagleson. Esposito inherited Mario Lemieux, the greatest player available in the 1980s, but alienated the sensitive star by referring to French Canadians as "frogs" and running them down for their laziness. He employed his old Sault Ste. Marie buddy Gene Ubriaco as coach, another move that backfired when he too clashed with Lemieux. Esposito was cashiered in 1990 for Craig Patrick; under his more sophisticated guidance, the Penguins promptly won back-to-back Stanley Cups.

While Bastien and Esposito may be extreme cases, they were not exceptions. In Toronto in 1988, Ballard promoted 30-year-old Gord Stellick from office manager to general manager when he tired of Gerry MacNamara. Stellick lasted less than two years. Detroit ran through five general managers in 11 years, including former heroes Alex Delvecchio and Ted Lindsay, as well as Jimmy Skinner, who'd previously coached the team almost a quarter century earlier. In the 16 seasons between 1970 and 1985, the Vancouver Canucks went through six different GMs, all of them old-time hockey men such as Bud Poile, Phil Maloney, and Jake Milford.

In this climate, it is easy to see how the wily management types churned out by Sam Pollock in Montreal had such success. Pollock ran the Habs like a business, not a hobby or a toy for owners, and his disciples — Torrey with the Islanders; Cliff Fletcher in Atlanta, later Calgary, and finally Toronto; Scotty Bowman in Pittsburgh and then Detroit; and Sather himself in Edmonton — were, like Pollock, simply more astute than the competition. Between 1964 and 1993, either Pollock or one of the men he influenced won 24 of the 30 Stanley Cups as either GM or director of player personnel.

Even today teams flounder because they entrust their operations to products of the old-boy network, whether deserving or not. In Tampa Bay, Phil and Tony Esposito have created a hockey backwater with the Lightning, squandering top draft picks and getting fleeced in a series of trades. The Lightning finished a deserving last overall in 1997–98, but new owner Art Williams, a first-time NHL owner from Alabama, renewed the Phil and Tony show for another season.

The Espositos are a dying breed, however. In recent years, notes Chris Chelios, NHL teams have changed their attitude toward the people they entrust with the care and running of their teams. "The game is 100 percent better than it was ten years ago," he says. "But we've got to keep going. You think all the teams are level but they're not. The GM has to have an education now."

For much of the 1990s, agents and lawyers — most with university degrees and business experience — have been outwitting traditional hockey people — most with little or no post-secondary education and no business experience. They find loopholes in the collective bargaining agreement, exploit them for their clients, renegotiate contracts, force trades, and otherwise engineer the business of hockey, while old time hockey men spit and mutter, like farmers watching the first Model T.

Sather, who straddles the old and new management eras, watched it happen with Coffey, Messier, and other players who fled Edmonton. More recently, in 1997, he was unwilling to sign Jason Arnott for the $1.8 million that agent Don Meehan was asking for his client; Sather thought $1 million was the right price for a "good player with lots of talent." Meehan knew that Sather needed the talented Arnott to sell tickets and convince Edmonton fans of the team's commitment to building a winner. Arnott got his deal and then performed poorly for the Oilers. "Meehan put our backs to the wall," Sather shrugs. "He had leverage, he used it. But hey, all's fair in love and war."

According to one agent, the firing of Pat Quinn as GM in Vancouver in 1997 came about because the veteran executive failed to recognize how much the business had changed. A disillusioned GM Bob Pulford resigned in Chicago when the money carousel began spinning too fast for him. Around the league, owners were desperately searching for bright young executives who could combat the salary spiral. Some of the best they identified — Pierre Lacroix, Brian Burke, Bill Watters — were once agents themselves. (Agents switching "teams" is a trend NHLPA boss Bob Goodenow, whose members have prospered in this climate, wishes would cease.)

Frustrated owners and GMs insist that, while they are not allowed to collude on salaries, the agents and the players' union share information. "Drivel," replies Tom Reich, who represents both hockey and baseball players. "The concept of the NHLPA controlling the agents is bunk. Bob Goodenow has done fine work, that's all. As for the agents, some talk, some don't. And don't believe for a minute that there isn't dialogue between the owners."

Like every other GM, Sather is also battling a time clock on star players they cannot control. In hockey's new economics, there are deadlines that force a GM's options. Teams have a narrow window after drafting and signing a player until he reaches salary arbitration or free agency with compensation. Under arbitration, a player with five years of NHL service can demand to be paid at the level of comparable players. Regardless of a team's financial wherewithal, it must pay market value to players who win before an arbitrator.

There are now many forms of free agency available to players, although most involve more agency than freedom. Under free agency with compensation, other teams can sign a player under 31 whose contract has expired, though the original team retains the right to match the offer. If it doesn't match, the original team is entitled to five first-round draft picks as compensation. It was this form of free agency that forced Detroit to match Carolina's huge offer sheet — which included a $14-million signing bonus and a $12-million playoff bonus — to their unsigned star Sergei Federov in February of 1998. The Red Wings swallowed hard and matched the offer.

While the Hurricanes' signing of Federov made plenty of noise, teams have traditionally been reluctant to sign restricted free agents from richer clubs. Anaheim's Paul Kariya, arguably the best young player in the game, received no offers in the summer of 1997 when his contract was up. Other teams feared reprisals from the Disney Corporation — owners of the Mighty Ducks — when one of their own top players was available. Working in a small market, Sather especially hates this gambit. He feels that Edmonton pays for a player's development, then a rich team swoops in and buys the prime of that player's career at a price he can't match. Sather thus often unloads a player before he hits this threshold in an effort to get some value for the millions the Oilers have paid to train him.

The next big deadline looms when a player turns 31 and is granted free agency without compensation. Any player without a contract at this point can go to the highest bidder. His former team has no matching rights and gets no compensation from the team signing this free agent. In such fashion, the Oilers lost defenseman Luke Richardson to Philadelphia in the summer of 1997 and Curtis Joseph to the Maple Leafs in the summer of 1998. These bidding wars with rich teams are the kind that Sather dreads. But one gets the feeling that, like Lee Trevino playing a $500 nassau with $5 in his pocket, he'll figure a way to beat the odds.

Because the cost of acquiring talent through free agency has risen precipitously, most organizations now take scouting and development more seriously. The erudite Ken Dryden, who played for Pollock in Montreal, has been charged with the task of modernizing the Toronto organization. As he stood by the bleachers at the Civic Centre on draft day 1997, he talked in his thoughtful fashion about perhaps the biggest change in how teams assess a prospect, the need to understand the whole person, not just the athlete.

"Whatever player you draft here," Dryden explained, "you're drafting somebody who needs developing. And how well that player is going to do is how well you do your job — treating him with the right circumstances, trying to understand him as a player, trying to understand him as a person. You'd better do a good job in the American Hockey League, and you'd better do a good job working with the kids you've drafted in junior. Because while they're playing for somebody else, they're also developing for you."

On the other side of the floor, near the Washington table, the Capitals coach Ron Wilson echoed Dryden. "I like to find out what a kid's dreams are. What he thinks about his teammates. If he talks 'we' instead of 'I.' How important his family is. And above all, his relationship with the coaches. Anyone can say the right things, but you have to know whether he's being sincere. And to do that you have to get the kid to relax. I mean, you've got kids who are nervous and shy, from a town of fifty people, and suddenly they've got seven people throwing questions at them. That's a special knack that scouts have — the good ones. They get the kids to relax."

It's Grey Cup week in Edmonton, November 1997, and the Oilers are hosting Carolina. The previous spring, the spirited young Oilers shocked the hockey world by upsetting Dallas, the Western Conference's top team in the regular season. With Doug Weight, Ryan Smith, Jason Arnott, Mike Grier, and Boris Mironov playing inspired hockey in front of the magnificent goaltending of Joseph, the Oilers beat the Stars in overtime of game seven. A miraculous save by Joseph on Mike Modano — some call it the best ever in Oilers playoff competition — had forced the overtime. One of the enduring images of that playoff series was an ebullient Sather leaping for joy in his shirt sleeves in the Oilers box high above the steaming ice of Reunion Arena after Todd Marchant sped around a stumbling Stars defenseman to beat former Oiler Andy Moog with the deciding shot. Sather looked like a man with the winning ticket in the Irish Sweepstakes.

The Oilers' playoff luck ran out in the next series against the powerful Colorado Avalanche, but the spring's remarkable events had lent
sweet promise to the 1997–98 season. That promise has quickly soured;
as the Hurricanes visit the Coliseum, the Oilers' record stands at 5–9–4.
They have just completed a winless six-game road trip, punctuated by
a racial incident involving the Oilers fine young American forward
Grier. During a melee, Chris Simon of Washington hurled racial epi-
thets at Grier, who is black. While racial taunting is hardly new, Simon's
comments were heard clearly by spectators. The newly sensitive NHL
suspended Simon for ten games. Ironically, a North American Indian
thus became the only NHL player ever suspended for issuing a racial
taunt during a game.

Only the abject futility of Vancouver and Calgary has kept the
Oilers out of the cellar in the Pacific Division so far. Just three NHL
clubs have scored fewer goals than Edmonton; only three have allowed
more. Worse, the young players who seemed to have come of age in the
playoffs versus Dallas — Arnott, Smith, Rem Murray, Andrei
Kovalenko — have reverted to their prior form. Kovalenko has no goals
in 15 games, Smith just four in 18 games. But it is Arnott — the tall,
rangy center who burst upon the NHL with 33 goals in his rookie season — who qualifies as the biggest conundrum for Sather and his
coach, Ron Low. Seemingly a franchise player, Arnott has just three
goals in 18 games, and a discouraging minus 10 plus-minus. His dedica-
tion has been questioned, too: he was thrown out in the first period of
a game against Boston when his jersey came off in a fight. Under NHL
rules, players must button down their jerseys to avoid the spectacle of
bare-chested warriors doing their Xena routine. It's a mundane detail
for certain, but necessary to avoid expulsion. Arnott's excuse? "I forgot."

Sather has been through the hockey wars long enough to know that
seasons are not lost in November. There is still time for the Oilers to hit

their stride. The question is, will it be Arnott and the young lions who turn the team around or is it time for new blood? Most of the talk around Edmonton is of the impending sale of the team. Pocklington has lost control, and local interests are forming to save it from the fate of the Winnipeg Jets (now Phoenix Coyotes) and Quebec Nordiques (now Colorado). After marathon talks about relocating the franchise, Edmonton seems to have rallied to the Oilers once more. "We've had 97 and 98 percent capacity," jokes Sather in a time-worn gag. "I'd have used 99, but we're not using that number anymore."

High above the Coliseum ice surface in his private box, Sather watches the game with his longtime assistant, Bruce MacGregor. Before, them lie the game notes prepared by publicist Bill Tuele's department. This is not a wet bar that never closes. It's a narrow booth with room for three or four people to watch a hockey game. The walls are bare, the desk standard industrial issue — no corporate schmoozing here. From this elevated perch Sather sees a larger picture than the one he used to see from behind the bench; he can better sense the flow — or, in tonight's case, the lack of flow — of the game. He can also comment freely on the inadequacies of his players without being overheard.

Like any red-blooded male, Sather has a TV remote in one hand and an unlit Cohiba cigar between the fingers of his other hand. He simultaneously surfs two monitors while watching the game below. One monitor has the Oilers game, the other NHL action elsewhere. Tonight, the game between the Rangers and the Devils draws most of Sather's scrutiny during breaks in the Edmonton game.

"This is one of the biggest changes in hockey," he says, jabbing the remote. "With the satellites and video, you know so much more about teams you're about to play or players you might be looking at in trades. How they're playing, what the local announcers — the guys who see them all the time — are saying. There are no more surprises in the

NHL, or there shouldn't be." It's hard to know from Sather's deadpan whether he considers this a good thing. (It's also hard to know what he may be looking for in the Devils-Rangers game. In six weeks, however, he will complete a major deal with New Jersey.)

On this night, the idea is for Jason Arnott to keep his Oilers sweater on and compete the way he did last spring. Doug Weight, the Oilers captain, is one of those prime NHL players who always compete, the sort of player Sather wishes Arnott would be. The smooth American center gives Edmonton a 1–0 lead on the power play eleven and a half minutes into the game. Swift and confident, the Oilers look like a team that just needed some home cooking. They easily control Carolina's forwards and keep the pressure on goaltender Sean Burke. Then Oilers defenseman Drake Berehowsky is called for interference, and the game's tone suddenly changes. Oilers nemesis Gary Roberts ties the score on the power play, beating Joseph between the pads. Just 73 seconds later, the Oilers foolishly lose track of sniper Geoff Sanderson, who gives Carolina a 2–1 lead at intermission.

The second Carolina goal seems to deflate an already docile crowd, and Sather grows restless in his perch. He is adept at disguising his frustration in front of the media, but one can see it in his eyes, his body language. If shoulders could talk, Sather's would be saying, "I've got no money to compete for players, I've got some young guys who won't compete, and I can't see things improving in a hurry."

There has been talk in the media that the Oilers will have to adopt the dreaded "trap" to compete seriously in the NHL of the 1990s. The team's attacking style seems to play into the hands of teams like the Devils and the Red Wings, teams built to exploit turnovers. And there is heat on Sather to dump Ron Low, his coach and a former Oilers goaltender. You might as well ask him to renounce his citizenship and sell his family into slavery.

"There's a lot of uncertainty in offensive players these days," he reflects. "There's a lot of uncertainty for coaches. That leads to conservatism. I like to see freewheeling, one-on-one hockey. When you get the opponent dumping it in all the time, it takes the creativity away. We'll have the effect of this for ten years. With expansion, there will be even fewer skilled players and it'll go more to defense than ever — like basketball has done. I mean, it's easier to teach defense, teach the trap, but young players won't develop fully if that's all you want them to do."

The Oilers longtime play-by-play voice Rod Phillips sticks his head in. Sather shoots him a killer look: "Lighten up on the radio, will ya?" Phillips, who evidently knows this scenario, smiles and comments caustically on Carolina's two quick goals at the end of the period. The two men exchange more mock insults, and Phillips returns to his microphone down the catwalk. When Phillips leaves, there is the hint of a smile on Sather's face. The exchange, the banter, clearly pleases him.

The game, however, does not. Just 43 seconds into the second period, the mercurial young Finn Sami Kapanen converts a pass from Curtis Leschyshyn at the left point. The shot beats Joseph to the glove side, just inside the post. 3–1 Carolina. Two minutes later, a couple of hits in the Hurricanes' zone force a turnover, and suddenly the Oilers find life once more. Rem Murray gives the crowd some hope with a shot that beats Sean Burke to make it 3–2. Sather does not cheer; he sits back in his chair and quietly grunts under his breath. The reaction is more relief than happiness.

No sooner has Sather got his hopes up than Kapanen puts the game out of reach. Seventy-one seconds after Murray's goal, he takes a feed from Roberts and wires another one-timer past Joseph. 4–2. Then a turnover by Boris Mironov in the third period leads to a third straight goal for Kapanen, a natural hat trick. This time he shows his range, deking Joseph and sliding the puck between the goaltender's pads. 5–2 Carolina.

Kapanen is the sort of offensive player on whom Sather built his great teams, a fast skater, offensively creative, with a nose for the goal. He's the kind of winger who'd fill the net playing alongside Gretzky. Whether he will do so alongside Keith Primeau or Jeff O'Neill in Carolina is hard to assess. But seeing him burn the Oilers while Jason Arnott skates large, lazy circles around the Coliseum ice must be galling for Sather. In the second period, Arnott misses a good chance and is slow coming back on defense. In frustration, he slashes Steve Chiasson.

"It's the same team as in the playoffs last year," says Sather, watching Arnott skate to the penalty box. "They just have to learn to compete." He has less to say when the Hurricanes score on the ensuing power play. It's now 6–2, and Sather's body language again tells the tale. Whenever the Oilers are on the defensive, he crosses his arms on his chest, the TV remote clutched tight; when Edmonton springs to the attack, his hands go to his hips and some indistinct squirming urges the puck toward the goal line. When things are going well for the Oilers, there is a contented stream of vituperation and asides for MacGregor.

There are few witty remarks this night. The Oilers mount a comeback in the third that makes it 6–4, but that is as far as they get. Carolina, one of the NHL's worst road teams, skates out of Edmonton with two points. Sather gathers himself, clearly unhappy. His team is losing for all the wrong reasons, and there is pressure to do something about it. Increasingly these days, he's asked whether he plans to resume coaching, go back behind the bench himself. On nights like this he must feel like quitting, right?

"They'll have to drag me out first," he growls.

CARL BREWER, THE FORMER NHL DEFENSEMAN, says, only partly in jest, that there have been just three schools of coaching over the years in hockey. "There was the Anatoli Tarasov school in the Soviet Union," says the iconoclastic Brewer, who also coached and played in Europe. "There was the Father David Bauer school with the Canadian National Team in the 1960s. Then there's the 'try harder' school used by everyone else."

Brewer describes the third approach: trailing after one period 2–0, the coach tells his team, "You're better than these guys, try harder." Trailing after two, the coach yells at the players, "You assholes aren't trying hard enough!" After the game, the coach sums up the loss for the press: "We simply didn't try hard enough."

While glib, Brewer's assessment has more than a little truth to it. Jung once observed that "a man who has not passed through the inferno of his passions has never overcome them." NHL coaches who don't know Carl Jung from Howie Young have unconsciously concurred for decades. Hockey was a game of intensity, went the thinking, and desire would take you through the inferno of your passions to victory. You just had to "try harder." In *The Game*, Dryden described how the NHL had evolved into "an adrenaline game," a game of energy, of try harder. Dryden should know, having played for both Father Bauer's National Team in the 1960s and the Canadiens of the mid-1970s.

Father Bauer believed in the mind controlling the heart; the NHL believes in the heart overriding the mind. As the National Team coach knew, there is a vast difference between controlled intensity and "trying harder." It's the difference between the North American and the European approaches — between a sledgehammer and a screwdriver. Canadians have long believed that the critical difference between them and the world lies in their "heart," the unquenchable desire to win that allowed them to come back against the Soviet Union in 1972. Heart was something the Canadians had and the Soviets didn't. Period.

It has, therefore, long been the NHL coach's priority to make sure his team's heart is emotionally charged for the game. "I think a lot of people who haven't coached for a living can't really understand the behavior," explains former NHL coach Tom Watt. "But you can't always control that emotion. If you expect your players to play with emotion, you'd better expect to show that you're as emotionally involved — or more emotionally involved — as you expect them to be." Jacques Demers is more succinct. "The players expect you to be a little cuckoo," he says. "And really, you have to be cuckoo to coach in the NHL. We're not all there."

The coaches' solution to every tactical problem faced by NHL hockey for 75 years was to pour more fuel on the fire, use more heart. When ratcheting up the intensity level failed to stop Valeri Kharlamov from speeding around a mediocre defenseman, "try harder" meant break his ankle, slash him in retaliation, high stick him to the ice. And the ethos became legend: witness Bobby Clarke's knowing wink as he described smashing Kharlamov's ankle on orders from the Canadian coaches, or commentator Don Cherry's approving grunts on TV. The approach involved strength and intimidation and an almost fanatical need to win. "We wanted very much to win," remembers Ulf Nilsson, the skillful Swede who played with Bobby Hull in Winnipeg. "But the Canadian guys *had* to win. They'd literally kill you to win."

As expansion watered down talent ever more, average players trying hard to stay in the league used whatever methods they could get away with to keep the skill players restrained: holding, hooking, hacking, fighting. And coaches played not to lose, to keep it close, to reduce the second guessing. "Try harder" could make the sport graceful — think of Peter Mahovlich's brilliant solo goal in game two of the 1972 series as he skated through the entire Soviet team — or disgraceful — think of the upraised stick of Jean Paul Parise poised to come down in frustration on a referee's skull in game eight.

On the rare occasions that coaches like Glen Sather modified that approach and turned out something beautiful, they would quickly be yanked back by the teeming throng of mediocrity below them in the

NHL. Compelled by reason of job security to win at all costs and stifled by generations of precedent, most coaches operated out of a survival instinct. Fred Shero in Philadelphia learned how to bend the rules through intimidation; Jacques Lemaire in New Jersey learned how to create a stalemate with the defensive game. (The Devils employed the Lemaire style even in the minors so that replacement parts would not need reprogramming.)

The game plan is familiar. Slow down the stars through obstruction and stick work. Clog up the neutral zone with five players looking for turnovers. Hit the puck carrier so hard he can't see straight. Coaches want two points, not style points. The virtues of speed and stickhandling, the virtues that characterized Sather's championship teams in the 1980s, were largely neutralized in this fashion, often through the acquiescence of the referees.

Referees don't call an NHL game so much as interpret it. The idea is to keep it close, prevent one team from gaining an unfair advantage through penalty calls. "Let the players decide the game, not the refs" was the slogan. In the NHL's interpretive school of refereeing, penalties should be more or less evenly distributed. But coaches also understand the reality: Evening up the penalties means a team can exceed its quotient of fouls, comfortable in the knowledge that few referees are willing to unbalance a game through their penalty calls. The secret is knowing who those referees are. While no one says it aloud, every team in the NHL knows the style of each referee and governs itself accordingly.

Among today's referees, Paul Stewart will give the players leeway. Don Marouelli has a short fuse. Terry Gregson will call everything in the first period. Kerry Fraser, unlike some, will call a penalty against the home team late in the game. "He's the best guy to have on the road," says Chelios. "When he's getting booed, I think Kerry loves it." Almost all refs will give a veteran the benefit of the doubt over a rookie.

No team made better use of such assessments than the Flyers of the 1970s. By the time they won two Stanley Cups under Shero, their bully-boy, adrenalin-pumping version of "try harder" had corrupted the flow of the NHL game. "They defied you," remembers referee Andy Van Hellemond. "If you called two penalties in a row on them, somebody would run at somebody to see if you'd call three. They won a lot of games on intimidation."

When Harry Neale coached in Vancouver, he'd find out if an eastern-based referee such as Van Hellemond was taking the red-eye flight home after the game. If he was, Neale would know that not many penalties would be called that night. The referee had a plane to catch. That meant the players could get away with more.

Sather was certainly not above trying to catch a break from the referees for the young Gretzky. In the WHA days, the Oilers coach had Gretzky show his battered and bruised body to referee-in chief Bill Friday. The league subsequently instituted face-off interference rules to reduce the punishment inflicted on Gretzky. It worked the other way, too. When Gretzky's "diving" showed up Friday, the veteran referee sent a message back via Oilers captain Al Hamilton. Any more half gainers and Gretzky would receive a ten-minute misconduct. At the next face-off, Gretzky — head bowed, looking away from the referee — said quietly, "It won't happen again, Mr. Friday."

"As for the game itself, its decline is painfully obvious. Sportsmanship, skill and beauty have been sacrificed for profit. Professional hockey has abandoned the grace and style so natural in a skating-passing game because, as everyone knows, winning teams sell more tickets than losing teams, and if you cannot win the way you are supposed to, win any way you can." Those words were written in 1972, by Bruce Kidd and John Macfarlane in *The Death of Hockey*. It's an old refrain. What's new is the way each generation seems to have to learn the lesson for itself.

UNTIL FAIRLY RECENTLY, NHL coaches were usually journeymen who'd had limited success. Like Sather or Al Arbour or Don Cherry, they tended to be role players who'd studied the game from the bench or in the minors. Scotty Bowman was severely injured as a junior player and turned to coaching as a way of staying in the sport. Coaches were equal measures drill sergeant, prison warden, and travel agent. In the 1980s, Boston GM Harry Sinden was reminding his new coaches that the three main areas of a coach's responsibility were discipline, motivation, and conditioning. With few options outside hockey, they weren't about to risk their jobs by trying anything radical. Working alone, they operated mostly by instinct; cunning strategy was the stuff of movies.

The venerable Hall of Fame coach Lester Patrick offered the coach's credo back in the 1920s: "It's very simple. I look for the best players and let them lead." With few exceptions, coaches in the first 60 years of the NHL largely confined their strategy to dumping pucks on the ice at practice and letting their stars dictate the pace and direction of games. Prodigies such as Doug Harvey or Bobby Orr transformed the game through their innovations; coaches simply rode their coat-tails and kept the other players in line. True innovators such as Lloyd Percival were looked on as rubes and amateurs who had no grasp of the "deep" interior heart of the NHL. "You haven't played the game" was the put-down of choice for NHL traditionalists.

The difference between bad coaches and good coaches was thought to lie in motivation — Brewer's "try harder" school. Punch Imlach and Toe Blake, for instance, vied for over a decade to see who could coax more from his team using intimidation and humiliation (Blake won the contest, six Stanley Cups to Imlach's four between 1958 and 1968). "In the old days, you coached a lot by using fear," admits former Islanders' coach Al Arbour, who played for Imlach.

The story of Jack Adams wandering through the Red Wings dressing room with train tickets to minor-league Omaha stuffed in his vest has become the stuff of legend — it worked efficiently at keeping players from questioning leadership. Players were expected to play in sickness or in health — and to keep quiet about it. "When I was a player," recalls Sather, "the coach might say two words to you in a month."

Strategy was a topic for the college boys. The most successful coaches of this era offered an authoritarian figure to players — stern but forgiving, like Arbour. "The coach has to be somebody you're afraid to let down," says Pat Flatley. "When you have a bad shift, you feel like you're freeloading. Al could come into a room, scream about a loss and never mention one name. But you knew he was talking about you. You were always thinking, 'I could have done more.'" Arbour's teams won four Stanley Cups, in large part to keep him happy.

Another weapon in the coach's arsenal is paranoia, used to promote team unity. Some coaches search long and hard in the newspapers for insulting quotes or slights that suit an "us against the world" agenda. The referees are against us, the league is against us, the media are against us, the gods are against us. In Edmonton's case, "finances are against us." While Sather chafes under financial restraint in the Alberta capital, he also sees the motivational aspects in taking on the big-budget teams with his economy model. "I sorta like that," he says. "I like the disadvantage."

Coaches have exercised their authority in more unorthodox ways as well. Fred Shero used to write letters to his players' wives at playoff time, telling them to keep their hands off their husbands so they could concentrate on the games. Players put up with all sorts of cruel treatment, for all sorts of reasons. Former Buffalo and Vancouver defenseman Mike Robitaille always felt that some people in his home town of Midland, Ontario, were jealously waiting for him to fail. As long as he could return home each summer wearing his NHL jacket, he proved them wrong. His NHL career gave him a positive identity among the folks he'd grown up with. To stay in the big time, however, he had to put up with heavy-handed treatment from coaches such as Punch Imlach and Phil Maloney. In Robitaille's case, this meant playing for Vancouver despite terrible neck and back pain in 1976. Maloney thought he was a hypochondriac; Robitaille actually had a broken neck. He later sued the Canucks for negligence and won.

Many believed that the establishment of the NHL Players' Association in 1967 would alter the power structure between players and coaches. But management continued its indolence and inefficiency when it became clear that executive director Eagleson was a paper tiger. He allowed the NHL incredible latitude in dealing with players he supposedly represented as union director. With no independent arbitration, the worst free-agency system in major pro sport, and a house union run in cahoots with team owners, players knew that, despite the union, they were just an impertinent word away from losing their careers.

Until the crystal ceiling imposed on players by Eagleson was finally shattered in 1991, most coaches continued to see their jobs as getting players to "try harder," not think smarter. Shero — who, ironically, later became an admirer of the European system — had an analogy. To illustrate the effort he wanted from his team he'd point to a plate of bacon and eggs. "The chicken, gentlemen, makes a contribution. The pig, however, makes a commitment."

It took an outsider to begin the push for smarter coaching. As the North American game grew more self-reverential in the 1950s and 1960s, a stagnant philosophy of play set in. Players skated in the grooves of those who'd come before them, up and down the wing, unwavering and unquestioning. Unchallenged from within, NHL coaches looked down at their rivals from Europe. That myth of superiority was first dented by the Olympic success of the USSR against Canada's national amateur team in 1954 and then crushed by the Soviets' unexpected brilliance in the 1972 series. Soviet hockey guru Anatoli Tarasov proved the NHL could no longer claim to be the only caretaker of the sport.

If the NHL was the Mother Church of hockey, Tarasov was its Martin Luther, a heretic crying in the wilderness. He felt the curators of the sport in North America had lost their way. "What I saw recently was the same thing I saw when we first toured Canada in 1957," he wrote in 1969. "Everything was practically identical. The contents of the training process is essentially unchanged. The teams have played an accustomed brand of hockey for many years, a brand that satisfies the clubs and the spectators, and therefore, the trainers have no intention of changing or modernizing their methods."

To Tarasov, hockey was speed and imagination on the attack, puck movement and coordination on defense. Getting your players to accept the message required psychology as well as emotion. Once the middle-aged coach decided that the best way to instill courage in players was to get them to dive head first into a swimming pool from a 16-foot diving board. He trooped his players to a pool and forced them up the ladder.

Team captain Boris Mayarov employed a little strategy. He asked Tarasov to demonstrate the proper technique. This prompted merriment, as no one expected the portly Tarasov to comply. Even though he had never made such a dive before and was frightened of heights, Tarasov waddled up the ladder, took his stance, and leapt into the water below. "Of course, he did a belly flop," Vladislav Tretiak recalled later. "But following him, everybody dived, and not only once. Even one player who couldn't swim climbed the tower." The only thing most NHL coaches ever dived into was a cold beer.

The psychiatrist Erich Fromm says that creative learning "requires the capacity to be puzzled. Children still have the capacity to be puzzled. But once they are through the process of learning, most people lose the capacity of wondering. They feel they ought to know every-thing, and hence it is a sign of ignorance to be surprised or puzzled by anything." Tarasov operated under no such inhibitions. He brought an unfettered approach to instilling those virtues. He took the sport into the lab and dissected it, creating athletes of remarkable fitness to over-come the physical advantages in the West. "Give us your conditions, your number of ice rinks and equipment and facilities and money, and we'll give you our conditions," Russian head coach Vladimir Yurzinov once suggested. "Then we'll see what level you'd be at with the training system you have."

Using limited resources, Tarasov created a team that was the equal of the greatest North American teams ever assembled. While his rivals approached hockey as a seasonal game, he made conditioning and skills improvement a 12-month process. The remarkable year-round fitness levels of Yzerman, Chelios, and almost all of today's NHL players is a direct tribute to his enduring influence.

His concept of offense also remains indelibly imprinted on the con-temporary style. Tarasov borrowed from soccer and tennis and track — even the theater of Stanislavsky — to create a system that could chal-lenge and beat the NHL. He brought the idea of lateral and criss-crossing patterns to the attack, and five-man units who all partic-ipated in the offense. He instilled the discipline to turn the other cheek when necessary. Indeed, the Soviets' rejection of fighting exposed how little tactical use fisticuffs actually were in the sport.

Tarasov's notions weren't infallible, of course. His teams' preoccu-pation with offense left them susceptible to determined forechecking in their own zones. They tended to be inflexible when the mood of a game changed. And the isolation of players from their families and friends for much of the year became untenable once Communism collapsed. But he had made North Americans question the NHL's omnipotence. No longer would fans have blind faith in NHL superiority the way they did before September 1972. By jolting the NHL from its torpor, he unlocked a curiosity and a wonder, a capacity for change, that had been missing in the heartland of the game.

Soviet victories against the WHA in 1974, at the 1979 Challenge Cup, and at the 1981 Canada Cup pushed the best and the brightest in North American hockey to respond. The analytical thoroughness of Scotty Bowman and his disciple Mike Keenan was inspired by the Soviet challenge. So was Sather's philosophy when he assembled and molded the creative Oilers teams of the mid-1980s that dominated the NHL and led Canada to successive wins in the 1987 and 1991 Canada Cups over those same teams from the USSR.

The axiom has always been that defense wins championships, offense wins compliments. Sather stood the conventional wisdom on its head. He dared you to out-score (or out-scrap) his team. His success now seems to have been as inevitable as Gretzky's assumption to greatness, but there were setbacks that would have caused less daring coaches to abandon the experiment. As his young club lurched forward and backward in the early 1980s, winning and losing by lopsided scores, critics sneered, "How could you blame their system when they had no system in the first place?" The Oilers' dramatic sweep of Montreal in 1981 was offset by their shocking 1982 loss to Los Angeles — a team that had finished 47 points behind them in the standings. "Weak-Kneed Wimps" the *Edmonton Sun* labeled them. There would be more back-and-forth swings before the Oilers finally nailed down their first Stanley Cup in 1984 against the Islanders.

It's easy to see why Sather's bombs-away approach rankled traditionalists. Most of the critics had never seen the free flow and the offensive participation of the defense corps in the NHL; like most mere mortals, they had trouble comprehending something new under the northern sun. And the system Sather devised was new. With Gretzky, Coffey, Kurri, and Messier leading the charge, NHL goals per game rose to heights never before seen. Within three years of the Oilers joining the NHL, the goals-per-game average jumped from 7.0 in 1977–78 to 8.3 in 1981–82. It never dipped below 7.3 the rest of the decade. Conversely, the best goals-against average rose from Ken Dryden's 2.05 in 1977–78 to Brian Hayward's 2.81 in 1986–87.

Sather appreciated the exceptional talents he'd been given, including a goalie in Fuhr who wasn't daunted by facing 35 to 40 shots while his teammates concentrated on storming the opposition end. In Sather's view, the system should express the players' abilities, not the other way around. If you had a Wayne Gretzky and played a dump-and-chase defensive system, you were not only cheating his potential, you were cheating your team's potential as well.

Bryan Trottier watched the Oilers dynasty overtake the one he'd captained with the Islanders. He credits Sather's latitude with Gretzky and Messier and the others for their success. "I think the best quality a coach can have is to allow his players to have some individualism," the Hall of Fame center remarked in 1993. "They [Gretzky and Messier] used to make sideways passes, drop passes, and I'd say to myself, 'That's creativity.' I'll bet they never practiced that. It was just guys doing their own thing."

"Glen allowed us to grow up without taking away any of our creativity on the ice," Messier agrees. "People talk about chemistry. Well, chemistry is good-quality people with talent working toward the same goals. Glen gathered the talent and let us play our way."

When Gretzky began setting up behind the opposition net, Sather let him. When he began hanging around the blue line instead of coming back on defense, Sather encouraged him, believing it intimidated the opposition. "Most people really don't like change," Sather once observed. "A lot of hockey is influenced by the older players who have graduated into becoming coaches, and they were trained by the guys they grew up with."

Unlike most of his apprehensive brethren in the NHL, Sather loved — and still loves — youth and skill and the inherent risk in giving free rein to players like Kurri and Messier and Anderson. Where others believe that trusting young skilled players is the fastest way to getting fired, Sather gives them every chance to succeed by employing them in situations in which they can succeed. In this fashion, he constructed an aggressive, attacking team that challenged the young players' creativity, not stifled it. Then, as now, other coaches usually demurred. "When I played," Sather says, "there were many players who had great skills, but really weren't able to use them, because they were confined in the way they had to play the game."

Later, when Gretzky was gone, Sather re-tooled his team, engineering a less flamboyant approach with Messier as his pole star, and won a fifth Cup with John Muckler behind the bench and Sather acting strictly as GM. That 1990 Cup was especially important to his reputation. "He looks and dresses like a star," Roy MacGregor and Ken Dryden wrote in their book *Home Game*. "He swaggers like a star. And being cocky and clever and witty enough, he has gathered to him an army of willing detractors, anxious for him to be exposed as over-rated and lucky, a Gretzky creation." That surprising win in 1990 removed the one-trick-pony stigma.

Scotty Bowman, the coach with the most wins in NHL history, had Sather as a player in Montreal. Part of Bowman's success has been his ability to adapt to modern players. He recognizes the conservative bent in fellow coaches, the instinct to trust only what has worked in the past. "There are some coaches who are obsessed with trying to get a certain player into a certain situation," Bowman told Dick Irvin for his book

Behind the Bench. "But you have to be ready to try things, to test the other coach."

The authors of a book called *Rekindling Commitment* describe four distinct types of employee. "Followers" are the good soldiers, running to keep their place on the treadmill. In hockey terms they are the second- and third-line players. "Drifters" are often burned-out followers; they tend to withdraw, stop trying, turn their brains off. The hockey equivalent would be a former high draft pick who now plays on the fourth line or sits in the press box. "Mavericks" are selfish and have their own agendas but are creative and energetic when it comes to their needs. The hockey equivalent might be the high-scoring winger who never backchecks — Brett Hull comes to mind. "Empowered Workers" strike an ideal balance between personal and team goals. The hockey equivalents might be Yzerman, Sakic, or, on Sather's team, Weight.

A successful coach and GM like Sather is adept at balancing the positive types and purging the negative ones. He seems always to be finding a complementary piece to add to the puzzle, the ingredient that makes an inert concoction explosive. "When Slats traded for me, I asked him what he wanted me to do," says Mark Napier. "He said, 'Keep on doing what you were doing in Montreal, that's all.' He knew what he needed from every spot on the roster, then went out and got a player to fit the spot."

The robust Marty McSorley, who joined the team after its first two Stanley Cups, had a similar experience. "They looked at players coming in to fill the holes and they accepted them," McSorley recalls. "Wayne always let everyone know how important they were to the organization, right to the twentieth guy. When I walked into the dressing room for the first time, he came over and congratulated me on coming to the team. It was like a family."

CREATING AND MAINTAINING PEACE AND HARMONY in a hockey family is a considerable challenge. Perhaps no one knows this better than Mike Keenan, the coach of Team Canada at the 1991 Canada Cup. How would he keep Gretzky happy without annoying Messier? Will Paul Coffey's ice time upset Eric Desjardins? Who kills penalties, who works the power play? Keenan gathered the stars of Canadian hockey before the chalk board and explained the math. How many minutes are there in a game, he asked. "Sixty." Wrong, said Keenan. On any given night, there were 360 minutes of ice time to be divided up — six positions times 60 minutes. Now, he said, goalie Bill Ranford gets 60 of those minutes right off the bat. That's 300 minutes left. Take away Gretzky's 30 minutes, Messier's 25, Coffey's 27 or so — down the list of players he went, the number of minutes left on the chalk board dwindling quickly. Star players were suddenly swallowing hard at the prospect of playing just three or four minutes a game.

Of course, Keenan added, penalties decrease the total. Ten penalty minutes leave only 350 minutes to divvy up. More groans. "What we're getting at here is that you're all stars on your own teams," he explained. "But here some of you will have to learn to accept six minutes, or eight minutes. You're now a role player, and that's the time a role player gets. You'll have a better appreciation for the role players on your own team."

As every great coach from Lester Patrick to Scotty Bowman will attest, the secret to coaching is getting your best players on the ice in crucial moments. That means assigning playing minutes in relative order of importance. What Keenan did in 1991 was to create an explicit pecking order, deciding which stars would take the important shifts and which wouldn't. He then dealt with the hurt feelings that ensued.

Such careful time management is what separates good from great coaches, Keenan believes. It shows a coach who is thinking ahead of the game, not with it. After a game, he says, Scotty Bowman can usually state within 15 seconds or so how much ice time each player logged (as can Keenan himself). In the days of two- or three-minute shifts and 14-man teams, those calculations were simple. Now, with 45-second shifts and 18 skaters to juggle, it is more like algebra.

"Watch how Keenan handles the players on his bench," says Tom Watt, who coached against him in university and the NHL. "When you're coaching, you know who knows what he's doing and who doesn't. You have to know your players, you have to know their skills. And you have to know what the opposing players can do in a certain situation. Keenan's a very good bench coach."

Being a good bench coach also means matching lines. Bowman is considered the greatest ever at getting the players he wants in favorable matchups with the opposition. On home ice, this is easier; the home team is allowed the final change. Bowman, Keenan, and Sather all made their mark on the road, finding ways to free their top shooters from the opponent's checking line. Sather would quick-shift a line, replacing it immediately after a face-off; he'd double-shift Gretzky so that the Great One's "shadow" was extended past his endurance. He'd match a defense pairing against a forward line. And he'd work on the referees, seeking to be allowed the latest possible substitution.

For the coach of a typical NHL team, of course, the assignment of minutes is less complex than what Keenan or Sather faced with Team Canada. Most NHL players may have been stars in minor hockey or in Europe, and the coach must be conscious of egos, but they have learned that their own team has definite stars and definite role players. Still, there's always conflict. "If the guy used to play regular shifts and then you don't play him regularly, you've got a problem," explains former Nordiques, Canadiens, and Rangers coach Michel Bergeron. "The same for tough guys. It's good to have them on the bench. But when they turn 29 or 30, they don't want to be on the bench anymore. Look at Tie Domi with Toronto. I think he's a fourth liner, but he wants to play third line or on the power play. It's hard for these guys."

Ice time is hard currency for NHL players. Agents plead for it, demand trades so their clients can get it, shake their heads when players squander it. Without ice time there are no goals or points. Without goals and points, there is no big contract. When Keenan or Bowman or Sather is deciding who will hop over the boards, he's also indirectly deciding who will make big money.

Until recently, an NHL coach answered only to upper management for these minutes, but that has changed. After the brief players' strike and the ouster of Eagleson and NHL president John Ziegler in 1991, coaches and GMs had to confront a new reality: players demanded to be consulted, comforted, and reassured about their ice time. With players sometimes earning ten or twenty times what the coach did, players increasingly dictated policy. Mark Messier's ouster of Roger Neilson in New York, Brett Hull's successful standoff with Keenan in St. Louis, and Dominik Hasek's power play against Ted Nolan in Buffalo are recent examples of players flexing muscle in the management of their teams.

As well, European players — who now predominate in the skill positions (check the top 25 scorers in 1997–98, or the list of finalists for individual awards) — brought different cultural demands to their jobs and, by extension, new demands on coaches. "In many ways, you have to see the European player differently," explains Dryden. "Somebody who comes over here at 23 or 24, he may not have a rookie's skills, but in many ways he has to be understood as a rookie and have a definite role created for him."

"It's a whole different package now," agrees Jacques Demers, who's been hired in five NHL cities, and fired in four. "Players know that you'll be gone in three years. It's not that they don't have any respect for the coach. The saying is 'Well, we're going to be here longer than the coach.' You can't ask them to win one for the Gipper. They're a whole lot more independent, there's a whole lot more money."

That money can mean trouble, too, as Sather learned when personal problems off the ice — including Grant Fuhr's notorious cocaine habit — derailed the Oilers express in the mid-80s. Sather believes that players, not clubs, must take responsibility for that part of their lives. "If they have personal problems we will work with them," he says. "But they must be mature enough to solve those problems for themselves. With what they're being paid and with their agents, they have to see that as professionals they must present themselves ready for work each day."

In Montreal, Pat Burns saw the evolution of this attitude first hand. Management wanted him to keep a close eye on what players did off the ice — as coaches had done in the old days — and Burns tried counting beers and making bed checks. By his own admission he became obsessed with spying on his players. Only when he realized that modern players responded better when treated like men did the bed checks stop. Like Sather, he understood that he had to define his role as employer, not drill sergeant or father confessor.

Sather was on the "cool" side of the scale as a coach, a player's coach. Burns, while he's had good relations with most of his players, is a "hot" coach, demanding and sometimes confrontational. For this reason, the two-time winner of the Jack Adams Trophy has had success coming into teams that were drifting or lacked passion. In both Toronto and Boston he brought purpose and structure to teams that had reached rock bottom. While Burns resents the other labels he's accumulated in his nine-year coaching career ("manipulative," "overbearing," "temperamental"), his methods have tended to lose their efficacy a few years into his tenure with each club. Sensing the overheated atmosphere he had created, both Montreal and Toronto replaced Burns with more conciliatory coaches. Still, Burns remains one of the top half dozen coaches in the game.

"There's two things you learn as a coach in this league," says Demers. "If you're an asshole, you're going to get fired. And if you're a players' coach, you're going to get fired. So just do your thing, be yourself, and do what you have to do to win." Demers adds that it's always inadvisable for an NHL coach to go to war with his best player.

What Sather has done brilliantly in Edmonton, and what all successful coaches must do, is foster a feeling of unity. "You've got to be able to sell your players that they should work together," says Ottawa coach Jacques Martin. "They have to understand that the individual players will benefit more from the team achieving than from an individual achieving."

For this reason, coaches must get to know — and program — their players early. "You've got four years to shape players," notes former Florida coach Doug MacLean, who's been hired to run the new Columbus expansion team. "When they're still playing junior, and in their first two years as a pro. That's when you and the coaches want to shape them into the players you want them to be. Their first two years in the league are so critical. Whether it's conditioning or attitude adjustment, they really need extra work."

When attitude adjustment was called for in the old days, Punch Imlach would peel the paint off the wall with a blistering harangue. Needless to say, that won't get it done in this day and age. "Remember there are 82 games in a season," says Watt. "That's 82 pre-games, 82 first intermissions, and 82 second intermissions. Plus overtimes. Harry Sinden had a great line. When he was coaching in Boston, he said he ran out of things to say by Christmas. You really have to pick your spots. There is a time to let it all hang out, but you can do it only so often."

Of course, Punch Imlach and Harry Sinden ran the show alone. Look behind the bench at an Oilers game in 1997–98 and there's a traffic jam. In addition to head coach Ron Low, trainer Ken Lowe, and equipment manager Barrie Stafford, assistant coaches Bob McCammon (former head coach of the Flyers and Canucks) and Ted Green (former Oilers head coach) were dispensing tips, changing the defense, and assisting with strategy. Imlach or Blake might have felt threatened by competing voices during a game or practice; their modern counterparts readily admit to needing help in handling all their duties.

When the Oilers ruled the NHL, they did so by sharing power among Sather and his assistants Muckler and Green. "Glen was the motivator, the bench coach," recalls Muckler, who worked as coach or co-coach from 1983 to 1991. "He didn't want any part of the practices, so I ran them. The longer I stayed there, the more authority I had at practice, and it worked out well."

"The combination of Muckler and Sather was the best I ever saw," recalls Napier. "Muck was the technician, the one who designed the strategy, while Slats handled motivation and getting the guys ready to play. One guy picked up where the other left off. It was great." Sather has never been above getting extra help as needed. For the first Cup win in 1984, he called in video wizard Roger Neilson to break down the tapes of New York Islander games and then followed Neilson's recommendation, employing an uncharacteristically conservative strategy to knock off the four-time champions.

Bowman, too, has been delegating responsibility to his assistants in Detroit. Dave Lewis and Barry Smith handle much of the day-to-day preparation while Bowman concentrates on other duties. Successful coaching in the NHL now requires a team approach. "You have to realize as a coach that you can't be a good communicator, you can't be a strong technician and you also can't lead the whole group of athletes to perfection," says Demers. "We acknowledge that there are some weaknesses we have; we just have to make the most of our strengths and go on." Typically, the head coach will deal with discipline, behind-the-bench strategy, the media, and liaison with team management. One assistant may be delegated to break down tape and plot strategy while the other conducts practice and does the on-ice teaching.

The ranks of assistants are constantly occupied by former head coaches waiting for a second chance — or in Roger Neilson's case, before he was hired by Philadelphia in 1998, a seventh chance. Penguins coach Kevin Constantine served a term as an assistant to Pierre Page in Calgary in 1997–98 after being fired by San Jose. "I certainly learned a lot being an assistant, watching a head coach and saying I was in the same boat a year ago," he recalled soon after being named Pittsburgh's coach. "I think of it as being a laundry detergent — you want to be new and improved compared to the first time around."

Bowman has found ways to be new and improved through 30 years and five head-coaching positions. When Mario Lemieux and other Pittsburgh players told him his coaching style had to change if he wanted to keep control of the Penguins, Bowman adjusted. "It was different ten years ago," says Red Wings defenseman Slava Fetisov. "But he's changed and stayed with the pace of the game and the times. That's why he's the greatest coach ever." Most coaches, however, lose touch or lose interest. In hockey parlance, their act wears thin and then wears out. It helps, notes Sather, that Bowman has moved around a bit. Players have a natural tendency to tune you out if you stay too long. Though Sather himself loved coaching even more than he loves being the GM, he also knew his days were numbered behind the bench with the Oilers. He made the move, replacing himself with Muckler, in 1989, before his act — and his enthusiasm — wore out.

The churn in coaches has been positively manic in the 1990s. At the conclusion of the 1997–98 season, Jacques Lemaire and Scotty Bowman had served the longest in their current jobs: five seasons. Lemaire promptly resigned in New Jersey while Bowman was told he should improve his health if he planned to continue subjecting himself to the stress of coaching. From January of 1997 to the end of the 1998 playoffs, 17 of the NHL clubs either fired their head coach or saw him resign. Besides Lemaire, who coached the Devils to the Stanley Cup in 1995, there was Ted Nolan in Buffalo, the coach of the year in 1996–97; MacLean, the 1995–96 runner-up for coach of the year, who took the Panthers to the finals; Terry Murray, who'd coached the Flyers to first or second place in the conference the previous three years; his successor, Wayne Cashman, who had the team in first in the Atlantic Division when he was gassed; and Ron Wilson, who'd won the World Cup with Team USA in the fall of 1996, but was fired in Anaheim. Wilson replaced the fired Jim Schoenfeld in Washington while Schoenfeld took Don Hay's job in Phoenix. Pierre Page quit twice in that period — once in Calgary, then in Anaheim.

"If you look at the guys who've been let go recently, the average person shakes his head and says 'Why?'," observes Constantine, who was fired in San Jose 18 months after leading the Sharks to their best playoff showing ever. "For Terry Murray to go the finals and not have a job, for Ron Wilson to go as far as he did and not have a job, for Scotty Bowman to be deciding whether to continue with the Stanley Cup champions — you shake your head and say, 'Where's the logic?'"

The logic is in the bank. With so much invested in player salaries — the average NHL salary has crept over $1 million — owners want to see instant results. Bosses who pay lip service to the notion of gradually building a core of talent often change their tune when faced with the cancellation of a few hundred season tickets. In the rush to cobble together an instant winner or to placate the ticket buyers, coaches get trampled underfoot.

Sather believes that disproportional salary scales are also partly to blame. "The mandate from owners isn't clear," he explains. "You can't sign players for $4 or $5 million, then pay others so much less. It creates internal problems. Coaches need to be more secure to try things out. Right now, as I say, they're just playing for ties."

And for plenty of guaranteed money. Bowman was the best-paid coach in the NHL in 1997–98 at $970,000, with New Jersey's Lemaire ($850,000), Boston's Burns ($750,000), Colorado's Marc Crawford ($750,000), and Los Angeles's Larry Robinson ($700,000) rounding out the Top Five. Down in the low-rent district sit Buffalo's Lindy Ruff ($275,000), Montreal's Alain Vigneault ($254,000), and Ottawa's Jacques Martin ($236,000).

Perhaps as compelling are the dollars being paid to coaches not to coach. Colin Campbell, fired at the Olympic break by the Rangers, collected the rest of his $750,000 salary and had another $800,000 due the next season when he opted to take a job with the NHL. Terry Crisp didn't make it to Christmas with Tampa but he still pocketed $515,000 for the season with another $550,000 due in 1998–99. When Doug MacLean took the bullet early in the campaign in Florida, he was due $425,000 for that season and $425,000 for the next. Makes you understand why Roger Neilson was hanging around for yet another head-coaching gig at the age of 60.

THE $400,000 SALARY earned in 1997–98 by Ken Hitchcock in Dallas puts him in the bottom third of NHL coaches' salaries. The Stars are getting a bargain. If Sather was the most interesting and innovative NHL coach in the 1980s, Hitchcock may be his counterpart in the 1990s. During the six seasons Hitchcock coached the Kamloops Blazers of the Western Hockey League, his club finished first in the Western Division five times. He was voted the top coach in Canadian junior hockey in 1990, and his lifetime winning percentage in the WHL is the best in history.

As head coach of the Stars, the 47-year-old Hitchcock has made a name for himself since Stars GM Bob Gainey wisely removed himself from behind the bench. Hitchcock turned a talented but underachieving team into the Central Division champions in 1996–97. After his team's disappointing playoff loss to the Oilers that season, he kept his injury-riddled team atop the Western Conference standings throughout the 1997–98 season, finishing first overall in the NHL before bowing in the playoffs to the eventual Stanley Cup repeat champions, the Red Wings.

Like Sather in the 1980s, Hitchcock has looked at traditional coaching values and found fresh approaches. In his case, this has meant drawing heavily from the business and academic worlds. "Try harder" has become "trust each other." Mission statements have replaced improvisational planning. His fresh insights, and his willingness to challenge and adapt the conventional wisdom, make him a prototype coach for the 1990s.

Unlike Sather, Hitchcock has no razzmatazz, no charisma. Watching him hold court with the media, you might be watching the local alderman. Having shed considerable weight several years ago, he might now be described as plump and unassuming. He doesn't have the swagger of Colorado's Marc Crawford or the forbidding presence of Mike Keenan. There's none of the rapid-fire repartee of Jacques Demers or the stony silences of Jacques Lemaire. With his amiable smile and hockey talk, he looks more like the secretary-treasurer of the Sherwood Park Hockey Association. Which is fitting, considering he began his coaching career in that Edmonton suburb guiding a Triple A midget team.

Still, reporters know that Hitchcock is good copy. Ask a hockey question and you'll get a good hockey answer, rather than the usual clichés. He's equally comfortable discussing Civil War generals ("I like Lee, Sherman, Grant — they thought that war was tough, and you had to be tougher than that. You needed to address it that way. I really respect those guys") or business leaders ("I look at people who've come through corporate America to become CEOs, really started on the ground floor and worked their way up. I like the fact that they are not afraid to communicate down to the level of the mailman or roll up their sleeves in a board meeting. I try to study them").

When Hitchcock rolled up his coaching sleeves in early 1996, his club had a reputation as a talented team that never quite produced to the level of its talent. Since 1993, when the franchise was moved from Minnesota to Texas, the Stars had never advanced past the conference semifinal. They seemed to have all the parts: a big, versatile defense; some handy scorers; solid goaltending; a franchise player in Mike Modano. So what was the problem? Around the NHL, the usual answer was that the team would go only as far as Modano took them. And to that point, the 6-foot-3 native of Livonia, Michigan, hadn't taken them — or himself — anywhere special. After a peak 50-goal season in 1993–94, he had trailed off to the 35-goal plateau. Respectable, but nothing that would lead the Stars to the Stanley Cup.

"The job of a leader is to help people see reality," says NBA coaching legend Pat Riley. Hitchcock set about helping Modano see the player he was and the player he could be. Hitchcock's mission statement was to cut down on the team's goals against, and getting the rangy center to buy into his plan was critical if the rest of the team was to accept the message. At first, though, Hitchcock found the team — and Modano — resisting his message. The Stars misssed the playoffs, and Hitchcock realized he had to retool his strategy. "I needed to think of each guy individually, what motivated him, where he fit in. I spent a lot of time that summer trying to change the thought processes of everyone."

Starting with Modano. When the team dispersed after the 1995–96 season, Hitchcock approached Modano about becoming a more committed two-way player. "He wasn't really convinced that he wanted to make the changes we thought were needed," Hitchcock recalls. "It took a lot away from his game, that's what he thought. He said he needed time to think about it. So he took the summer, then said he'd give it a try. He didn't have really good point production early, but the team was winning. And he was out there at the start and end of every game. I think he really bought into what we were doing."

With just half a season as an NHL head coach behind him, Hitchcock was gambling by asking for a strong defensive commitment from a veteran team, especially from offensive specialists like Modano, Joe Nieuwendyk, and Pat Verbeek. "It's a tough thing to do. When you ask for a lot and they give it, and it doesn't work, it becomes a problem. What happened with us was that we asked a lot, they gave it, and we won early. That made it easier. Now I don't sell the program; our group of veteran leaders sell it themselves."

The Stars started strong and finished strong in the 1996–97 regular season, cruising to a ten-point win over Detroit in the Central Conference and almost knocking off Colorado, the defending Stanley Cup champs, for the Western Conference title. Then they hit the Edmonton speed bump in the playoffs. Inspired by Curtis Joseph's superb goaltending, Sather's carefully assembled group of speedy, hungry, upset-minded youngsters knocked the Stars out with that overtime victory in game seven. In the summer, Dallas picked up veteran goalie Ed Belfour and bolted out of the blocks again in the fall of 1997. By the time of the all-star break in January 1998, Dallas was comfortably atop the Western Conference; the Stars finished the season ranking among the top three NHL teams in both goals scored and goals allowed.

It's a mild surprise for a defense-first team to lead the NHL in scoring. Hitchcock traces the improvement partly to an innovation he made. It seems deceptively simple at first. Watch the Stars practice their rushes and offensive drills and you'll notice that he insists on the players continuing the two-on-one or five-on-five until a goal is scored. At first the players looked upon this as a castigation; after all, nearly every other coach blows the whistle and lets the players skate off to try the drill again. Not Hitchcock: "Let 'em play. Let the drill flow, let them figure it out themselves." He believes scoring in practice breeds confidence to score in games. The drill also promotes the idea of doing it till it works.

"You have to have confidence in the players," Hitchcock says. "I think too many of us try to micro-manage our teams. We try to correct and handle every problem, every detail. We don't let the players handle it. That's when the trust breaks down. A lot of football coaches manage too much, and they end up being stereotyped as a certain type of coach. That wears on people."

Encouraging players to learn themselves, rather than being instructed every few moments, allows coaches to set expectation levels higher as well. A study in *The Journal of Applied Psychology* described how expectations affect people. Army combat instructors were told that certain trainees among their recruits were gifted with superior leadership skills. After a 15-week course, the study concluded, the trainees from whom instructors had been told to expect better results had indeed scored higher on leadership and achievement than the rest of the group. Told that the superior students had in fact been randomly selected, the dumbfounded instructors refused to believe that these trainees were not gifted in the first place. Higher expectations produced higher results.

Conversely, believes Hitchcock, setting the expectation bar at the level of your average player doesn't work for a team. Neither does yelling "Try harder!" Hitchcock points out, "People think it's a sport where the coach provides the intensity level. That's completely wrong. The players provide the intensity level. Your job is to make them responsible and accountable to each other."

Hitchcock doesn't subscribe to the notion of a coach being "a little cuckoo" in the manner of Jacques Demers. "The other thing that's very difficult is not allowing yourself to get caught up in that emotion," he says. "Let the players provide the emotion. We've got to be the ones to right the ship, to smooth things out, and that's very difficult. But if you stay on an even keel, you can be pretty successful" — as Hitchcock is demonstrating these days, as Glen Sather demonstrated before him, and as Scotty Bowman has been demonstrating for almost three decades.

AFTER 30 YEARS of being situated on a windswept, isolated patch of the Canadian National Exhibition grounds in Toronto, the Hockey Hall of Fame was moved in 1996 to a former bank building in downtown Toronto. It's a beautiful edifice, the facade of the historic Yonge and Front streets branch of the Bank of Montreal grafted onto a modern office tower. The bank was said to be haunted by the ghost of a former employee who jumped to her death from the cupola when her lover — who was also her boss — turned out to be a cad.

More recently the building has been home to cads of a different kind. Alan Eagleson was inducted as a builder in 1989, at the height of his powers; the NHLPA boss was subsequently disgraced when he pleaded guilty to fraud and embezzlement involving the players' union, his personal clients, and international hockey. Eighteen of his fellow members vowed to resign if the Board of Governors allowed him to remain. The showdown threatened to wreck the Hall's credibility until, just five days before a scheduled vote on whether to purge him, Eagleson resigned.

Almost as controversial was the time Kings owner Bruce McNall talked then-NHL president Gil Stein into putting Stein's name up for election to the Hall in 1992. Stein's credentials were marginally better than those of Harold Ballard, who was convicted of stealing from Maple Leaf Gardens, or Bruce Norris, who ran the Detroit Red Wings into the ground for two decades. But the public saw it as an insider trying to force his way into the Hall under false pretenses. In the uproar that followed, Stein withdrew his name from consideration, and the Hall took a public-relations black eye.

Tonight, it's the annual Hall of Fame induction ceremony. To call this gathering a shining moment is to understate the voltage. Some of the greatest names in the sport, men whose illustrious accomplishments are described on the plaques mounted on the walls, occupy seats in the auditorium. Naturally, NHL commissioner Gary Bettman and other suits from the league also have prime seats. In the front row await this year's inductees. Mario Lemieux — flanked by his wife, parents, and agents Tom and Steve Reich — is seated near his former Pittsburgh teammate Bryan Trottier, captain of the Islanders dynasty in the 1980s. Trottier's family is arrayed around him. Glen Sather, in a tuxedo, sits across the aisle with his wife and sons. Tonight the inductees are Sather, Lemieux, Trottier, and two media people, Ken McKenzie of *The Hockey News* and longtime Flyers announcer Gene Hart.

The Hockey Hall of Fame is a capricious organization. While it requires that playing members be retired for three years before induction, it is making an exception in the case of Lemieux, who retired only the previous summer. Perhaps they feared Mario's 613 goals or six Art Ross Trophies or three Hart Trophies would evaporate, or that Lemieux might move to a distant planet. One would think they'd learn patience. The Hall had previously enshrined Guy Lafleur and Gordie Howe, only to have them emerge like Lazarus from retirement to resume their careers as honorary playing enshrinees.

Getting in while you're still active, Sather says with a smirk, "puts a lot of pressure on you to keep your nose clean so you can stay in there." He's making light of the Eagleson fiasco. And while the Hall of Fame was designed to honor the immortals of the business, its criteria for induction have sometimes made the institution more like the Hockey

Hall of the Well-Known. Where baseball has chosen to enshrine only the true legends of the game, hockey has had a more generous interpretation of greatness. This has allowed popular players such as Bob Pulford, Buddy O'Connor, Leo Boivin, Edgar Laprade, and George Armstrong to win places alongside immortals such as Howe, Hull, Richard, and Orr.

The 1991 election of Pulford, a journeyman player and later a powerful management figure in Chicago, particularly rankled those who felt that Eagleson had engineered the installation and that Paul Henderson was more deserving of a spot. Perhaps as a result of the controversy, the voters seem to have raised the bar for player inductees of late, permitting just one new member in some years.

There are no quibbles with Sather's nomination. The few people in hockey who do not like him personally certainly respect his credentials as a builder of the sport. Tonight, among the media people and his management colleagues and the players who've been on his teams, the Sather stories are flying fast and furious. Sather himself, surrounded by media hounds probing the latest financial woes of his Edmonton club, digresses into a tale about the time he was rooming with Bobby Rousseau in their days with the Rangers.

Seems Slats was bored one day and decided to go to work in their hotel room with Limburger cheese. The fun began when Rousseau got his first helping of the stinking Limburger on the handle of the hotel door. Attempting to wash his hands, Rousseau acquired a second coat of the pungent cheese from the taps. The third booby trap was the hand towel he reached for. And the pièce de résistance came when he lay his weary head on the pillow — Limburger hair mousse. The gathered entourage is still laughing when Oilers PR man Bill Tuele spirits his boss away; only after Sather has gone do they realize that their question about Edmonton's future went unanswered.

Sather is used to speaking to groups about everything but Glen Sather. "I don't feel comfortable with a bunch of people making a fuss over me. I'm more comfortable in the background. It's a humbling thing to be recognized, to receive the peer acceptance from all those great people who've been there before." This is a challenge for a man who enjoys challenges. All day he has wrestled with his script, adding and dropping names, dates, and anecdotes. He wants to sound like the Slats everyone knows, confident and cocky, but he knows that if he looks at his family.... He decides he won't thank them, but as he gets to his feet he changes his mind again. He'll thank them but he won't look their way.

"When Scotty Morrison told me that I'd been selected into the Hall of Fame in the Builder Category," Sather begins his speech, "I told him I thought he'd been mistaken, that I should have been in the players' category. Somehow he convinced me I was in the right spot."

He singles out Harry Sinden. "Harry used to help me in the minors, he used to call me Tomato Face. In fact he called me Tomato Face last night. The time I spent in the minor leagues was always remembered as a struggle to reach the top. While hell at times, it paid off with the realization that nothing is ever accomplished without sacrifice. There's no escalator to success, only stairs."

He pokes fun at himself: "After we won our first Stanley Cup in Edmonton, John Ziegler asked me what I was going to do. I asked him if he'd ever seen the movie *Saturday Night Fever*. In the movie John Travolta said he was going to strut. Well, that summer I strutted."

And he talks about love. "The survival of hockey teams in any community depends on the love of the fans, and ours have been and — I hope — will be a lasting affair. Speaking of long affairs, I need to stand here and say how lucky I am to be accompanied" — he makes the mistake of looking at his wife and the speech comes to a halt — pause for breath — a moment of self-composure — "accompanied on this journey by my wife, Ann. The strength and understanding that she's provided has helped greatly through these times with me. My two sons, Shannon and Justin, if there was a Hall of Fame for sons, you're already in it, and have been since the moment I laid eyes on you. It's not easy being the wife or son of somebody you read about in the newspaper on an ongoing basis. But Ann and Shannon and Justin have persevered."

And, as usual, a quip to end it: "To the Hall of Fame and the selection committee, I also express my gratitude. Especially since this is not being presented posthumously."

GLEN SATHER HAS REASON TO SMILE as he sits in the gold seats at Maple Leaf Gardens a couple of months later, watching his team practice. It's not just El Niño–inspired early spring that has him feeling frisky. He's been recognized once again at a reception for Oilers' corporate sponsors at the Hockey Hall of Fame, and he's about to be named to the Board of Governors of the Hall. Meanwhile, a consortium of 36 community leaders has met the deadline imposed by the Alberta Treasury Branches to match an offer for the Oilers from Houston Rockets owner Les Alexander. It looks as if — once again — the Oilers will be saved for Edmonton. Sather jokes that he might have to assign name tags to the members of the unwieldy consortium when they meet. He's less glib when he says he won't be taking advice from the new "experts." "The guys all have their own businesses to run," he says. Whether the team will have the cash flow to compete for free agents after robbing the piggy bank is another matter. Still, the option of staying or leaving Edmonton will be Sather's, and he'll receive a handsome sum to ease his pain at leaving Edmonton if it comes to that.

He's also smiling because it's looking like he's turned a sow's ear into a silk purse yet again. He started the year with one of the youngest teams in the NHL, a team built with speed and skill — and not much money. The new season began with great expectations. But after the loss to Carolina in Edmonton, with his young team reeling, the Oilers GM reached out for help. In a series of deals over three months he has added defenseman Roman Hamrlik from Tampa Bay, a talented 23-year-old Czech who'd got lost in the disaster wrought by Phil Esposito; unheralded Russian forward Valeri Zelepukhin, who'd been shackled in the New Jersey defensive system; Bill Guerin, the speedy American forward who'd been battered in a contract hassle with the Devils; and defenseman Janne Ninimaa, a Finnish prodigy who'd been sacrificed by Bobby Clarke in Philadelphia in Clarke's quest for a more physical defenseman. Sather has also resurrected veteran defensemen Frank Musil and Bobby Dollas as well as forward Tony Hrkac from Dallas via Europe.

What Sather has given up from his current roster in all these deals is Jason Arnott, whose woes have continued in New Jersey; Kelly McGillis, who was fighting for ice time at training camp; Jason Bonsignore and Steve Kelly, who are doing little to help Tampa Bay; Bryan Marchment, who's already been dispatched by the Lightning to San Jose; and some draft choices. Sather's only misstep may have been letting go of little Ray Whitney, who's having a fine season in Florida.

Colleagues in the league just shake their heads at his deal making. Most didn't know that the coveted Ninimaa was even available. Sather found out and he had the right price. "How does he do it?" asks a befuddled Ken Hitchcock. "It's robbery."

Since the Arnott trade, the Oilers have recovered from their early season swoon. Arnott's replacements, Guerin and Zelepukhin, are fitting in nicely (Guerin has 21 points in 20 games for Edmonton). "Jason was under a huge burden," says Sather, rolling an unlit stogie in his mouth. "The media was on his ass. The fans were on his ass. The coaches were on his ass. He was under a lot of pressure to perform after signing that big deal. We did him a favor trading him."

Hamrlik, meanwhile, is averaging close to a point a game on the Oilers' blue line. Oilers scout Gilles Leger had scouted him over the course of several weeks for Sather. "You know what kind of player he likes, a guy with skills, a guy with some vision," says Leger. "He asked me just one question about Hamrlik — 'Should we make the deal?' Then he pulled the trigger." The young defenseman now has an Olympic gold medal, thanks to the Czechs' unexpected victory in Nagano. "The Olympics reaffirmed his skills as a player," says Sather. "When we got him from Tampa, he was questioning whether he was the player he'd always thought he was. The success he's had with us has re-established that confidence. The Olympics was a further affirmation."

Adding to Sather's buoyant mood, the Oilers are now in possession of a playoff spot, having played winning hockey since losing to Carolina in November. "Leadership," he says with a nod toward the players on the ice. "That's the biggest change from earlier in the year. We drafted lots of young guys, waited a few years for them to develop so we could move them for the necessary ingredients to compete better."

When they figure out how to implant a cell phone in the human ear, Sather will be first in line. The constant ringing of his phone this day is a reminder of the impending NHL trade deadline, but he's always on the phone, deadline or not — in airports and coffee shops, while shaving in the morning or barbecuing for friends at night. His assistants guard the number fervently — "Glen doesn't want media guys calling him on this line" — but Sather is rarely less than cordial when you reach him at his portable office.

Today the "office" is in Toronto, where the Oilers have an important game with the Leafs. Edmonton holds down the final Western playoff spot, eight points ahead of the Leafs, who are launching another of their late-season, let's-try-to-squeeze-into-the-post-season efforts. Like the school break, it's a March tradition that never fails to grip the long-suffering Leaf fans. Coach Mike Murphy has his meagerly appointed squad working hard, but even in the parity of the NHL, teams need more than one talented players (in the Leafs' case, Mats Sundin) to make the playoffs. As usual, the late charge will fall short, but it will spark optimism for next season — an annual fall tradition in Toronto.

Congratulated on the Oilers' improved play, Sather says, "If you'd seen us against Anaheim [a 4–0 loss] there wasn't a guy out there who looked like he could play. Who knows where they go sometimes? Before the Olympic break we won seven in a row and then dropped three in a row. They were brutal. But they're a bunch of guys finding themselves in life, finding their roles, and they've started to come together as a team."

This is vintage Sather, talking about players "finding themselves in life." In his acceptance speech at the Hall of Fame, he had made a point of saying how he enjoyed playing a role in the non-hockey part of the lives of his young Oilers, instilling confidence in "how they dressed, how they lived, how they acted away from the rink." Many former players talk about the Sather Finishing School, the crash course he offers his players in grooming, dressing, and dining like a champion. In a sport where fashion goes to die, Sather's teams have always had a GQ look about them.

"We were basically a bunch of hayseeds," recalls Kevin Lowe, of the great Edmonton teams of the 1980s, "and here was Slats, a fairly cosmopolitan guy. He encouraged the dressing up thing, the good restaurants thing. He taught us it wasn't just a business, it was also a game to be enjoyed."

A reporter gingerly asks Sather about the Olympics and the American players' destruction of hotel property in Nagano. This is ticklish ground for Sather as Guerin, one of his players, is a rumored culprit. Sather is annoyed at the distraction over what he feels was an over-blown prank. He recalls an occasion when two of the early Oilers flooded an entire floor of a hotel with hoses — a practical joke that cost $10,000, a sum coughed up by the entire team. Or the time Tim Horton — then a Pittsburgh Penguin — put a Coca-Cola dispensing machine in the elevator, blocking all traffic to the upstairs floor. It took six men to undo what Horton had alone wrought. Silliness under stress is a hockey tradition, he says, and when some of media guys disagree, he just shrugs.

Sather has never coached an Olympic team, but he has coached Canadian teams at the World Cup (1996), the Canada Cup (1984), and the World Championships (1994). He's also been the general manager for several teams of Canadian NHL stars in these tournaments. He's reluctant to second-guess the Canadian team assembled by general manager Bobby Clarke and coach Marc Crawford. "I don't want to get into that stuff."

The reporter takes a different tack. How would you have approached the bigger Olympic ice surface? "Speed," Sather replies instantly. "I'd have taken more speed. Coffey, Niedermayer, Messier, I'd have taken them. Clarke wanted to put a stamp on the team, naming Lindros as captain, but what's more important, his stamp or the ability of the team to win? The first mistake was the leadership role, not giving Gretzky the C. That put a lot of weight on Eric's shoulders. Here's Gretzky, the greatest player of the past 20 years, it's his first and last Olympics. Wayne was the leader of the team anyway, on and off the ice. Eric's a great player, but…"

Should Gretzky have had a chance in the shootout against Hasek in the game against the Czechs? "Of course," says Sather. "But those are the things everybody's going to second-guess in Canada. One thing, though, I didn't understand — the defensemen for Canada never put any pressure on. The defense never rushed the puck, just fired it in, turned it over, and the other team would fire it out on the boards. They never had anybody pinch off on the right-hand side. Hasek always shoots the puck that way. They never had a guy on the wall because the coaches wouldn't let the defense come down. They never put any pressure on the other team.

"The Americans, too, they didn't move up on the play. The big ice is like an optical illusion. With the extra 20 feet you think you've got to be careful. My experience has been you've got to cut down the gap between the forwards and defense. If the defensemen don't move up and the forwards move back at the same speed, you're going to have those gaps. That's why you've got to get guys who can skate. They have to be guys who are technically sound."

Sather looks at Curtis Joseph, his goalie, kicking aside pucks in practice. Joseph will become a free agent at season's end, and Sather will come close to trading him this day to get some compensation for his anticipated loss. None of that matters for a moment. "The fact that they didn't dress Curtis was ridiculous. It's okay to be sold on your number one guy in Roy, but there's three guys, why not rotate the back-up goalie? He goes all that way just to sit in the stands?"

The cell phone rings, and Sather engages in deep discourse. The media types lean closer, hoping to overhear a snippet about a trade, or an agent with a big-contract demand. On the ice, players steal a quick glance at their boss — am I going? Is Slats picking up another steal? No such luck — Sather's making plans to drive to Hamilton to see the Oilers' farm team, the Bulldogs, play that evening.

"The Olympics was a great experience for the players," he continues, "the experience of a lifetime. I thought it was great for the game. It's the skill of the players that develops the speed, not the size of the ice. I like our size ice, it creates more action, but I loved what I saw in Japan. I know some people had problems because Canada, the U.S., or

Sweden didn't win, but that's just sour grapes. I loved the hockey I saw, that up-tempo style."

Of course. Just like old times.

THE SPRING OF 1998 saw the re-tooled Oilers claim the seventh spot in the playoffs and a date with Patrick Roy and the Avalanche, champions of the Pacific conference. On paper, it was a mismatch; Colorado was just two years removed from winning the Stanley Cup and had eliminated the Oilers the previous year. But the late additions of Hamrlick, Ninimaa, Guerin, and rookie Scott Fraser plus veterans Hrkac, Musil, and Dollas had propelled the Oilers to a 15–9 mark after the Olympics. The Oilers were heading into the post-season playing their best hockey of the year. "There wasn't an awful lot of resemblance between the team that started the season and the team that entered the playoffs," Sather allowed. "These new guys have a second nature about the style we want to play. They look for the good pass, they don't just chip it out or ring it around the boards." Adding to the optimism in northern Alberta was the memory of the underdog Oilers upsetting highly ranked Dallas a year earlier.

Sather was at his manipulative best prior to game one with the Avalanche, protesting the short visitor's bench at McNichols Arena in Denver. In his most indignant tone, he hinted that the Avalanche might be forced to sit on chaises longues, or worse, when the series shifted to Edmonton. It was balderdash, of course, but it diverted attention away from the young Oilers and relieved the pressure — the desired result of the protest.

Meanwhile, the Avalanche — which sent eight players plus head coach Marc Crawford to the Olympics — had suffered a letdown after Nagano, winning only nine of their final twenty-three regular-season contests. The team had suffered key injuries to Peter Forsberg and Joe

Sakic and was said to be racked with dissension — Crawford and Roy had been at odds since Canada's Olympic loss and Crawford's future in Colorado was uncertain.

In the finest Oilers tradition, the team Sather built and Ron Low coached was based on speed and skill and the solo goaltending of Curtis Joseph. The Oilers used an aggressive forecheck, attempting to deny the Colorado defense clear passing lanes to their superior forwards. The Oilers' young defense would try not to cough up the puck under pressure from the menacing likes of Claude Lemieux, and Joseph would be left to clean up their mistakes in his final games before becoming a free agent.

It was a laudable formula, but when Colorado won game four in Edmonton to take a 3–1 series lead, it seemed like cold comfort for Oilers fans. The highly praised Ninimaa had handed away the winning goal in overtime of game three while Joseph had surrendered 15 goals in four games. Heading into Denver for game five, it looked like the Oilers would shortly be on the golf course.

At that point, Joseph took matters into his own hands. In the final three games of the series, he surrendered just one goal, shutting out the Avalanche in the final two games, including the clincher on Colorado's home ice. The 4–0 final in Denver may have been less dramatic than the Oilers' overtime win against Dallas a year earlier, but for sheer satisfaction it served the purpose. The speedy combination of Guerin and Weight teamed up for six goals in the series, including four on the power play.

Even as the exhausted Oilers pounded congratulations on Joseph at game's end, however, Sather knew the price they had paid. "We were spent," he observed as he relaxed in his Palm Springs retreat after the playoffs. "They were big, fast, and tough, and it took a lot out of us to get past them. What we have to do is get by the first round without playing a team like them, so that we have something left. And we have to get bigger forwards and another couple of tough defensemen."

Sure enough, the Oilers' next opponents, the Dallas Stars, were big, fast, tough, and — critically — too deep for Edmonton in the next round. While the Oilers sent out three competent forward lines, the Stars rotated four lines, wearing down their young opponents as the series moved along. Edmonton lasted just five games against Hitchcock's well-coached club, surrendering to goalie Ed Belfour and the Stars' defensive specialists. But it was not the trap that caused his club's downfall, Sather knew — it was depth and dollars.

"They picked up a lot of players like [Brian] Skrudland and [Mike] Keane, because they had more money than us," he lamented. "They sort of rent them for a couple of months. There aren't a lot of teams who can afford to do that. It's an unfair advantage, and if you ask me, that's more frustrating than playing against the trap. When you don't have much mental and physical energy left after a tough series, that kind of advantage can kill you."

Money was an advantage not even the vaunted Sather could overcome within the Oilers' rigid financial framework. And money was the reason he listened carefully when Vancouver, Toronto, Atlanta, and other clubs phoned him in Palm Springs to see if he'd be willing to run their well-financed clubs for the next few years. Though he still had a year remaining on his Edmonton contract, he was working for someone other than Peter Pocklington for the first time in 20 years.

"IS THAT ALL SWIRLS?" Sather asks. "Or is it a mixture?" He's buying ice-cream cones for his scouting staff at the 1998 NHL Entry Draft at Buffalo's Marine Midland Arena. The young runner assigned to the Oilers, a kid barely in his teens and rendered dumb to be so close to famous hockey people, summons up the pluck to respond: "Swirls, Mr. Sather."

"Okay, swirls all around," Sather tells the attendant at the snack bar. A reporter is seconded to carry the melting treats back to Barry Fraser and his sidekicks at the Oilers' draft table located along the boards. It's been three weeks since the Sabres skated off this surface after losing to Washington, five weeks since the Oilers were eliminated by Dallas. The Red Wings are once again Stanley Cup champions, having swept the Capitals in four straight.

Sather has seen the Maple Leafs, of all people, scoop his sleeper prospect, center Nikolai Antropov of Kazakhstan, with the tenth pick of the first round. ("They made a real smart pick there," Sather concedes. "He's got great vision.") But he's elated that powerful young Michael Henrich of the Barrie Colts has somehow dropped to the Oilers at the thirteenth pick. "We had him rated fourth overall," says Sather, picking his way through the crowds hovering next to the draft tables. "Good speed, good size [6-foot-2], fits right in with us. Of course, it's a real pot shot, you won't know for two years with these kids."

An autograph seeker delays Sather. He hands the cone in his right hand to the reporter so he can sign a ratty napkin. Cone safely back in hand, he gestures across the rows of blue seats filled with parents, agents, and hangers-on. "Some of these kids have big-time skills, some have great vision, but there's so much time that passes before a guy can play or perform. It's not two or three months, it's two or three years."

Another draft, another day of dreams for an arena full of young players, another turn on the carousel for Sather. People he's known for decades, like the perpetually tanned Phil Esposito, drop by for a chat or to cook up a deal. The master builder is in the Oilers house. While he hasn't confirmed that he will remain for the final year of his contract, he's certainly acting as if he intends to stay, selecting players he hopes will bring a sixth Stanley Cup to Edmonton. "At this point, I don't anticipate any problems," he says as he reaches the Oilers table. "We'll talk after all this is over." (Sure enough, he will confirm a multi-year deal to remain with the Oilers a few days later.)

Coach Ron Low, head scout Fraser, assistant GM Bruce MacGregor, and scouts Harry Howell, Kent Nilsson, and Dave Semenko crowd around for their ice cream. The team's draft evaluation meetings in the past weeks render the presence of so many bodies moot. Key decisions have already been finalized. When the Leafs picked Fraser's pet pick Antopov, for instance, the Oilers simply crossed him off their list and went to the next-rated player. There's no time for lamenting lost opportunities. Still, the Oilers and the other clubs dutifully bring their scouting staffs to sit at the team's table for the eight or ten hours of the draft. A random cameo on the TV broadcast is a harmless perk for the faded stars and rink rats who spend the rest of their lives in dingy arenas, away from the spotlight.

As this year's draft grinds along, Sather is asked about last year's first pick, the young Swiss forward Michael Riesen, who had his jaw broken playing in the Swiss League earlier in the season. Are the Oilers having second thoughts? Will he be another Jason Bonsignore or Jason Soules, a first-round flop? "A big-time talent, he can play," says Sather forcefully. "The biggest improvement is his intensity; coming to our camp last fall was a learning experience for him. He learned how hard these guys work, how hard they train. It takes a couple of training camps for these guys to find out what it takes. We'll bring him into camp again, we may sign him. A big-time talent."

At the podium, commissioner Bettman calls on home-town Buffalo to select. With the eighteenth pick of the first round, the Sabres take 6-foot-2 defenseman Dmitri Kalinin from Chelyabinsk, Russia. The reaction from the Sabres fans is muted, but this is considered a coup for Buffalo as Kalinin was rated the number one European prospect in the draft by the NHL's Central Scouting Bureau. As it turns out, he's the fourth European selected. This news is greeted with an impressed grunt from Sather. The willingness of other teams to trust their own instincts pleases him.

Sather is pleased with any positive developments in the game he has given his life to. "Hockey's been a great sport, a great entertainment, the greatest game in the world, but for some reason we've gotten away from the excitement. I mean, the penalty killing is so good that teams can get away with hooking or holding or other penalties. The league has to make some fundamental changes to open up the game again, and I hope the ones we're trying next year work."

What about shortening the endless season and playoffs? "That's the easiest problem to solve," Sather says. "There's absolutely no way we can't shorten the season to make it more effective." He's got everyone's attention now. "All we have to do is call up Bob Goodenow at the NHLPA and say if the players want only 60 games, we'll pay them 80 percent of their salaries." He's enjoying this. "Just call him up and say six million instead of eight million. It's quick, it works for everybody, I'm sure he'd agree. Call him up."

The crowd's lapping it up when Lou Lamoriello of New Jersey suddenly hoves into view behind the scrum. Sather's hooded eyes flash like those of a hawk that's just caught sight of a rabbit in the field below. "Sorry guys, gotta go," he shrugs. "I'm making a trade." It's not the off-season for the master builder of the Oilers. It's hunting season.

Dominik Hasek
IRON
BUTTERFLY

"Dad was thoroughly Czech. He always did his duty conscientiously while thinking the opposite of what he was expected to think."

JOSEF SKVORECKY, THE ENGINEER OF HUMAN SOULS

"I WAS BORN WITH VERY FLEXIBLE LEGS," says Dominik Hasek. "When I was ten years old, I could do almost a 180-degree split. I lost a little flexibility when my body matured, but I don't think I lost a lot." Hasek is lounging on an immense leather sofa in the living room of his bright spacious home in a subdivision off the Millersport Highway east of Buffalo. It's a gray, threatening day in late June 1997, not long after Steve Yzerman and the Red Wings have swept Philadelphia to win their first Stanley Cup since 1955. Hasek's wife, Alena, is out shopping, and their two children are due home from school at any moment. The only interruption is a phone call from the doctor who's been treating the knee he injured a month earlier.

During the NHL schedule, this pleasant corner of upstate New York is home to the best goaltender on the planet. Except for the Robert Watson art prints on the walls, there are virtually no signs that a wealthy hockey star lives here. Hasek's Olympic and NHL memorabilia are confined to his cluttered office upstairs; the only videos in sight by the TV are not highlight films but *The Lion King* and *Pocahontas*. The decor and layout of the house could be those of any middle-class family. In part this reflects the taste of Hasek and his wife, but it's also a reminder that they arrived in this part of the world with virtually nothing.

Hasek reflexively stretches his hamstrings, then settles back on the couch. Simply put, he is a rubber man. Lloyd Percival, the late fitness expert, would have called him "ecto-medial" — muscular and wiry, very active and agile, with terrific coordination in high-skills activities. In contrast to the mesomorph and meso-medial body types of most of his teammates, Hasek has a compact torso with long arms and legs. Instead of the bulging, chiseled musculature common in NHL dressing rooms, he sports a slender build and long, smooth, rounded muscles. In chinos and T-shirt, he looks as if he might be the star of Cirque du Soleil, not the Buffalo Sabres.

Body type, extraordinary flexibility, and lightning reflexes partly explain how Hasek has baffled and frustrated the NHL's best shooters for the past five years, but his excellence owes much to his Czech upbringing as well. Like the other great European goaltender, Vladislav Tretiak, Hasek is the product of unorthodox training methods — at least by North American standards of the day. Growing up in Pardubice, a Czech town of 100,000 souls between Prague and the Polish border, he played hockey from the age of four. "When we went outside on the lawn or the ice," he recalls, "the trees were my net. I was always the one in the net." That much is traditional. But Hasek also played soccer and a Czech game called nohy ball — a combination of soccer and volleyball — in which you kick a ball over a net about a meter high. The results are obvious. "He's got the quickest legs of anybody," says former NHL sniper Joey Mullen. "His legs are always moving. You know, down and out and to the side, in different positions."

Like many superior athletes, Hasek played with older, more experienced players through much of his youth, accelerating his development. And in the best tradition of old-time goalies, he was largely self-taught. "My parents supported me, but they never forced me. It wasn't like Walter Gretzky making an ice rink in the back and shooting the puck at me. When I was coming up, there was no one who said, 'Don't do this' or 'Don't do that.' They told me to keep my stick on the ice, to hold it hard, and some people said I was on my knees too much. But my numbers were good and so they didn't say much. I watched all my peers back home in goal; I never missed a game. I tried some of the things they did, but my style was almost automatic — I couldn't play like them."

Hasek's lightning-quick hands owe a debt to Anatoli Tarasov, the great Soviet coach. "My hands come from playing tennis," says Hasek. "My brother Martin and I built a tennis court in our rooms with the tape and the beds. Whenever we had time, we played tennis." Hasek was a junior champion in Eastern Bohemia and continues to play tennis in the off-season, refining his hand-eye coordination. Martin — four years Dominik's junior — is now a forward playing First Division soccer with Sparta Prague in the Czech league. For a while, Dominik played goalie in soccer against him and his friends. "Until I was ten years old I played goal in soccer. Since then, nobody gets me in goal in soccer. No chance!" Hockey was his passion even then. "I liked the challenge of stopping the puck. I won't say I wasn't afraid of the puck, but I was always the youngest on the team, and I liked stopping the older guys, challenging them."

While his writhing, flaying style in net was still a work in progress, Hasek was as baffling for young players in Pardubice as he is today for NHLers. But Hasek as a youth had few illusions of greatness. "I remember it was just one year till I played in the First Division. They asked me about my future. My mother and father were there. I said I didn't think I was good enough. There were too many other good goalies."

Not good enough? At 16, he was starting games in the Czech First Division. By the time he was 18 he was battling Jiri Kralik for the job as national team goalie for Czechoslovakia. By the time he was 21, he was the number one goalie on the national team, playing in the world championships and the Olympics, refining his style against the vaunted — and, to a Czech, hated — Soviet hockey machine.

He doesn't want to discuss the Olympics or the Soviets on this humid afternoon. Instead, he wants to talk about pulling himself from a game even though he was not injured. It was an important game, he admits, gazing out into the backyard. He knew the consequences of bailing out on his team would be severe, but in his heart he simply couldn't continue. He had to live by his principles. So, at the first opportunity, he scooted to the bench with a bogus injury.

Now, before someone tells his former Buffalo coach, Ted Nolan, that Hasek admits that he faked an injury, understand that he's not referring to *that* game, the one against the Ottawa Senators when he skated off the ice after injuring his knee in the playoffs. No, Hasek is referring to a First Division match played in Czechoslovakia in 1990, before he moved to North America. He was the goalie for the powerful army team Dukla Jihlava; his opponents were his old teammates from his home town. Hasek had been drafted into the army when he completed college; that meant he was also drafted to play for the army's hockey team.

But his heart belonged to Pardubice, where he'd been born in 1965. (Jiri Crha, who played briefly for the Maple Leafs, was an earlier product of the town's hockey program.) Hasek's father, Jan, a miner, worked away from home most of the week, and Hasek grew up watching the Pardubice team at the local arena with his grandfather. "I was always crying when our team lost," he recalls. "My grandpa would bring a handkerchief for my tears."

Hasek's unorthodox goaltending had kept Pardubice solidly in the First Division for seven years. And he expected to play for them again when his army hitch ended. Now, here he was, playing for the powerful army team against his old club. To make matters worse, Pardubice was in danger of being relegated to the Second Division if it lost to Hasek's new team.

"In the Second Division, there was no money, you had to work, you couldn't play on the national team, you'd ruin your career," he says. "I told the coach on the army team, a few of us, we couldn't play because we had to go back to our old team after the army. But he said the army had ordered us to play. It was easier for the other guys, because they played forward or defense, they didn't have to look as bad as me. I didn't want to look like an idiot and lose my career. But I didn't want our old team to lose, either.

"So I told some of the older guys, don't be surprised if I leave the game. The first time I stopped the puck, ten or twenty seconds into the game, I took myself out with an 'injury.' It was stupid, I guess. The army suspended me, sent me to a camp in the mountains for two weeks, an army camp. I don't know why I did it."

The tale is classic Hasek. He's the Czech version of Jacques Plante, an eccentric original with a highly independent nature and, friends say, an IQ in the genius range. Like many bright people, he's also forgetful. He leaves his wallet in the dressing room, arrives at the rink for an important playoff game without his goalie pads, shows up in Toronto for the NHL awards without his tuxedo. No wonder his teammates call him Kramer, after the eccentric "Seinfeld" character. Luckily for Kramer, conditions behind the Iron Curtain in 1990 were being liberalized; the Czech revolution had overthrown the Communists, and Václav Havel was leading the former satellite state into freedom. Hasek would not be made to disappear into a hockey gulag; in fact, he would

finally be allowed to sign with the Blackhawks, the team that had drafted him seven years earlier, in 1983.

"I had started thinking about the NHL back in 1984," he recalls.
"Someone said you can make $150,000 a year and get a big BMW car
just for signing. But before the revolution, if you leave the country, you
can't go back. You leave your parents and everything behind. I didn't
want to do that. It would cause great problems for my parents."

Under the new liberalized system, he was able to obtain his release.
Some NHL people, well aware of how good he was, were urging their
teams to get him. Former Czech star David Volek, for instance, was
telling everyone he met about the acrobatic goalie from Pardubice with
the lightning reflexes. Pat Flatley, Volek's teammate with the Islanders,
remembers hearing Volek sing Hasek's praises. "Every time I saw Hasek
against us I just said, 'Damn, we could have had him,'" recalls Flatley.
"He was available. We had some lean years with the Islanders there, and
he could have been the difference. He's the key to the Buffalo franchise."

Hasek's circuitous route to the Sabres is instructive. Though he
arrived in Chicago with a great reputation, the NHL was not about to
fall at his feet. He may have been the Czech Goalie of the Year five times
in succcession and the Czech Player of the Year in 1987, 1989, and 1990,
but this was the big time, sonny. In Chicago he found himself buried
behind another eccentric, all-star Ed Belfour; a dependable back-up,
Greg Millen; and a hotshot rookie, Jimmy Waite. He couldn't even wear
his favorite number nine from back home. League rules and Millen's
ownership of 29 meant he had to settle for 39, a multiple of unlucky 13.
Hasek quickly found himself toiling for Indianapolis of the
International Hockey League. In part, his unique style — sprawling,
flopping, smothering pucks with his stick hand — distracted traditional
hockey people. He just didn't *look* right in the net. The unconvention-
ality extended to his personality. Chicago captain Chris Chelios,

however, had seen enough to make an assessment. "I told everybody, he's the best goalie in the world. Who cares if a goalie's crazy? Like Eddie Belfour's not?"

After two years of bouncing unhappily between Indianapolis and Chicago, Hasek was ready to chuck the North American dream. "Knowing Dominik and his competitiveness, it must have been very hard for him," says Oilers defenseman Frank Musil, who grew up in Pardubice with Hasek. "You can find all the excuses to quit. But he stuck with it and was determined to prove everybody wrong." Another Czech friend, journalist Jiri Kolis, believes that Hasek's time in the minors — however painful — helped him make the transition from European star to NHL legend. "He learned to concentrate so much better," notes Kolis. "And he gained the confidence to try different things like playing on his back or without the stick, things he hadn't done as much in Europe."

"Mike Keenan called me [at the end of the 1991–92 season]," Hasek remembers, "and said that Jimmy Waite had the starting job. I began to think maybe I wasn't so good. I told Keenan I didn't want to stay."

Before returning to Europe, though, he had made a favorable impression on at least one other astute hockey man: former coach and current "Hockey Night in Canada" analyst Harry Neale. "When Chicago played Pittsburgh in the finals in 1992, and the Penguins beat them four straight," Neale recalls, "Keenan replaced Belfour with Hasek in the last half of game four. Hasek stopped Lemieux one on one three times. We all thought, 'Oh, what's the big deal? Lemieux's not trying, and who is this guy anyhow?' Then they made the deal to send him to Buffalo. The Sabres didn't know what they were getting, and Chicago didn't know what they were giving up."

The trade that summer — Hasek for marginal goaltender Stephane Beauregard and a fourth-round draft pick — was little more than a giveaway by Keenan and Bob Pulford, the Hawks general manager, a blip on the transactions report. Hasek himself was unimpressed when he learned he was being moved. After battling to beat out Belfour, he now had former Edmonton all-star Grant Fuhr ahead of him as the Sabres' number one goalie.

In Buffalo, however, Hasek soon made believers of coaches and fans alike. After sharing the goalies' job — and the Jennings Trophy, for the lowest team goals-against average — with Fuhr that first season, he made Fuhr redundant with a stunning performance in 1993–94. He won the Vezina Trophy and earned the first-team all-star berth while registering a league-high seven shutouts and a microscopic 1.95 goals-against average — the first sub-2.00 average since Bernie Parent in 1973–74. And he'd done it for a team — unlike Parent's Flyers — of decidedly modest talent. In one playoff game that spring, Hasek stopped 70 shots in a 1–0 win over New Jersey that went to four overtime periods. It was one of the great goaltending performances in Stanley Cup history.

He repeated his brilliance during the lockout-shortened season of 1994–95, winning the Vezina, being named first all-star, tying for the league lead in goals-against average, leading in shutouts (with five), and again posting the best save percentage. Fuhr could see the writing on the wall; he showed up at training camp the following September wearing generic white goalie pads that wouldn't be out of place on any team. In February 1995, Fuhr was dispatched to Los Angeles. Hasek never missed a beat, winning the Vezina and another berth on the first all-star team on a club best described as mediocre without him.

After a mildly disappointing season the following year, Hasek rebounded with his best year to date in 1996–97. He won his third Vezina, his third selection as the first all-star goalie, and his fourth straight save percentage title. Save percentage is probably the most reliable index of a goaltender's worth. A strong defensive team can help a good goaltender to an impressive win total, shut-out total, or goals-against average. And it can help an excellent goaltender to join the elite. Martin Brodeur is undeniably an excellent goaltender, but New Jersey's superb balance and brilliant defensive style contribute enormously to his success. That's why, game after game, season after season, the most telling stat kept by the NHL is probably save percentage. In 1995–96, Hasek stopped 1,850 of the 2,011 shots he faced, a save percentage of .920; in 1996–97 he let in only 153 goals in 2,177 chances — an otherwordly .930 save percentage.

This time he also added the Hart Trophy as NHL MVP — the first goaltender to do so since Plante back in 1962 — and the Lester B. Pearson Award, which honors the best player in the league as voted by the players themselves, as well as the Sporting News NHL Player of the Year Award and other minor honors. On perhaps the weakest Buffalo team in four years, he posted 37 wins (second only to Patrick Roy of the mighty Avalanche) and registered five shutouts as the Sabres, against all odds, won the Northeast Division title.

But the luster came off that spectacular season in the first round of the playoffs. Perhaps the only blemish on Hasek's reputation heading into that spring's post-season was a losing record in the playoffs. The night he started the memorable game three against the Senators in Ottawa during the first round in 1997, his playoff record stood at 6–11, despite a tidy 2.36 goals-against average. As he skated into the crease at the Corel Centre that night, he was also at odds privately with Nolan. Recently, Hasek had angrily smashed a washroom in Boston's Fleet Center, and he had left the ice on occasion during practice — a rarity for the hardest-working goalie in the NHL. Hasek felt Nolan was undermining him behind his back, with his Sabres teammates. He also felt the coach was putting his own ego ahead of the good of the team.

In the first period, Hasek was in his butterfly stance — so-called because the goalie's legs are spread out at right angles like the wings of a butterfly — when Sergei Zholtok of the Senators crashed into him. He suffered a grade one sprain of the medial collateral ligament in his right knee and left the game.

"My problem was I was down on the ice, and I couldn't protect my knee," he remembers. "I didn't see him. I could feel it crack. It's the first time I hurt my knee like this. Once or twice I missed a practice or a game, but never like this. I knew right away I was going to be out. With a player maybe you could put a brace on, or tape the knee, but with a goalie you can't go post-to-post with this injury. You can't go down in a butterfly. I called my wife from the locker room and said four weeks."

Hasek's first mistake was breaking the time-honored playoff code by frankly discussing the injury with the press after the game. In the post-season, players are expected to hide every injury this side of amputation. He compounded his image problems by going that night to visit (with the permission of general manager John Muckler) his boyhood friend Musil, then of the Senators, who was out with an injury of his own.

"I knew I was out of the playoffs for a couple of weeks at least," says Hasek, "so why not visit him? He had a new baby. I didn't think I was doing anything wrong. Then they said I was going to talk about our strategy! Maybe I could have learned their strategy, but nobody said that."

"North Americans look at it differently," says Musil. "I'm not saying it's right or it's wrong, but we had a different opinion. Knowing Dominik, he'd never turn away from his team. That's just not his personality. He's driven by success. Believe me, he was hurt."

Hasek's matter-of-fact attitude further annoyed the traditionalists. How could he have stood behind the Buffalo bench the next game if he was so badly hurt? And why wasn't he consumed with guilt and anxiety? "I'm the kind of person who, if he's not going to play, I don't want to show up in the locker room. I don't want to distract the guys," he explains. "What can I give to them?" (Plante, too, adopted this aloof attitude when he was hurt.)

Stories began circulating that Hasek's injury wasn't as severe as he was making out, that the player of the year was trying to make his coach look bad, even that he was drinking too much. On the surface, the accusations sounded ludicrous against a man who had played so hard and given so much to his team for the past four seasons. But the play-offs are an emotional time, the NHL still has dark corners of xenophobia, and Hasek was walking a fine line with his unconventional response to the injury.

The backlash crystallized in an article in the *Buffalo News* by Jim Kelley that intimated Hasek was bailing out on his team. The radio phone-in shows, sensing blood, took it a step further, accusing Hasek of faking his injury, of not being a team player, and perhaps of causing the McKinley assassination as well. Hasek let his emotions get the better of him; he confronted Kelley in the hallway of the Buffalo Auditorium and grabbed him by the throat, ripping Kelley's shirt. The two had to be separated by Sabres officials.

Hasek quickly apologized for his behavior. At a press conference arranged by his agent, Rich Winter, he accepted responsibility for his actions, while taking pains to point out that the offending article had been inaccurate. The NHL suspended him, but the injury precluded him from returning to the playoffs before the Sabres were eliminated by Philadelphia in the second round.

Two months later, gazing out at his backyard, Hasek was still seething over the incident. "I don't mind when they write about my play on the ice," he said with a shrug. "They can say whatever they want. Back home, we got lots of pressure — maybe more — when we played against the Russians. But when they talk about things off the ice, like I show up late or I don't want to play, I don't like that. I can forget almost everything, but I cannot forget that he said I was sprinting out of the rink that night [in Ottawa]. It was a lie. He's a professional writer. He cannot say I was sprinting when I was limping. I don't know why he did it."

That day as he watched Michael and Dominika, home from school, chasing each other around the yard, Hasek had a little surprise for his detractors. He had already chosen his parting words about Nolan, words he'd deliver to the Buffalo media on his way back to the Czech Republic a few days later. At the time, Nolan was engaged in a cold war against not only Hasek but general manager John Muckler as well. Hasek was about to turn up the heat.

"I don't believe in him," Hasek confided. "I'll be happy if he's not back in Buffalo. I think in my heart I did a very good job for him. I didn't like the things he did, but the whole season I did the best for him and the team. I couldn't do anything else. But I don't respect him, and I don't want him back."

True to his word, Hasek delivered his piece as he left for his summer home in Pardubice. Nolan would be named NHL coach of the year (the same night Hasek would win the Hart Trophy), but would lose his job to Lindy Ruff. The widow of club founder Seymour Knox would protest the decision not to rehire Nolan. Muckler would be fired as GM and be replaced by Darcy Regier. And club president Larry Quinn would make a clumsy attempt to cut the Sabres' payroll by trying to force Pat Lafontaine into retirement, a move that would backfire when Lafontaine starred for the Rangers instead. Quinn would be fired halfway through the next season. By the time the smoke cleared, only Hasek would be left standing in Buffalo — and even his future with the Sabres would be in doubt.

A GOALIE AT THE CENTER OF CONTROVERSY should come as no surprise. Perhaps because the position makes such extraordinary demands in pain and uncertainty, it has always attracted unique personalities. The image of 38-year-old Terry Sawchuk, eyes sunken, body bruised grape-jelly purple, drawing silently on a cigarette while his Toronto teammates celebrate the Stanley Cup in 1967, somehow epitomizes the position. An acerbic loner, Sawchuk was once pictured with the hundreds of stitches he'd taken in his face superimposed all at once like a Frankenstein figure. One of the greatest goalies ever, he died in a scuffle with a teammate after winning his final Stanley Cup.

Then there were the miseries of Glenn Hall, who pioneered the modern school of "butterfly" goalies. Hall once compiled an astounding 502 consecutive complete games, though he was sick to his stomach before many of them. "Playing goal is a winter of torture for me," he once said. "I often look at the guys who can whistle before a game and shake my head. You'd think they didn't have a care in the world. Me? I'm just plain miserable before every game." Virtually every summer, Hall held lengthy contract holdouts from Chicago, and then St. Louis, to forestall the inevitable day of reckoning with the job.

Hockey commentator John Davidson, a former goaltender, remembers being stopped by the Rangers' team doctor after playing back-to-back games. The doctor was concerned that Davidson was so bruised by the shelling he'd taken the previous two nights that he might have internal bleeding. And few who saw former Washington goaltender Clint Malarchuk's gruesome injury will ever forget it. Malarchuk was on the ice when a skate blade slashed his throat. In a scene right out of M*A*S*H, the Capitals' trainer staunched the gushing flow of blood, saving the goaltender's life as a hushed crowd watched in horror.

No wonder goalies have had unconventional attitudes. Look down the list of those who've played in the NHL and you'll find a number who managed just one game. Robbie Irons of St. Louis holds the brevity record — his NHL career lasted exactly two minutes and 59 seconds on the night of November 13, 1968. Whatever happened to Al Shields, who gave up nine goals in his 41 minutes of fame with the New York Americans in 1931–32? Or Greg Redquest, who surrendered three goals in 13 minutes in 1977–78 for Pittsburgh?

No matter how long a goalie plays, the job leaves its mark. Over the years, goaltenders have dealt with the loneliness and uncertainty in their own ways. Gary "Suitcase" Smith — who played for eight different NHL clubs — used to peel off his equipment and shower between periods. Gary Inness had to have an exact number of Dixie cups lined up on a table in front of him, ice on the right side, water on the left. Gilles Gratton, who played in the World Hockey Association, believed in reincarnation and considered his job punishment for having stoned people to death in biblical days.

The superstitions today may be less dramatic, but they're still very much in evidence. Patrick Roy of Colorado never touches the red or blue lines, bounces the same puck on the floor of the dressing room all season, puts his sweater and gloves on precisely seven minutes before the start of each period, and insists that the same player takes the first shot in every pre-game warmup. The same shooter must then stand beside Roy during the national anthem — at least, until his luck runs out, when another "charmed" teammate gets the assignment.

It used to be more than the rabbit's foot that helped you tell the goalie in a crowd of hockey players in a hotel lobby. The goalie was the guy with the patchwork face and black eyes. A classic photo from the 1940s shows a battered, bleeding Maurice Richard shaking hands with Boston goalie "Sugar" Jim Henry, who surpasses the Rocket in gore: both of Henry's eyes are blackened and his nose is smashed, too.

Today, thanks to modern masks and bulletproof materials in their padding — and to a greater recklessness on the part of forwards and defensemen — goalies are the ones with all their teeth. And while

Hasek and Ed Belfour may perpetuate the time-honored reputation of "flaky" goalies, the men in pads are now better scouted, trained, and equipped than their predecessors. Teams that once treated goalies as if they had communicable diseases now employ specialty coaches and advisers to work with them. And why not? "Goaltending is to hockey what putting is to golf," says Boston general manager Harry Sinden. Detroit's legendary GM Jack Adams chose a different sporting analogy. "What pitching is in a short series in baseball," he said, "goaltending is in the playoffs." Punch Imlach made the same point when his Maple Leafs confronted a skinny 21-year-old named Rogatien Vachon in the Montreal net for the 1967 playoffs: "Do they think they can win with a Junior B goalie?" he sneered.

No position has evolved more, but only recently has it evolved in the goaltender's favor. In pre-war days, men like Roy "Shrimp" Worters of the New York Americans could tend the net at a majestic 5-foot-3 and 135 pounds. Charlie Gardiner, who's in the Hall of Fame, was only 5-foot-5. The slapshot had not been invented, and the arts of screening and running into the goalie in his crease had yet to be perfected. Freed from ancient rules that forbade a goalie from falling to his knees, Worters and his brethren stopped most low shots by stacking their leg pads toward the shooter and keeping their head out of harm's way.

New leg pads pioneered by Emil "Pops" Kenesky in the mid-1920s were a quantum leap in protection for goalies, making it easier for them to remain standing and direct low shots away from the net using their legs. High shots were handled with the gloves or deflected away with the stick. The lightly padded chest and arms were used only as a last resort. As opposed to the bullet drives and screen shots Hasek must cope with today, most pre-war goalies faced only wrist shots and back-handers from relatively close in, and goalies had a good idea where the puck was going. The simple nature of the sticks also restricted the force

with which a Charlie Conacher might unleash his "bullet" wrist shot
— at a leisurely 50 miles an hour. With goalies on their feet much of
the time, players generally aimed low and to the corners. (The preference for beating goalies between the legs — the so-called five hole, [so
named because it's one of the five holes in a goalie's coverage of the net]
— is a by-product of modern goalies who spend more of their time on
their knees.) Until the advent of the red line and the two-line offside
pass during the Second World War, games were generally low-scoring
and dominated by passing and skating, rather than shooting.

Occasionally a goalie suffered a gash or broken nose for his pains
and was stitched up while everyone waited. But the gravity of these
wounds did not warrant major changes in equipment or rules. Besides,
coaches of that era also might have considered it a sign of puck shyness
if their goalie started worrying about how hard he was getting hit.

As the war years ended, however, star goalies such as Bill Durnan
and Gerry McNeil started getting hit harder as players grew bigger and
stronger than their war-time counterparts. Rocket Richard and Ted
Lindsay crashed toward the net and were not loath to run into goalies.
Richard, in particular, liked to be led on passes so he could break past
his checker with some momentum toward the net. Even the fixed posts
of the net did not discourage him from rushing the goalies of the day.

As a result, the 1950s brought a generation of bigger, more agile
goalies, like Sawchuk, whose deep crouch allowed him to peer through
the increasing traffic now clogging the front of the net. Sawchuk could
bounce up and down from this position with great dexterity for a man
5-foot-11 and 180 pounds. And no one could go post to post like the
brilliant Detroit netminder. Hall, meanwhile, advanced this low-down
strategy by adopting the now-common butterfly position, spreading his
legs to stop pucks at ice level from post to post. Hall's idea was to get
low to maximize coverage in what was becoming an increasingly sight-

less position. "In the pre-mask days," he recalled, "you stacked the pads and tried to get the head on the opposite side from where the shot was coming. The recovery was so difficult from the stacked-pads position. I found that if the shooter was far enough in, I could split out and cover both corners and still tighten up the five hole." While Hasek and his brethren today have the security of the mask and helmet when they drop to the ice, Hall's cohorts were understandably skittish about pucks at eye height. "If we fell down," remembers Johnny Bower, "we got up real quick."

Goalies were also now faced with widespread use of the slapshot. This shot had been around for years, but stronger players and curved sticks took it to a new level. "My first professional camp was in Toronto in 1961," Gerry Cheevers once recalled. "The first time Frank Mahovlich hit my shoulder with a shot, I staggered back, and my shoulder hit the cross bar. It was as much from surprise as the force of the shot. I just hadn't expected a puck could feel like that." The slapper was also less accurate. "When the curved stick came in, the people sitting behind me in the fifteenth row had more trouble than I did," Gump Worsley told Dick Irvin in *In the Crease*. "The guy shooting it had no real idea where the puck was going. That was the biggest worry for a goaltender."

A slapshot off a curved blade from someone like the unbelievably muscular, 195-pound Hull was a considerable threat. A 96-mile-per-hour Hull slapshot traveled 60 feet in 0.42 seconds. This left the goalie precious little time to react. If he was ten feet out of his net, cutting down the angle, that same slapshot would reach him in 0.34 seconds — just time enough for the goalie to let the puck hit him, hopefully in a padded place.

The added range of the slapshot forced the goalie into a Hobson's choice: move out to cut down the angles and the rising power of the shot, or stay back to gain a nanosecond more reaction time for tips, deflections, and screened drives. Here he needed help from teammates. The goalie who moved out had to be assured that his defensemen would direct the shooters toward a bad angle and cut down on cross-ice passes to fellow wingers. The goalie who stayed back had to hope his defensemen would block or deflect shots while he anticipated a pass. Ed Giacomin, a five-time all-star in this era, approached his position with equal measures of cunning and survival instinct. "We would first position our body, then we'd worry about our head," he recalled. "If I knew I had the angle cut off, I'd start to look for my defenseman's rear end. I'd tuck my head in behind it and wait for the puck to hit me." It must have worked — Giacomin never lost a tooth in his career despite not wearing a mask much of the time.

The goalie's work was aided by the complementary skills of such unspectacular but effective defensemen as Marcel Pronovost, Bill Gadsby, and Jacques Laperriere, masters at deflecting shots with a nimble pokecheck. Indeed, after watching the likes of Allan Stanley perform in front of him, Johnny Bower of the Leafs himself became a master of the pokecheck — lunging out with his stick to knock the puck off the stick of an onrushing forward as he made his move. Hasek's deft stick work — at least when he has a stick in his hand — owes much to Bower's clever checking 30 years earlier.

Plante, meanwhile, created another legacy that Hasek exploits by coming out of the net to assist his defensemen. Much to the consternation of his Canadiens coach Toe Blake, Plante began clearing pucks behind his net and in the corners, formerly forbidden territory. This allowed defensemen to commit to the attack for a longer time before retreating to their own zone. Like the goalie mask, this roaming style is one of Plante's legacies to the modern game. Not that he ever converted Blake to the idea, as former Habs goalie Rick Wamsley, now goalie consultant with Toronto, discovered after a game at the Montreal Forum in which he himself had roamed far and wide. "Do you mind if I ask you a question?" Blake inquired. "When you're in the corner with the puck, who's playing goal?"

While Hasek holds down one of the 54 full-time jobs in today's NHL, there were only six full-time goaltending jobs in the 1950s and 1960s, and plenty of willing replacements. Coaches like Blake and "Fiery" Phil Watson of the Rangers expected their netminders to be self-sustaining and indestructible. Watson regularly flayed Gump Worsley for being a "flopper" during their years in New York. While these coaches liked to criticize, however, they were loath to instruct, merely tapping that night's starter on the pads and pointing to the net. Worsley recalled once trying to discuss with Blake a goal Worsley thought he should've stopped. Blake turned away muttering, "Don't ask me. I know nothing about it."

The advice goalies did get often seemed extraneous. "I was told: 'Don't stop a puck that's going to miss the net. You might deflect it,'" says Glenn Hall in Douglas Hunter's book *A Breed Apart*. "Well, if you're that bad, you shouldn't be playing. The goalkeeper's idea of how the position should be played often varied quite a bit from management's idea." Gump Worsley said of coaches: "They tell you never to kick at a puck with your skates because you might kick it backwards into the net. What do they know?" Plante, never one to hide his feelings, said simply, "Nobody among them is capable of understanding what the goaltender goes through before and during a game."

Perhaps only Eddie Shore, the Hall of Fame defenseman who became the mad coaching genius at Springfield in the American Hockey League, tried to coach his goalies to any great extent. Shore was famous for keeping his goalies on their feet by tying a belt around their throats that would choke them if they went down. Other Shore techniques included tying a goalie's knees together to prevent a goal between the legs, putting a steel bar between the posts to prevent him from backing in too far, and putting him on a leash to prevent him from wandering too far from the crease.

The final — and most painful — indignity for goalies of the 1950s and 1960s was the increasing technology gap between the scorers and themselves. "The shots got harder before the equipment got better" is how John Davidson puts it. As a result, goalies were continually tinkering with their equipment to give themselves greater protection and service. The trapper — or catching glove — originated with Emile Francis in the 1940s; as a junior goalie, he devised a method of adding a padded cuff to a first baseman's mitt. Today, Hasek's trapper is the size of a skillet. Likewise, the blocker — or stick glove — evolved from a padded defenseman's glove; Frankie Brimsek used padding with bamboo ribs to reinforce it. Finally, the rectangular "waffle" board became standard, and a much-improved version of it is still in use today.

The leg pads devised by "Pops" Kenesky in Hamilton were probably the best single innovation in goalie equipment, but they too were altered by Harry Lumley, who created a horizontal crease that allowed the pads to deflect pucks down to the goalie's feet. And Turk Broda extended the padding down the sides to improve blocking — and comfort — around the skates. Plante and then Sawchuk adopted the mask to protect the face, but it did little other than prevent cutting. The masked men who followed kept adapting the shape and design until goalies can take the full force of a shot today without injury.

Until fairly recently, the padding on a goalie's arms and chest was made of leather or felt stuffed with cotton or other light materials. "I remember when Bobby Hull was shooting the puck," recalls Francois Allaire, the goaltending guru now responsible for coaching the "Block Quebecois" of Patrick Roy, Felix Potvin, Martin Brodeur, and others. "Most of the goalies were trying to catch the puck. They wouldn't stop it with their upper body, because it was too painful."

Former Boston goalie Eddie Johnston played with some bad teams in the 1960s. One season he played every minute of all 70 games; the Bruins won just 18 of them. Bad as the team was, his protection was even worse. "All we wore on our arms was just a little padding and our underwear. I had no protection at all on my skates," he recalled. "My toes were always hurt. I'd walk around the whole year with swollen toes. The year I played every game [1963–64] I broke my nose three times and had the lobe of my ear sliced off. But with only one goalkeeper you were afraid to come out of the net. Somebody would step in and you might be gone."

Sawchuk and Worsley both wore the same shoulder pads they'd worn in junior throughout their careers. Worsley remembers unpacking his goalie kit in front of Blake when he arrived in Montreal. "Is that all there is?" asked an incredulous Blake. Assured that it was, Blake said simply, "You're nuts."

Plante wore as much padding as possible, but his peers kept their gear to a minimum, seeking mobility. John Davidson recalls being shocked by the padding of fellow netminder Don Edwards, one of Hasek's predecessors in Buffalo. "He used to wear pads so flimsy I wouldn't have worn them even as a kid," says Davidson. "He used to say he wanted to feel the puck." Weight was another factor. Goalies' leather pads and gauntlets, and the cotton underpads, took on tremendous volumes of water from the ice and sweat. Ed Giacomin remembers losing 13 pounds the first time he faced his old teammates after being traded to Detroit. Losing seven or eight pounds during a game was typical. "It (the weight) was unbelievable," former Canadiens goalie Gerry McNeil told Douglas Hunter. "The felt got wet and stayed wet for a long time, and just about doubled the weight of the pads. I would love to start over and try the new equipment." So would Worsley, who got to try on some modern padding for a TV commercial. He was shocked by the feeling of the lighter, synthetic materials. "No wonder they just stand there and let the puck hit them," he said. "They can't get hurt."

Many of the goalies who came later in this era had long careers — in part due to expansion from six to twelve and later to eighteen teams. The World Hockey Association, formed in 1972, created even more jobs. Sawchuk and Worsley both lasted 21 seasons, Plante and Hall 18, and Bower 15. But many others cracked under the pressure. "Steady strain, that is the fate of us goaltenders," Plante once intoned to a youthful Vladislav Tretiak, who himself discovered the "joys" of goaltending as his career progressed. "During the last years of my goaltending career," Tretiak wrote, "I experienced many of those unpleasant sensations which Plante had described: upset stomach, insomnia, pain, I felt there was not a single healthy spot on my body."

As the NHL expanded, and the two-goalie system became common, goalies were no longer expected to carry the entire burden for their teams. As Sawchuk and Bower proved in winning the Stanley Cup for Toronto in 1967, a tandem had definite advantages. The sharing of duties — and blame — helped relieve the stress immeasurably as Bobby Orr and his imitators pushed scoring levels to new heights in the 1970s and 1980s. Hall and Plante thrived together in St. Louis, despite their vastly different personalities. Cesare Maniago learned to partner with Worsley in Minnesota. Maniago recalled that when Worsley didn't feel like playing he developed "flu" or a "pulled muscle." "Once I got to know him, I told him that was okay with me," Maniago said. "But I asked him to let me know. I didn't want any surprises, and it worked out pretty well."

"Nobody really knows what a goalie goes through other than another goalie," says Bobby Taylor, now a TV commentator. "For the number one guy, it can be like Alcoholics Anonymous. When you're on AA and you're struggling, you make a phone call and somebody comes over to talk to you. Well, if you're struggling in goal you can go over to the back-up and talk to him. That helps."

Phil Myre and Daniel Bouchard split goaltending duties in Atlanta for six years. Their competition for playing time stimulated them both. "We hid our injuries, because we had a real good competition going," Myre told Dick Irvin. "We knew if one guy had a chance to take over, the other guy might not be back in there for a long time. So we both played hurt, we both played sick, but for six years nobody else ever dressed for a game." Hasek shares Myre's reluctance to take a night off — he's played three-quarters of the Sabres games since 1993–94.

Another man who bucked the trend to job-sharing was the pre-eminent goalie of the 1970s: Bernie Parent of the two-time Stanley Cup champion Flyers. After returning to the NHL from the WHA in 1973–74, Parent played 50 or more games in four of the next five seasons, four times posting goals-against averages of less than 2.40 in an era when goals per game were soaring toward seven. "I played in two old-timers' games," joked Taylor, the Flyers' other goalie in those years. "That's more than I played as Bernie's back-up."

Tending goal in the 1970s was a matter of angles and of dealing with the increasing onslaught of bodies in the crease. The crossover offensive patterns popular in Europe — introduced to most Canadian fans during the 1972 Canada-Russia series — had yet to transform the game in North America, and goalies were able to range far out of the net, safe in the knowledge that shooters were unlikely to move to better angles. Parent, the quintessential stand-up goaltender, combined a trigonometric understanding of angles and deft coordination with his defensemen. While stalwarts like Jimmy Watson and Ed Van Impe were rudely riding opposition forwards off to bad angles, Parent was kicking aside shots. He rarely dropped to the ice or gave out rebounds, and seemed to look calmest in the most pressure-filled moments. In his prime, says former Leafs and Flyers goalie Jeff Reese, Parent "was just poetry to watch."

Ken Dryden of the Canadiens, not Parent, was the most successful goalie of the 1970s, winning six Stanley Cups. But he's often discounted for playing with the Canadiens teams of the late 1970s — among the greatest ever — and for some disappointing international performances, in particular the first game of the 1972 series. At 6-foot-4, he never looked as composed or as fluid as Parent; his size seemed to magnify his awkwardness when he was beaten. Cheevers, who won just two Cups with the great Orr teams in Boston, was considered a better "money" goalie than Dryden. Yet Dryden's work in helping an underrated Montreal team steal a pair of Stanley Cups from Boston earlier in the decade was among the most impressive goaltending ever. The goalie he defeated those two seasons? None other than Cheevers.

With his diving, swooping, smothering style, Dryden helped usher in the era of the big goalie. Unlike Parent, he was also effective on the ice, virtually blotting out the bottom of the goal with his long arms and lanky frame. While no one would describe him as a butterfly-style goalie, he may have been the most effective "sprawler" before Hasek arrived, reaching along the ice with his catching glove or extending his stick across the crease as if it were a telescope — "a thieving giraffe" is how a frustrated Phil Esposito described him after watching him snare the puck, coming out of nowhere, during the 1971 playoffs.

Dryden was also the most articulate purveyor of the goalie's craft, explaining the vagaries of his job in his landmark 1983 book *The Game*. "Playing goal is not fun," he wrote when his career had ended. "Behind a mask there are no smiling faces, no timely sweaty grins of satisfaction. It is a grim, humorless position, largely uncreative, requiring little physical movement, giving little physical pleasure in return."

Dryden benefited from the improved padding in the 1970s, but he also graphically communicated the physical price of the slow, steady beating administered by the puck over a season. "I catch few shots now, perhaps only two or three a game," he wrote. "I should catch more but years of concussion have left the bones in my hand and wrist often tender and sore, and learning to substitute a leg or a stick to save my hand, my catching glove, reprogrammed and out of practice, often remains at my side."

His teammate on Team Canada in 1972, Tony Esposito, could empathize with Dryden. He tried to alleviate the sting of the puck by rubbing a heating balm on his skin before games. He found the psychological wounds more difficult. His former Blackhawks roommate Gilles Meloche once described Esposito's pre-game trials. "The whole afternoon of a game he would walk back and forth in the room, sweating, saying he hated hockey and wished he was doing something else for a living. Then he'd get in the game that night and they couldn't get a pea past him." Esposito was a first-team all-star three times in his career, twice winner of the Vezina, and a recipient of the Calder Trophy in his rookie year to boot. He recorded 76 shutouts in 886 career games — one for every 8.5 games he started, much of it during an offensive explosion in the league. In his rookie season, 1969–70, he posted a remarkable 15 shutouts, a record never challenged until the 1997–98 season, when Hasek had 13.

The other goalie who changed the position in the 1970s and 1980s was Tretiak, netminder of the great Soviet teams. His preparation and fitness level awakened hockey people to the fact that a fit goalie was a better goalie. His lightning reflexes had been honed by racket sports and soccer, activities no self-respecting NHL goalie would have dreamed of playing at the time. Tarasov, the father of Soviet hockey, insisted that his goalies play tennis to develop their hand-eye coordination. He made

Tretiak carry a tennis ball with him at all times; when Tretiak balked at taking the ball swimming, Tarasov had him sew a pocket on his swimming trunks to enable him to take it with him.

Tretiak's coolness under fire, combined with his technical skill, gave him a formidable psychological advantage. He had also studied the game and his own position with painstaking thoroughness. He realized that once the shot leaves a player's stick, the goalie cannot follow the puck, so he mentally constructed trajectories of the shot and positioned himself at the best possible spot to intersect its flight. This allowed him to get as much of his 6-foot-1 frame in the way of the shot as possible.

Another technique he developed through game experience was playing shooters by reading their eyes. "If, at the last moment, he looked at me and then at the puck, I knew he was going to shoot. Then I could forget his partner and fight him one on one. But if he looked for a moment at his teammate and then at the puck, I knew he would pass to his partner and I was ready for it." Tretiak tried without success to pass on his eye-ball technique to others.

While most goalies kept their arms fairly tight to the body, Tretiak kept his at a 90-degree angle to increase the area for blocking the puck, a technique emulated by Hasek and Patrick Roy in the 1990s. And, like Dryden, he dispelled the notion that a big goalie could not be nimble and move well laterally.

WHEN DOMINIK HASEK DRESSES today for the Sabres, he's the product of nearly 50 years of pain and punishment inflicted on his forerunners. Training methods like Tretiak's are now established practice. Space-age nylons and Kevlar have replaced felt and cotton. "The puck doesn't really hurt goalies when they're hit in the protected areas," says Steve Bessel, pro rep for Vaughn Sports, a major manufacturer of goalie equipment. "If they get deflections, they're going to feel a bit of a bite. But the equipment and the technology is so advanced with layered foams and high-density foams and all the light nylons, they're basically blocking the puck as opposed to catching it."

Rick Wamsley agrees: "The improvement in the goaltending equipment has probably led a lot to the style of goaltending you're seeing today. The pads are real big, the blockers are real big. You've got four or five pads on top of your shoulders, and bubbles in the arm protector." Allaire puts it this way: "The goalies today can perform better than the guys before because they are not afraid. Now a goalie can have a guy shoot a one-timer from 15 feet away, and he'll put his body in front of it without any problem."

"The goalies have been cheating the past couple of years," laments Glen Sather. "Roy has been the forerunner in all that. He's got those little deflection pads that angle down, and [Garth] Snow's got things going up. They should put a little cup on them so the puck goes back and hits the shooter in the face."

Watching Hasek waddle to the ice from the dressing room is like watching a little boy dressed up in his father's clothes. He and Roy, in particular, seem to be swimming in enormous sweaters. Allaire says they have no choice but to wear the gigantic sweaters. "Koho Canada put the new shoulder pads with the big protection for the elbow, and you cannot wear the old sweater with it," he says. "You have to wear the 'goalie cut,' and that gives the impression that the goalie is bigger than he really is."

When one goalie comes up with an innovation, his colleagues quickly try it out as well. One Wednesday night in Toronto, Roy was spotted with a new piece of padding: a small pad on his right hip, designed to stop pucks that squeeze between his stick arm and his body. Days later, while Curtis Joseph of Edmonton was dressing for practice, an observer remarked the absence of Roy's new device. "I've got to get one of those," said Joseph. "There's no rule against them."

(In the summer of 1998, to Joseph's chagrin, the NHL let it be known they would implement new rules governing equipment size and placement.)

Perhaps the only downside to the new technology comes in practice. In the old days, goalies would field perhaps 50 shots in a practice — most of them easy lobs. Shots above the waist were considered rude and brusque behavior. Nowadays, goalies field up to 300 shots in a practice, and shooters who once respected a goalie's vulnerability blast away mercilessly. "There isn't as much respect for goaltenders as there was in the old days," notes a rueful Glenn Healy.

Perhaps more than any other goalie, Hasek exploits the seeming invulnerability produced by the new technology. "If you watch him, he plays a different style," points out Bessel. "In an awkward position, he'll throw any part of his body at the puck — including his head. So if you're a shooter, you've got to bury the puck when you get a chance. Otherwise he'll throw something at you because he's not afraid to get hurt."

"If you see Hasek play two or three times," says Harry Neale, "you go away from the rink thinking he was lucky. He didn't have his stick, he didn't catch a lot of pucks, he comes out of his net on a partial breakaway, he couldn't get away with that every night. He's a bit of a sprawler. I used to think he was a gambler, but I've come to the conclusion that they're pretty calculated gambles. He certainly doesn't have much grace or style, it seems like it's all reaction. But we know you can't survive in the NHL just on reaction. He's much smarter than we give him credit for. You don't score many goals below two feet on him. I know that he spends a lot of time studying shooters, the way a baseball pitcher studies hitters. He doesn't give them what they want to see very often."

"His awkward style fools a lot of people," agrees Senators coach Jacques Martin. "But probably his biggest asset is his concentration. He's always focused on the puck. And he's aware of the people around him."

"Focus" is a word that comes up repeatedly in descriptions of Hasek, but what, exactly, does it mean? In Hasek's case, it refers to his total awareness of where he is in the game, who's on the ice, how he feels physically. It's the by-product of a mental re-creation of game situations, a practiced art. Perhaps the best illustration of focus in a sport is the case of Major James Nesmeth, a U.S. serviceman imprisoned for seven years in Viet Nam in the 1960s. Nesmeth was a golfer who shot in the mid-90s. To keep his sanity in the brutal prison conditions, he imagined himself playing golf at his favorite club. Mentally he chose his wardrobe, selected his clubs, took swings, followed the flight of the ball, and then walked to the next shot. In this fashion, Nesmeth envisioned himself playing 18 holes in real time. He considered weather conditions, course conditions, his grip, how his swing felt, how the ball sounded dropping in the hole. He did this for seven years. When he was finally liberated, he played a round of golf at his club and shot a remarkable 74 — 20 shots better than his previous average. His mental preparation, his focus, had made him a better golfer. Through this sort of visualization, many Olympic and professional athletes vastly improve their performance. Hasek is one of them.

Sabres captain Mike Peca sees the exasperation from opponents when "the Dominator" is focused on the job. "There was a save he made against Mario in Mario's final year, nobody could believe it," recalls Peca. "Mario was bearing down on Dom, and Dom was on the ice. Mario went up top with the shot — Dom somehow caught it in mid-air. You could see Mario just shake his head."

Anyone acquainted with road hockey recognizes Hasek's style. In road hockey, where the sting of the ball lasts only a moment, a smart goalie will sprawl across the crease, throwing just about any part of his body at the shot, confident he will not be badly hurt. This imperviousness to pain, encouraged by the new equipment, is what Hasek seemingly has in common with the other top goalies of the day, such as Brodeur of New Jersey and Roy of Colorado. Where earlier goalies sought to direct pucks to the available pads, catching the puck whenever possible, today's goalie will take the puck where it hits him, confident that rebounds will be controlled and his defensemen will clear players from the front of the net. Better skaters than their old counterparts, modern goalies like Hasek and Roy and Brodeur are unafraid to challenge a shooter.

"A goalie has to learn to relax, to accept the puck," says Jim Bedard, goalie consultant for the Detroit Red Wings. "Sometimes the temptation is to go out and get the puck before it hits you. That's what they did in the old days. Today, I tell our goalies, with the new equipment, just let it hit you."

LIKE MANY HOCKEY FANS, Dominik Hasek learns a lot about NHL scorers by watching highlights. During a late after-game dinner at Mother's, a Buffalo restaurant, he's constantly peeking at the TV monitor in the corner. Halfway through a thought, he sees Montreal score in Pittsburgh against Ken Wregget. He pauses, enters the data in his mental hard drive — Mark Recchi, off-wing, low shot, stick side — then continues the conversation. Then a highlight from Detroit: Doug Brown of the Red Wings goes five hole on Felix Potvin of the Leafs. Once again, there's a pause as Hasek records details of the goal for another time, another rink.

Back in the final days of Soviet-occupied Czechoslovakia, information on opposing players was hard to come by. "Before the satellites, I never saw players in the NHL," he says. "We just saw the Canada Cup or the world championships. I knew that in the NHL they challenged more, came out of the net. That's because they shot more. In Europe, the players were playing with the puck more, making more passes, using more skills, trying to put the puck into an open side. Sometimes the people over there like the guy who makes nice goals, pretty goals, not always the guy who scores 30 goals."

In North America, Rangers goalie Mike Richter was making similar observations. "Guys used to come at you in lanes," he explained in 1995. "Now guys are coming in weaving. If I go out and he passes it to a guy behind me, I have a long way to go and not enough time to get there." Richter began staying back and staying low. So did Roy, and Belfour, and a growing number of other NHL goaltenders.

Living half a world away in Eastern Europe and never seeing NHL hockey, Hasek was coming to the same conclusions about modern shooters and adopting the same techniques as NHL goalies. He observed that as the game got faster, the accuracy of shooters dropped, and the bulk of the shots came along the ice. His solution was to use the butterfly stance, keeping his shoulders square to the shooter, staying in the middle of the net, and laying the paddle along the ice to protect low, trying to make as big a target as possible.

The Sabres goalie knows the statistics: most shots come along the ice. So he creates a barricade against the entire lower part of the net and takes his chances with the minority of shots that come in high. It's a calculated gamble that works for another of today's best goalies, says former netminder Chico Resch. "They say Patrick Roy goes down in the butterfly all the time and it's true. He's giving you a few inches at the top of the net and he's saying you can beat me up there, but under pressure that's a tough shot."

"The war is on the ice for goalies," agrees Anaheim goalie consultant Allaire, echoing Lloyd Percival's data from the 1950s. "What we find is that in every big event in hockey, 60 to 70 percent of the shots go along the ice now. I don't think we have any choice, we have to use the butterfly style." The reason so many shots are low is simple. "Right now, the play is so fast in the NHL that the guy really doesn't have one, two, three seconds to say, 'Okay, I'm going to pick the corner.' It's speed against speed. That's why mobility is so important."

As Allaire can attest, a butterfly goalie must be able to skate well and move quickly. One of the liabilities of the style is that skillful players can force the goalie to his knees with a fake shot, then circle the net and tuck the puck into the opposite side before the goalie can recover — the so-called wraparound. Like most shots, though, it requires time to execute, and time is in short supply with defensemen hanging all over the shooter. "A lot of pucks are just getting thrown at the net due to the speed of the game," acknowledges Wamsley. "If you're in any kind of position at all, you stand a good chance of getting hit."

Increasing the odds of getting hit has meant increasing the average size of goalies in the NHL. At 5-foot-11, Terry Sawchuk dwarfed Roy Worters; this current generation of goalies would tower over Sawchuk. More than half the starters in the NHL measure 6-foot-1 or taller; half a dozen (Sean Burke, Olaf Kolzig, Garth Snow, Tom Barrasso, Darren Puppa, Trevor Kidd, Mikhail Shtalenkov) are 6-foot-3 or taller. And with the predominance of the butterfly style — a long torso and long arms are essential — the increase in size won't end soon. Roberto Luongo, the top goaltending prospect in junior hockey, is 6-foot-4. "I don't say that smaller guys can't play the style," says Allaire. "Jocelyn Thibault is a good example of that. But in the long run, guys who are taller have a better chance of covering the whole net."

"It's going to be much more difficult when you're down and out, and you're small," says Glenn Hall. "You're going to have a big problem. The big goalie can just reach out, and he can stay in the play even if he's down on the ice."

Of course, big goalie or small, there is still the issue of the so-called five hole flaw in the butterfly style. It drives old-timers crazy to see so many goals going between the goalies' legs. A sample of goals from any weekend in the NHL would show as many as half finding their way between the goalie's legs. Flyers goalie Ron Hextall often hears the wrath of his father, former NHLer Bryan Hextall, about pucks scooting between the pads.

"He says, 'Just keep your damn legs together.' But I tell *him* to put his knees together and try to move laterally. You can't do it. Mario [Lemieux] just waited for you to come across with him, and as soon as your legs opened up, he had the puck through them. Unless it's from the blue line, a five-hole goal isn't necessarily a bad goal."

Goaltending is also changing in the way it attracts better athletes. In the old days, small players, bad skaters, and unstable characters ended up in the net. But with the success of Roy, Thibalt, Brodeur, and the other members of the "Block Quebecois," says Allaire, many good athletes in French Canada are giving goaltending a chance. "They can see the stars in the league, and they want to do the same thing. I think the kids realize they have a chance in hockey after watching Patrick. That brings in quality athletes in goal now." Allaire works with agent Gilles Lupien in developing goalie talent in Quebec.

Goalies are getting better instruction at an earlier age, too. Percival observed that lack of coaching and organized practice meant that goalies were the last players to mature in the NHL. The high level of coordination needed to play at the top level required repeated practice, but such practice for goaltenders was missing in the old days. It was an area that Tarasov addressed systematically in the Soviet Union but that has only recently been addressed in North America. "There's no doubt that we spend more time with our goalies now," says Senators coach Jacques Martin. "We realize how important goalies are to our hockey club, and finally we've spent time improving their physical skill and their mental skill. They can be such an asset for the organization."

Hall once tutored Wamsley in Calgary and their relationship speaks volumes about how the art of goaltending has improved. "We had sort of a father-son relationship," remembers Wamsley. "One time I went to Glenn with a specific problem about getting from point to point and staying square to the shooter. We talked for almost an hour, a great talk, and it really helped me."

Allaire's reputation was made when he guided Roy from an outstanding junior in Granby to one of the top goalies in the NHL. Their symbiosis was so powerful that Allaire's firing by the Canadiens helped precipitate Roy's confrontation with then-Montreal coach Mario Tremblay during a game at the Forum in late 1995. Roy was being buried by Detroit at the Forum; when the score reached 7–1, the Habs fans gave their hero a derisive cheer for stopping an easy shot. Roy responded by holding his arms aloft in mock celebration.

At the next whistle, Tremblay finally excused Roy for the night. Instead of taking a place at the end of the Habs bench, Roy stomped past Tremblay to confront Montreal president Ronald Corey, sitting directly behind the bench. Roy told Corey, "I've played my last game as a Montreal Canadien," or four-letter words to that effect. On December 5, 1995, the Canadiens traded perhaps their greatest goalie ever to Colorado.

Allaire and other goalie coaches such as Ian Young also contribute to summer camps that cater to goalies exclusively, always on the lookout for the next Roy or Brodeur. "To be a better goalie right now in hockey, you have to be a good skater first of all. If you're just big and you've got no mobility, that's no good. You have to be big and quick and a good skater. And the big guys need more practice to develop their quickness than the smaller guys."

Mitch Korn is the Sabres' goalie consultant, but like most of the men who make their living coaching goalies, he only periodically visits Dominik Hasek, commuting from his home in Oxford, Ohio, to see him and the Sabres' back-up netminders. The rest of the time, he's on the road to see the Sabres' goalies in the minor leagues and junior hockey. The theory seems to be that you can easily spoil a goalie by micro-managing his game. With a self-taught goalie such as Hasek, the risk of getting him thinking too much is amplified. The Red Wings also employ a "commuting" coach. Jim Bedard travels from Niagara Falls to monitor the progress of the Wings' goalies and prospects. But with younger, less experienced goalies than Hasek, there is more teaching to do.

"Don't fight the puck, let it hit you" is Bedard's mantra as he sits high in the press box at Maple Leaf Gardens, watching pupil Kevin Hodson in action for the Red Wings. In front of him, he calmly scribbles notes to himself as the action unfolds below. The Leafs are on the power play, swirling around Hodson in the net. At six foot and 182 pounds, Hodson has the size of the prototype goalie of the nineties. But the 25-year-old needs good positional play to make up for average reflexes and movement. It's his first start of the season in place of the principal goalie, Chris Osgood. Last season, Osgood was Detroit's busiest goalie, but he was then passed over by Scotty Bowman in the playoffs. Mike Vernon won the Conn Smythe Trophy as the playoff MVP, leading Detroit to the Cup; Osgood played in just two games in the playoffs, and those were when Vernon was bombed early. Now with Vernon in San Jose, Osgood must carry the Wings most of the way. And Bedard must soothe his confidence, bruised by the snub in the playoffs. Hodson, meanwhile, must stay ready for those infrequent nights when Bowman decides to give his number one goalie a rest.

"Don't get caught up in the action, move out of your crease," urges Bedard under his breath, as Wendel Clark jostles Hodson in the crease. The puck moves to the point, Hodson slides smoothly to the front of the crease, away from where Clark and the Red Wings defense are battling for position. The shot comes through unscreened, and Hodson is in perfect position to gather the shot into his body. "Good, good..." Bedard says.

The puck is dropped again to Hodson's left — or glove side. But Steve Yzerman wins the draw, and the Red Wings clear the defensive zone. Hodson relaxes; a hundred feet above him in the press box, Bedard watches dispassionately, like a scientist studying slides under the microscope. Soon, the Leafs counter and Bedard leans forward. "Square up, now," he says to Hodson. "Top of the crease, side to side...." The puck is shot toward the net; in falling, Hodson commits both legs to the right side of the net. But the defense can't control the rebound, and the puck slides across to his left. Down on his goal line, all he has left to stop the puck is his head and a flailing trapper. It's not enough, and Steve Sullivan ties the game.

Bedard scribbles notes in the cacophony of Leafs fans cheering an infrequent goal by their team. "He committed too soon," explains Bedard. "When he put both pads to one side he was stuck..." It's one of only two goals that will elude Hodson this night, however; the Red Wings score three and escape with a road win. Hodson stops 30 shots, including Mats Sundin on a stick save from point-blank range with just 4:30 left in the game. In all, a relatively successful night for Hodson and for Bedard, who makes his way to the Detroit dressing room after the game for a quick post mortem with Bowman.

IT'S MID-DECEMBER 1997 in Buffalo, and this snow magnet of a city is covered in white. It's been a trying couple of months since the 1997–98 season began. The Buffalo fans started booing Hasek when he stepped on the ice for his team's first home game in October against Dallas, after the team's summer of discontent and Hasek's annual sojourn in Pardubice. There weren't the usual 18,000 of them, either; many had canceled their season's tickets in a media-inspired protest over the tumult in the Buffalo front office. Forward Matthew Barnaby had threatened to flatten his own star goalie in the team's first practice of the season for badmouthing Nolan. Hasek had clearly gone from golden boy to vile ingrate in the span of a few months. ("I knew that probably some people wouldn't like what I said," he shrugged after the opening-night loss to Dallas in which he seemed torpid and uninspired. "I believe I was right. I had lots of time to think of it. There's nothing you can do. All you can do is your job.")

Whether it was the booing, or perhaps the brace protecting his damaged knee, Hasek had got off to an unusually slow start in 1997–98, which meant that the Sabres did too. After 23 games, he sported a goals-against average of 3.11 and a save percentage of .898 — respectable numbers by any standard except his. The Sabres, meanwhile, were a ghastly 6–12–5, tied for last in the Northeast. More recently, however, Hasek seems to have regained his impeccable form, though the Sabres remain in last place in the Northeast, the NHL's weakest division.

Tonight they host the team just ahead of them in the standings, the Carolina Hurricanes (née Hartford Whalers). It will be Hasek's twelfth straight start, a streak that has seen him chalk up three shutouts while posting a 1.80 goals-against average and a sparkling .940 save percentage. In that span, he has set a team record by holding the opposition scoreless for almost 176 consecutive minutes over three games. Hasek has whittled his goals-against average down to 2.68, raised his save percentage to .911, and is in the midst of racking up an NHL record six shutouts in December.

Since the team skate in the morning, Hasek has been relaxing at home with his family. He's less intense in game-day practices, say his teammates, who are regularly hauled back to the ice for more work by the perfectionist Hasek. "He's done that to me numerous times," says Peca. "Either I've had a good practice and scored on him, or we've done some breakaways and I score three out of five. I've got my equipment off and he's forcing me to come back out and take some breakaways. He's a very competitive guy."

Every goalie prepares for a game in his own way. "We never talked in the car going to the game, never," recalled Tony Esposito, the Hall of Fame netminder with Chicago. "Even when the kids started to drive down with us, no talking. If I was going to fail, it wasn't going to be because I wasn't mentally prepared. If I ever had a roommate it was the same thing. No talking." Hasek takes a more relaxed approach to the prospect of doing battle.

Hasek drives his Ford Explorer through the snow to the Marine Midland Center, arriving at 5:30 p.m. for the 7:30 p.m. game. Perhaps because he's weighted down with his equipment all game, behind the wheel Hasek likes to fly like a forward. Following him through the slushy streets of Buffalo sometimes requires a succession of daring turns on amber lights and distant sightings as he breaks away. The drive to the rink this evening is conducted at a more sedate pace.

Like many new NHL buildings, the Marine Midland Center has an outside dressing room, where the players put on their equipment, hold meetings, and meet the media after the game; and, beyond that, a second room, where they shower, dress, and sometimes hide out from the media. When Hasek arrives in the dressing room, he puts on his blue hockey underwear, then prepares one or two sticks for the game, carefully wrapping tape around the slightly curved left-hand blade, before heading for the team meeting. The Sabres coaches go over what they've noticed on the tape they've been studying. Sean Burke (who will be traded to Vancouver in three weeks) is the goalie for the Hurricanes, a tall (6-foot-4), mobile man who has yet to play for a contender that would allow him to showcase his skills. The secret to Burke, the coaches agree, is to create traffic in front of him and to get him moving, to open those long legs and go five hole.

Of more interest to Hasek are the Hurricanes' line combinations. Though an inveterate watcher of highlights, he spends little time watching raw videotape. Indeed, he likes to suggest that everything comes by instinct although, as Harry Neale points out, you can't get by just on instinct in the NHL. "Maybe I'm lazy, I don't know," says Hasek. "I don't say it's good, but I don't watch tape."

Asked who the toughest shooters are for him in the NHL, Hasek has a surprising reply. With only a few exceptions — Gretzky, Hull, Lemieux when he played — he concerns himself more with who his defensemen are and where they're positioned than with the opposition forward. He takes his positioning from his defensemen and constantly communicates with them. (Teammates say he is an inveterate chatterbox during games, constantly shouting encouragement and instructions.) If the defensemen are taking away the rush, Hasek prepares for the shot. If they're standing up, forcing the shot, he anticipates a possible deke.

(Other goalies have their own styles, and these can affect the way the defense plays as well. In Dallas, Ken Hitchcock had his defensemen staying low, taking away the low shots and leaving the rest to Andy Moog. Then the Stars signed Ed Belfour to replace Moog. Belfour hates players to block shots in front of him. Thus the Stars changed their style to suit their new goalie. Belfour takes the shots while the defense tries to clean up rebounds.)

Carolina has struggled almost as badly as the Sabres, but they have some good scorers and are unbeaten in three games, looking to make a run at Ottawa and Boston in the standings above them. Their big line is Keith Primeau, a tough, lanky center; Gary Roberts, attempting a comeback from serious neck problems in Calgary; and Sami Kapanen, a Finn who's off to a good start with 15 goals thus far.

After the team meeting, Hasek relaxes with a cup of coffee. There are no Glenn Hall upheavals of lunch, no banging of the head against the wall, no stony silences. He chats amiably with teammates — countryman Michal Grosek is perhaps his closest friend on the Sabres — and then, 30 minutes before the warm-up skate, begins his stretching routine, uncoiling the remarkably limber muscles in his long legs and back. He seems always to be stretching; staying flexible appears to be virtually a full-time job. "I stretch before games and practices. And when I'm watching TV or just around the house. Sometimes two minutes, sometimes five, sometimes ten. Just to keep loose. And I work out more, especially in the new building, because we have a full gym just ten steps away." Though he hits the gym frequently, it's not to bulk up. "When I first came to Chicago, Mike Keenan used to have us do reps — press your weight. I couldn't do that," he says sheepishly. "I did 135 pounds three times, and I'm 160 pounds. So next time I said no way!"

Hasek slips the brace on the knee he injured against Ottawa and begins dressing. After putting on an oversized protective cup, he slides on his goalie pants, with their extra padding , the bulky black upper body protector with arm pads that resembles a knight's armor, the goalie skates with their reinforced toe caps (left skate first), his lightweight red and white Bauer "Reactor" leg pads (he keeps two sets in his locker), the goalie-cut sweater, number 39, his Bauer catching and stick gloves, and finally his neck protector and the old-fashioned birdcage mask he's worn for eight years. He grabs his white goalie stick and joins his teammates for the warmup.

After their turbulent summer and slow start, the Sabres are having trouble drawing in their expensive new home. Even on a Friday night at holiday time, the Hurricanes clearly don't appeal to many fans on the Niagara frontier. The house will be announced as 12,321, but the warmup music blaring from the sound system echoes off empty rows of blue seats. This cacophonous pre-game laser show is an annoying reminder of the intrusion of NBA-style marketing in the NHL, courtesy of commissioner Gary Bettman, a former vice-president of the basektball league. Next, the anthem singer mangles not just the words but the tune to "O Canada." The "soulful stylings" on "The Star-Spangled Banner" are only marginally better.

Unlike the crowd at the season-opening Dallas game, this modest gathering reserves its loudest cheer for the announcement of Hasek as starting goalie. His improved play of late has them warming up to the Dominator again. The Sabres, as usual, will need him at his best tonight — Buffalo's offense without the traded Lafontaine is fifth worst in the NHL, their penalty killing third worst in the league.

The first chance of the game goes to Robert Kron of the Hurricanes. Trying to force the action, Buffalo's defense pinches at the Carolina blue line. As Kron comes in alone off the left wing, Hasek moves out to cut down the angle on his countryman. Kron has no option but to shoot. There is a sound of puck hitting plastic, but it's difficult to tell just what part of Hasek has made the stop. ("It hit my head," he'll explain at dinner after the game. "He had the breakaway and the shot hit my cage. I've been wearing this same helmet for 18 years and I've never been cut. Never. I've had a couple of hard shots, too.")

The Sabres get the first power play of the night when Steve Chiasson takes a hooking penalty. Buffalo's power play looks dreadful for the first 1:55 of the penalty, exerting no pressure whatsoever. Then, with Chiasson just two seconds from returning, a beautiful pass from Richard Smehlik finds Peca alone to one side of Burke. The Sabres captain, who missed Buffalo's first 14 games in a contract dispute, deposits his fifth goal of the season.

The rest of the period bogs down in missed passes, errant shots, endless play in the neutral zone. Hasek's only real challenge comes with 30 seconds left, when he's caught behind the net as his clearing pass gets back to Jeff Brown on the point. Scrambling back in position, he adopts the paddle-down, butterfly stance. He makes one save, the puck squirts loose, and suddenly Hasek, lying on the ice, has his back to the play. The Hurricane forwards flail at the puck, which hits Hasek and slides to the side of the net, where Alexei Zhitnik sits on it, drawing a whistle. ("Even though I was down, I saw it the whole way," Hasek will explain later. "I was afraid Zhitnik was sitting on the puck in the crease and we'd have a penalty shot.")

The period ends with the Sabres leading 1–0; Hasek has faced seven shots, but only two real scoring chances. In the second period, however, the Hurricanes open up. They pelt Hasek with 17 shots, many of them dangerous, and take the flow of this erratic game away from the Sabres, who seem content to protect a 1–0 lead. This is Hasek's habit, defying the opponent for long stretches; unfortunately for him, it is the Sabres' habit to think that one goal can stand up. The previous night in Boston, he stoned the Bruins for 52 minutes, only to have them score twice late in the game to steal a 2–1 win.

Against Carolina in the second period, Hasek robs Kevin Dineen on a two-on-one with a lovely pad save, stops Curtis Leschyshyn's tough shot from the point using his blocker, foils Roberts from the right circle with the blocker again, then confounds Kapanen with a trapper save on a two-on-one. Twice he roams to the corners, deftly clearing pucks for his defense. Some opponents believe that puck handling is one of his few weaknesses, but a veteran foe disagrees. "At one time, we thought we should get on him when he's got the puck, that he was weak with the puck. But I don't see that at all. He's good with the puck."

Playing the puck for his defensemen is something Hasek has mastered since arriving in the smaller rinks of the NHL. "It's very difficult to stop the puck behind the net [on the larger European ice surfaces]. Once you go to the corner or behind the net, it's too far. If somebody puts the puck along the boards, you've got to get the defensemen to get it. There they have more room. On this rink [in Buffalo] there is no room."

Hasek is perhaps the most active goalie in leaving his net to play the puck. Particularly when the Sabres are killing a penalty, he'll stray daringly to clear it to safety, often having to scramble back to make spectacular saves. He's as close to a defenseman as any goalie this side of Ron Hextall in Philadelphia. His boyhood friend Frank Musil says that back home Hasek even ranged far and wide to bodycheck opponents, a practice he's discontinued in North America. A superior skater, he's expert at corralling "shootarounds" behind the net. Roaming in this guerrilla fashion invites contact by opposing forwards who seem to believe that Hasek can be intimidated. In fact, he's fearless.

The Sabres take the 1–0 lead into the third period. The Hurricanes outshoot them by a considerable margin in the third — 18–3 — but Hasek holds them at bay. After one long point shot from Chiasson on the power play, he quickly skates to the right of his net, then serves the puck tennis-style into the neutral zone. The exasperated fans cheer as Hasek takes matters into his own hands. ("It wasn't frustration, I just wanted to get the puck into the neutral zone. I didn't want to drop the puck in front of me for a whistle. I hit it off the paddle of the stick. I do it [the tennis serve] once in a while. I used to do it more in Europe. The only problem is that when you miss, it drops right next to you.")

Midway through the third, referee Paul Devorski leans against the Sabres' net during a stoppage. What do referees and players talk about in those private moments? Was Devorski warning Hasek about delay of game? Commiserating about the foul Buffalo weather? "We were talking about my play," he says. "He was joking that I always try to play the puck, and I told him he was right. I like to play the puck, but it's not easy for me. I am so slow. I don't like to talk to the refs too much. It hurts my concentration." Maybe so. When Devorski whistles the play back in, Paul Ranheim passes from the left boards. Dineen grabs the puck and shoots. Hasek, in the butterfly position, saves with the toe of his left skate, but the puck bounces to his left. He slides across the ice, extending his trapper as far as he can. Dineen has the Sabres 6-foot-6 Mike Wilson draped all over him, but manages to sweep the puck around Hasek's glove and into the empty net. Suddenly, it's 1–1. (Hasek's eyes grow animated when he discusses the goal. "Yeah, I made the save, but the puck was getting away from me to the side. I could've made the save, but I thought he was covered by my teammate. All of a sudden, nobody was there. I couldn't believe he made it to the rebound. I had to make an adjustment but it was too late. I depended too much on my teammate.")

Sensing a swing in momentum, Carolina turns up the attack. A minute later, Stu Grimson — who played with Hasek in Chicago — sets up a screen. Although he can't see the initial shot, Hasek makes the save. Then, with the 6-foot-6, 220-pound Grimson jamming at the puck, he covers up. Grimson is knocked to the ice, two Sabres defensemen collapsing in a heap on top of him. With the volatile Grimson this could be an invitation to trouble, but he understands this is no time to disrupt his team's momentum. There are words but nothing else as the players unpile.

Buffalo's Bob Boughner takes an interference penalty halfway through the period. Behind the bench, Sabres coach Lindy Ruff drops his head in resignation. The Sabres force the puck into the Carolina zone on the penalty kill and, for reasons known only to himself, Alexei Zhitnik tries to pinch at the Hurricanes' blue line. Carolina chips the puck past him, and Jeff O'Neill, an erratic young center benched for indifferent play early in the season, breaks down the left side with the veteran Nelson Emerson on the right. Richard Smehlik is the only Sabre between them and the net.

It's a classic two on one. Does O'Neill, a prolific junior scorer, shoot, or does he pass to Emerson, who's more in the center of the rink? ("I thought he'd shoot," Hasek recalls afterwards. "In the NHL, I know that if you have a shooter, the defense cuts off the pass. But I like my defense to be more aggressive and try to force the shooter. Even if he passes, I can still make the play. I was disappointed in my defenseman, because he was so much in the middle of the rink. It was like 'I've got the pass, you've got the player.' The defenseman let O'Neill come to the middle too much.") As O'Neill crosses the face-off circle, he lets go a quick snap shot. The low drive beats Hasek through the legs as he moves to guard against the pass. ("He made a good shot in my five hole. There was a big hole and he hit it.")

Seeing their team blow a lead late in the third period for a second straight night, the fans boo lustily. ("How would you like it," Jacques Plante once asked reporters in Montreal, "if every time you made a mistake at work, a red light went on behind your desk and 15,000 people started booing?") For the next few minutes, the Hurricanes pin the Sabres in their own zone, forechecking effectively with Primeau, Kron, and O'Neill. The booing intensifies. Carolina's checking gets even more effective. Pucks deflect off Buffalo sticks, passes go astray — this is losing hockey personified. ("I was also disappointed with the way we played. We could not get anything going. The reporters asked after the game why the guys could not get together. I told them to go ask the coach.")

With 1:38 left in the third and the puck being cycled harmlessly along the boards in the Carolina end, Sabres defenseman Jason Woolley pinches in from the point. He takes the puck and throws it in front to Slovakian forward Miroslav Satan. The previous season, Satan was dumped by a frustrated Glen Sather in Edmonton for his ambivalent approach to the game. With Buffalo, however, he has come to life. He shoves the sweet pass behind Sean Burke and the game, incredibly, is headed for overtime, despite the fact that the Sabres have been outshot 34–20. Give thanks once again, O Lord, for the Dominator.

In overtime, things do not improve measurably. With 30 seconds left to play, Hasek is forced to make a tough save off his upper arm on a shot by O'Neill. He plays the puck up the wing at the moment the Carolina defense changes on the fly. (As Hurricanes coach Paul Maurice will say later, "For some reason our two defensemen decided they needed to change with 14 seconds left in the game.") Smehlik feeds the puck to Matthew Barnaby — he of the idle threat against Hasek earlier in the season — who breaks up the ice on a two on one with Grosek. At this point Barnaby has 0 goals, 4 assists, and 100 penalty minutes. The laws of the hockey universe dictate that he give Grosek, a more talented scorer, the chance to win the game. But Barnaby has clearly not studied law. He gets within 35 feet and tees up a Brett Hull-like drive that rips over Burke's shoulder into the net. The Sabres win 3–2, and Hasek leaps joyously in the air, again and again, as if he's won the Stanley Cup instead of a tedious December match in the NHL's long regular season.

"It's the best feeling of the year," Hasek gushes in the media scrum around his locker. Later, with a little reflection and his adrenalin slowing, he modifies his assessment of the man who wanted to take his head off months before. "It *might* be the best feeling. I didn't believe Barnaby could score like that. He can handle the puck but he's not really a play maker."

In his post-game news conference, the final word goes to the coach, Lindy Ruff, who says of Hasek, "He gives you what you want from your goalie — big saves and a chance to win." Or, as an opponent will later put it, "He'll give up a soft goal sometimes — a blooper over his shoulder, or a long shot through the five hole — but the goal Hasek almost never gives up is the one you really need, the one that means the game."

IT'S JANUARY 1998, and it's raining in Vancouver. Inside GM Place, Dominik Hasek wears the sunny smile of a man writing headlines with his play on the ice. After their tepid start, the Sabres are again looking like the team that won the Northeast Division the season before. Since the overtime win against Carolina, Buffalo has gone 9–7–1, with Hasek leading the way. His numbers are back in line with the ones that earned him the Hart Trophy, no one's mentioned Ted Nolan in the longest while, and the Sabres, despite their offensive limitations, have become a team that can knock off anybody on a given night. In a couple of weeks Hasek will head to Japan to play for the Czech Republic in the Olympics, a tournament he's keenly looking forward to. All in all, he has plenty of reasons to smile.

Hasek has brought his ten-year-old son Michael to watch him tend nets for the World Team against the North American all-stars. While Dad, in the white World Team jersey with the Czech flag on the shoulder, fields questions from the media, Michael stands at his side, dressed in a black Sabres jersey with HASEK across the back. It's a family holiday paid for by the NHL, though the all-star game itself is no holiday for goalies. The previous year, Hasek was peppered with 21 shots in the third period by the Western team; he stopped 20 of them, preserving a 5–4 win for the Eastern Conference (or was it the Wales?). The year before, he stopped 12 of 13 shots in a scrimmage that ended up 11–7 for the East (or was it the Campbells?). The game is a contact-free shooting gallery for the best snipers in the NHL.

So is the skills competition, staged before the game. Here the NHL's best compete in contests for the hardest shot, most accurate shot, fastest skater, and two goalie categories: rapid-fire saves and the breakaway relay contest. Hasek teams with Olaf Kolzig of Washington and Nikolai Khabibulin of Phoenix to win the rapid-fire event for the World team.

Then he takes on North America's best shooters alone in the breakaway contest: Six of the top marksmen from North America go head to head with him in a 20-second onslaught, rebounds allowed.

Most NHL players consider Hasek the toughest goaltender to beat on a breakaway. What makes him so difficult? Joey Mullen, the top American-born goal scorer of all time, points to Hasek's unpredictable style. "You don't know what to do, because he does everything so different from a normal goalie. Usually you have a guy's movement, but Hasek falls so differently you don't know which way he's going to go. That confused me particularly; he stops it with the back of his head or something."

"Dominik never lets too much distance come between himself and the puck," says the journalist Jiri Kolis, himself a former amateur goalie. "He's such a good skater he can move in and back fast to crowd the shooter and prevent him from shooting up high, where he doesn't have as much of the net covered."

"He's an acrobat, a contortionist," agrees Hasek's teammate Peca. "He's got no set style. And he outsmarts the shooter. You can see when a lot of younger guys come in, especially in close, Dominik's got the psychological advantage. They're hurrying up the play. He's got the upper hand."

"It's intimidating playing against him in the NHL," says Roman Hamrlik. "It must be a great feeling for him to be so intimidating, to do it against great players."

This psychological mastery, says Chico Resch, the former Islanders goalie, is what defines great goaltenders. They intimidate shooters in breakaway situations. "Great goalies have one thing in common. Under pressure, the puck doesn't go through them. Under pressure, they continue to play up to their standards. The great ones don't self-destruct."

Certainly nobody in the skills competition qualifies as a nervous young guy, shivering in his boots. The North American and World teams are tied when Brian Leetch, Scott Niedermayer, Joe Sakic, Mark Recchi, Wayne Gretzky, and Theo Fleury each put their Sunday-best move on Hasek. One after another, in rapid-fire succession, they swoop down the ice, and one after another he stones them using virtually every piece of his equipment. At the other end of the ice, Patrick Roy is just as hot and the competition moves to a tie breaker. The corporate crowd at Vancouver's new sports palace is primed for the showdown; the North American skaters simply hope that Hasek won't make them look too bad. Joe Sakic moves in first. As he closes in, he moves the puck to his backhand and then back to his forehand. The deke eludes Hasek's glove.

When Peter Bondra scores for the World, it comes down to Hasek versus Mike Modano of Dallas. Modano chooses to shoot, but Hasek's lightning-fast trapper snatches the shot. Hasek wins the competition for the World and the top goalie award for himself.

There is genuine warmth in the fans' response to Hasek, but it will never approach the adoration felt by Canadians for the likes of Gretzky, Roy, and Messier. Still, the mere acceptance of the World vs. North America format in 1998 speaks volumes about the changing ethos of the NHL. Only a few years ago, the idea of Europeans taking on the heroes of this continent would have been laughed at. To say that the gradual erosion of Canada's NHL monopoly by high-priced foreign imports has been a sore point in some quarters is like saying the *Titanic*'s demise messed up some travel plans. With fervent nationalists like Don Cherry leading the chorus, European players have been blamed for everything from higher ticket prices to the increase in stick work in the league. In his self-anointed role as keeper of the flame, Cherry has become the Al Sharpton of hockey, a ubiquitous, dandified buffoon who panders to the basest fears of his frightened, disempowered constituents.

"They talk about all the things that foreign players have brought to the game," says Cherry. "Well, let's see, what have they brought? The helmet, the visor, the dive." Hey, Don, don't forget lack of loyalty, disrespect for coaches, longer games, fewer Canadians in junior hockey — all this and more Cherry has laid at the door of the imported players. Cherry, of course, is not alone. Andy Van Hellemond, a respected NHL referee for many years, summed up the stereotype of European players for Dick Irvin: "They come over here and soon find out that you make $2 million for playing 82 games and $60,000 for playing 21 or 25 playoff games. What are you gonna do? I mean, they're not stupid. Playoffs are tough, man-to-man hockey. You go out there and get hit and pounded. And what does the Stanley Cup mean to a kid from across the ocean? He knows he'll make another $2 million next year if he stays healthy.

"In my years in hockey, that's been the biggest change. A Canadian or an American will take a bump, a hit, a smack in the mouth and keep playing. Now you see those guys from Europe fall down and grab their mouth and get a five-minute power play and a few of them start to do it, too. Big money and too many Europeans."

No doubt, Van Hellemond — who pines for the good old days — had anecdotal evidence on which to base his observations. Harold Ballard loved to say similar things, and there was some truth to his assertion that one of the Swedes on the Maple Leafs could go into the corner with a dozen eggs and come out with them intact. But that was 20 years ago, and the current depiction of European players as cowards, cheats, and ingrates is outdated, pernicious, and xenophobic. Ask any defenseman who's taken a run at Pavel Bure whether Bure's a coward. Ask players who had their teeth loosened by Vladimir Konstantinov if European players avoid physical play. Ask any player if Peter Forsberg's in it for the money or if Teemu Selanne is a wimp.

The "Chicken Swede" characterizations represent little more than nostalgia for the days of the 99 percent Canadian NHL, days when claims of superior mental and physical toughness could be safely made but never tested. Call it national pride, or human nature. "The Victorian idea that physical and mental toughness meant national superiority came back to haunt the British," the American sports sociologist John Hoberman noted, "when the outstanding performances of the Australian and New Zealand soldiers in both the Boer War and World War I were contrasted with the alleged passivity of [the British] troops."

While the myth of Canadians' moral and competitive superiority has been largely repudiated, the old perceptions fanned by Cherry and others still have a powerful influence on the hockey culture. Mike Bell of the OHL's Ottawa 67's was singing from the Cherry hymn book in May 1998 when he told TV interviewer Michael Landsberg that Europeans in his league "get hit a lot. And they get sticked. And you know, sometimes they deserve it. We don't like them. The entire hockey league [doesn't] like them."

The demonization of foreign players also fails to take into account the extraordinary challenge of cultural assimilation faced by players coming from Europe — particularly those, like Hasek, from formerly communist parts of the world. Jaromir Jagr of the Penguins was faced with the full range of challenges, from language to finances to style of play, when he came to North America as an 18-year-old product of Czech hockey. Despite diligently taking English lessons, he was often unable to understand coaches and teammates, which made him depressed and moody — Van Hellemond's stereotype. The situation was not resolved until the Penguins got him a Czech teammate to talk to. (In 1997–98 the Penguins had five Czechs on their roster, and Jagr won the Art Ross Trophy as the NHL's top scorer.) Today, he acknowledges that the simple task of comprehending English may be the biggest obstacle faced by foreign players.

"We interviewed one player from Europe who had a brother in the NHL already," remembers Ken Dryden, president of the Leafs. "One of the things his brother had told him was quite interesting. He said so much of the sports life is the practice of it, the playing of it, and the hanging around it — 'And I can't hang around. I can't get across what I feel well enough to be comfortable hanging around.' His brother was finding it lonely. That's part of the challenge of drafting a European player. You're drafting somebody who's got certain skills, but how those skills are going to be used depends on how comfortable he is. If he feels like an outsider, a hired hand, then you're going to get a hired-hand performance."

Certainly the cultural gap between Hasek and the people of Buffalo had a bearing on his problems at the end of the 1997 playoffs. Unlike many European players today, who come in their teens to play junior hockey, Hasek was 25 when he arrived, more set in his ways. (In 1997–98 he was the oldest player, at 33, on the youngest team in the NHL.) His accented English, his awkwardness with the cultural assumptions made by the likes of Nolan, Barnaby, and Kelley, and the stigma of coming from a country recently considered "the enemy" all fed the firestorm. (An earlier impaired driving charge didn't help matters either.) The function of the media in reporting such things also has different implications for Hasek, who was brought up with a controlled press. In short, he and other European players who plan to leave North America at the end of their careers make easy targets.

"A couple of the Swedish guys I played with — Tomas Jonsson and Mats Hallin — were two of the funniest guys in the league, and well respected," recalls Pat Flatley. "What hurts many European players is that they can sense the perception of them. If there's negative feeling, spoken or not, they feel it and react accordingly. That's what made some Russian players go to a 'screw you' attitude. The onus is on the North American players to make them feel welcome. And if they're treated fairly, the key is for the Europeans to learn to speak the language and integrate. There's a perception that the Europeans only understand what they want to understand. Tell them something good and they'll understand. Tell them something bad, they don't speak English. So they have to make an effort to integrate."

These language problems occasionally have an amusing side. Former Flames coach Terry Crisp was asked in 1993 how Russian rookie German Titov was picking up the team's system. "The scary part is, a guy who doesn't understand me is doing exactly what we want," said Crisp. "And some other guys who clearly do understand me haven't got it yet."

The xenophobia is also undoubtedly a spillover from the paranoia felt when Canada faced the dark and dastardly Soviet empire in 1972. "We really felt like we were playing to save our system," recalls Wayne Cashman, who'd been encouraged by his Boston mates to "get a Swede" in an exhibition match on the way to Moscow. "Since then we've come to learn that they are great players and good people who can make a real contribution to our hockey teams."

Most NHL players agree. "Look at the impact the Russian Five (Kozlov, Fetisov, Larionov, Federov, and Konstantinov) had in a market like Detroit," says Hurricanes winger Grimson. "They've brought a real flavor to the North American fan. And the North American players have not been exposed to much going back into the seventies and eighties." Even a traditionalist like Chelios of the Blackhawks appreciates the grit of the Soviet players. "I respect guys like Fetisov and Larionov," he says. "You watch them play in the Canada Cup and the World Cup and these guys are tough. They just keep coming at you, and they beat you. And they had an old-school guy like Konstantinov. Our guy Krivokrasov is also a tough little guy. The Russians are tough."

Not that the boorish behavior has disappeared completely. Tod Hartje, an American, played a season in the Russian Elite League in the early 1990s and remembers an exhibition game against some Canadians in Finland. No sooner had the game begun than the Canadians started tossing insults. "When's the last time you had a bath, dickhead?" one of them yelled at Hartje's teammate. Another noticed the condition of a Soviet player's teeth — "'You ever hear of toothpaste?' he yelled. The Canadians kept up the boorish abuse the whole game — to the point where I was embarrassed to be a North American."

Sometimes the skepticism about European players extends to NHL coaches. Despite Hasek's success, he's only one of three European starting goalies in the NHL. When it comes to the most crucial man on the ice, most NHL coaches, all of whom are North American, prefer to entrust the game's fate to one of their own.

EVEN HERE, in a dank hallway at the Big Hat arena in Nagano, Japan, Vladislav Tretiak's wide-set eyes, hawk-like nose, broad shoulders, and shock of sandy brown hair are unmistakable. Watching the Czech players take the ice for practice at the 1998 Winter Olympics, Tretiak — wearing a trenchcoat, sipping coffee — still resembles the stoic young soldier who burst into the Canadian hockey consciousness a quarter century ago. This was the face that haunted the first Team Canada, the man who, Canadian scouts assured their team, would be "the weakest link on the Soviet team" when they met in 1972, the goalie who became a legend during that tournament.

Tretiak is in Nagano to watch Russia's starting goalie, Mikhail Shtalenkov of the Mighty Ducks. The best Russian goalie these days, Nikolai Khabibulin of Phoenix, is passing up the Olympics, and Shtalenkov can use some pointers. But Tretiak also has more than a passing interest in the man who has superceded him as the greatest goalie in European history. The Russian helped coach the nervous young Czech when Hasek arrived in Chicago to play for the Blackhawks.

There's a certain irony in Tretiak's having coached Hasek. "I don't recommend blocking shots by falling down or kneeling," Tretiak wrote in his 1988 book *Tretiak: The Legend.* "Stand confidently on your feet. It is easier to fool a goalkeeper when he is lying down. Falling is often a sign of poor skills or no confidence." To his credit, Tretiak knew enough to ignore his own advice in Chicago when he encountered Hasek, who broke all the rules.

"How to describe his style?" Tretiak muses, cradling his steaming coffee. "Hasek style like no one else. He works very, very hard in practice. He falls down more than me. If you ask me what is his strongest part of game, I think it is his gloves. But again, he works so hard in practice. That is his secret. I think Shtalenkov is a very good goalie. But Hasek" — Tretiak's English fails him briefly — "Hasek is Hasek."

No one knows better than Tretiak that a goalie can steal a medal, or sink his team, in the brief Olympic tournament. He himself won the gold with the Soviet Union in 1972, 1976, and 1984. In between he experienced the desolation of losing to the United States at Lake Placid in 1980 (he was pulled after two periods of the final game by an irate Viktor Tikhonov). He knows there is no better goalie in the world these past four years than Hasek. Still, nobody really gives the Czech Republic much chance at this tournament. Canada, the United States, Sweden, and the Russians also have good goaltending, as well as offensive depth that the Czechs — who boast Jagr up front but not much else — can only envy. With just 12 NHL players on their roster, the Czechs are considered undermanned. Hasek in peak form, goes the thinking, might cause an upset or two, but you can get long odds betting on the Czechs.

Not that Hasek is perturbed. He is upbeat as he clomps up the hallway from the dressing room, bulked up like the Michelin man in his enormous protective shell of equipment. He feels, coming into the Games, that he's playing as well as he ever has. Buffalo is unbeaten in nine games. Since the Carolina game in December, Hasek has lowered his goals-against average by almost half a goal. His save percentage has improved from .910 to .924, and he has tacked on four more shutouts. He's gone 12–6–6 in that span, playing virtually every game for the Sabres. Pausing in the hallway, he greets Tretiak fondly and pauses long enough to share a joke in Russian before stepping on the ice.

The Czechs and the Russians have been grouped with Finland and Kazakhstan in one division of the round robin. This is considered a break for the Czechs, because they won't meet the three presumed heavyweights of the tournament — Canada, the United States, and Sweden — until they've played a few games.

Hasek chose to sit out the 1996 World Cup, and the Czechs vaporized without him. The dressing room was filled with arguments over style of play and ice time; while their former countrymen from Slovakia headed to North America for the final stage of that tournament, the Czechs stayed home to brood. The national program seemed in ruins. But former national hero Ivan Hlinka has taken over as coach and has convinced Hasek and Jagr to play. He has also named respected Vladimir Ruzicka captain. After five years in the NHL, Ruzicka returned to play in Europe where his offensive talents are celebrated, instead of his defensive liabilities criticized. He and Jagr will key the offense, along with Martin Rucinsky of Montreal and Robert Reichel of the Islanders. Unfortunately for the Czechs, hard-nosed center Bobby Holik of New Jersey has been ruled ineligible to play since taking out American citizenship.

On defense, Hasek will have help from his underappreciated Sabres teammate Robert Smehlik, along with veterans Petr Svoboda of the Flyers, Jiri Slegr of Pittsburgh, and youngster Roman Hamrlik of Edmonton. The rest of the Czech names are either dimly known or completely new — Jaroslav Spacek, Jiri Dopita, Pavel Patera. "You know, I recognize many of the players in the dressing room," Hasek says, smiling sheepishly, "but I'll have to learn some names. There are four or five guys, I don't know their name in there. But it will be a team that wins here, not one goalie. I can't stop everything, and we have guys who can score."

Jan Caloun, one of those Czech "names," is playing in Sweden after three unsuccessful tries at making the San Jose Sharks. He is awestruck to be playing with Hasek. "My favorite save is the way he can turn his shoulders around when he's on the ice and catch the puck behind his head," says Caloun. "If I score against him in practice, I know I've done something. He doesn't lose, even in practice. He must win at everything. He's a great advantage for us."

How much of an advantage quickly becomes clear in the Czechs' opening game against Finland, played two days later at the smaller Aqua Wing arena. Hasek shuts down Teemu Selanne, Saku Koivu, and the other offensively gifted Finns in a 3–0 shutout. Against lowly qualifier Kazakhstan the next day, Hasek is ordinary, perhaps bored, but the Czechs run their record to 2–0 with a convincing 8–2 win. This sets up a showdown with the Russians to decide top spot in their division. The winner gets Belarus (the other qualifying team); the loser draws either the powerful Swedes or the talented Americans.

The contrast between the Russian team Hasek faces in Japan and the Soviet juggernaut he played against in the 1988 Calgary Olympics is stark. Calgary was the last hurrah for all things Soviet in sport, the heyday of the Soviets' brilliant Krutov-Larionov-Makarov line. The three men finished 1–2–6 in Olympic scoring that year, and their defense comrade Viacheslav Fetisov finished third. The Soviets lost just once in nine games under the cranky Tikhonov to win their second straight gold, and sixth in seven Olympic Games.

The Russian team that has shown up in 1998 is considered a mere postscript to the glory days. In the past, participation in such tournaments was compulsory. In 1988, many players have opted out, citing age (Fetisov, Larionov), disenchantment with bureaucracy (Slava Kozlov, Khabibulin), or "new priorities" (Sandis Ozolinsh, Sergei Zubov). One player who has shown up, Sergei Federov, is thought to have attended more out of a desire to spark stalled contract talks with Detroit than out of patriotism.

Still, the Russians have iced a highly talented, threatening team. The Bure brothers, Federov, Alexei Yashin, Valeri Kamensky, and Alexei Zhamnov provide a flashy offensive attack; the Mironov brothers, Darius Kaspartitis, and Alexei Zhitnik have the makings of a stalwart defense. Shtalenkov — who backstopped the so-called Unified Team to the gold medal in 1992 — can be expected to make at least the routine saves. And a vast improvement over the 1996 World Cup team that flamed out in the semifinals is the installation of Vladimir Yurzinov as coach. The much-loathed Boris Mikhailov had alienated many of the top stars in Russian hockey, but Yurzinov placated most of them in time for these Games.

One thing has not changed with the Russians. Their pace is blinding when their stars are in gear, and they start the game against the Czechs as if something urgent awaits them right after the game. In the first period, they fire 14 shots at Hasek, including a bullet drive by Kamensky as he tears in off the right wing. When the puck hits Hasek's head, shards of blue plastic fly one way; the puck goes off the other. Like a fighter who's taken Mike Tyson's best punch, Hasek staggers but won't go down. He plays the remainder of the game with the battered head gear flopping loosely around his ears. Several of his saves in the first period are spectacular. Alexei Morozov of the Penguins is sent in alone on a give-and-go pass. His shot looks perfect — low to the stick side — until Hasek, with his extraordinarily quick legs, flicks out the toe of his right skate. A few minutes later his Buffalo teammate Zhitnik tries to cut in off the wing after taking a perfect pass. Hasek stacks the pads so suddenly that Zhitnik has no option but to jam the puck uselessly into them. The period ends scoreless.

The second period starts the same way, with Hasek frustrating the dangerously free-wheeling Pavel Bure, captain of the Russians. Then the Czechs get a break on the power play: Reichel tips a shot from Patera between the pads of Shtalenkov. Despite outplaying the Czechs at every turn, the Russians are suddenly behind 1–0. Hasek takes a quick skate around his net to celebrate Reichel's clever score, seemingly psyching himself up for the onslaught to come. Sure enough, by the end of the second period, the Russians have tried 21 times to beat Hasek, and 21 times they've failed. The Czech fans are giddy at the prospect that maybe, just maybe, Hasek can pull off a miracle.

There will indeed be miracles in Nagano, but not this day. Less than four minutes into the third period, the Russians generate a lightning-fast counter-attack. Valeri Bure moves just inside the blue line one on one with Smehlik. He threads a wrist shot through the defenseman's legs. Hasek, screened, reacts too late, and the puck beats him stick side. (After the game, he will call it a good goal, but his unhappiness on the ice makes it obvious that he believed he should have stopped it.) He's clearly still thinking about Bure's shot ten seconds later, when Zhamnov is hauled down on his way to Hasek's net. As he falls, Zhamnov manages to scoop the puck in the air. Hasek, down on all fours to smother what he thinks will be a rolling puck, reacts too quickly as the shot, like a change-up in baseball, sails lazily over his shoulder and into the net. Two goals in ten seconds have suddenly, cruelly, turned a Czech upset win into a loss. The red, white, and blue flags and banners that have danced all day in the crowd suddenly go limp. Kasparitis levels Jagr with a powerful check at the blue line, a statement. Hasek recovers his poise in time to make several more great saves, but the Czech offense simply cannot overcome the Russian defensive scheme. Counter-attacking beautifully, the Russians hang on for a 2–1 win and a date with the Belarussians.

It is a hard loss for Hasek to accept. He believes the first shot was stoppable, and he knows the second had to be stopped by a goalie of his caliber. But the gloom of loss gives way to a crucial realization: Hasek and his teammates understand that they can be more than simply competitive with the Russians. They can beat them, they believe, if the two teams happen to meet again in Nagano. In the subdued atmosphere of the dressing room, the Czechs metamorphose from a raggedy band of dreamers into a team with a goal and a growing assurance they can reach it.

First to discover this quiet determination are the overconfident Americans, who run up against Hasek's best single performance of the Games. He turns aside shot after shot; many saves are of the "Did you see that?" variety. On the U.S. bench, captain Chelios, the Rangers' Leetch, the Stars' Modano, and the rest of the individually gifted Americans can only watch as their gold-medal dreams evaporate. Up in the corner of Big Hat where the families of the Czech players are seated, meanwhile, Alena Hasek cheers alongside Jaromir Jagr's mother, Petr Svoboda's wife, and other friends and family, all of them wearing their gaudy red Czech jerseys, linked in an exquisite rapture, alternately terrified and exultant. When the Czechs take the lead in the second period, Alena notices her husband bow his neck in the resolute way he sometimes does, and takes heart. It's Dominik's silent version of "They shall not pass."

After the game, a 4–1 victory that eliminates the Americans, Hasek stands in the media zone, half dressed, dripping sweat. The Czech reporters look dazed, screaming out his name for a quote, a sound bite, anything. "To play for a little country like the Czech Republic and win is great," he tells CBC Radio above the shrieks of his countrymen. "I feel tired but good. I think for me this is the greatest moment of my career."

Not for long. Two days later, against mighty Canada, the Czechs demonstrate the truth of a widely mouthed platitude. Before the

Games, all the coaches and players said the same thing: with so much individual talent on display, the secret of success would be playing as a team. Much thought went into line combinations; both Canada and the United States took great care to assemble groupings that would gel immediately. But the Czechs prove to be the ones who have best assembled and melded a squad that's more than the sum of its parts.

While not given many scenes in the early part of the Czechs' game against Canada, Hasek steals the movie in the final reel. Regulation ends with the score 1–1. In an uncanny replay of the skills competition at the all-star game, he's again forced to face some of the NHL's top shooters one on one. Hasek had shut down the best North American snipers in a fun format in Vancouver, but how would he do in hockey's ultimate cliffhanger, with the whole world watching?

Of the six men who tested him at the all-star game, only Theo Fleury gets a chance for revenge in Nagano. Mark Recchi and Wayne Gretzky remain on the Canadian bench this time. Joe Sakic, the only player to solve Hasek in Vancouver, sits morosely in the upper deck of Big Hat, his injured knee taped beneath street clothes. In five minutes of the highest drama, Hasek duels the goaltender many consider his only peer, Patrick Roy of the Canadian team.

Watching the shootout, the parents, wives, and families of both teams sit uncomfortably close to each other in the upper reaches of Big Hat. Team jerseys, emblazoned with the name of a son or a husband, are now soaked with perspiration. The spectators sit oddly poised, suspended in the moment. Many, like Gretzky on the Canadian bench, find the drama impossible to watch. Others cling together for support. Down on the ice, meanwhile, in his flopping, sprawling style, Hasek repels each of the Canadian shooters in turn. Roy plays brilliantly himself, but he's beaten once, by Robert Reichel. When it's finally over — when Hasek leaps skyward after turning aside Brendan Shanahan, propelling his club into history and relegating Canada to a 1998 footnote — the Czech fans ignite, hugging and hollering and flag-waving. The Canadian fans, distraught and tired, quietly file out with barely a backward glance.

In the interview area, Hasek wears a dazzled, almost disbelieving smile as he makes the rounds of TV and radio positions. The emotional peak two days earlier against the Americans is now a molehill compared to the mountain he and the Czech team have climbed. A silver medal is assured, the gold not out of reach — Russia will play Finland in the other semifinal, with the Czechs playing the winner. Back home, Hasek knows, the entire Czech Republic is following every move the team makes. The shouting, pleading media mob is glorious vindication for the man accused of pulling himself from the playoffs the previous spring to dodge the pressure. Pressure? He has allowed just six goals in the five games so far in the tournament.

Midway through an interview with Czech TV, Hasek abruptly bolts down the hallway. The interviewer and cameraman shoot perplexed glances at each other. Was it something someone said? Nerves? As it turns out, it's doping control; Hasek has realized he's late for giving a urine sample to the IOC drug police. While he attends to his Olympian task, the other ecstatic Czechs begin to grasp the extent of their upset. It turns out that the IIHF brain trust, like almost everyone else, has underestimated the Czechs, too, and booked them on flights out of Nagano the next morning. It's one flight Hasek is happy to be bumped from.

GOING INTO THE OLYMPICS, Hasek believed that the road to a gold medal, unlikely as it was, would lead through the United States, Canada, and Russia. Now only one of those teams remains, the team that symbolizes something far greater than just hockey, the team on whom the Czechs would love to exact revenge: Russia. Not simply for the 2–1 loss earlier in the tournament, but for all the painful losses through the years at the Olympics and world championships. Perhaps the most agonizing hockey loss was the gold-medal game at the 1976 Olympics in Innsbruck. Leading 4–3 late in the third period, Czechoslovakia allowed two quick goals, dashing what would have been their first gold-medal triumph at the Olympics. Instead of celebrating victory, the Czechs watched in agony as Maltsev, Kharlamov, Yakushev, and company triumphed again.

For some, of course, any meeting between the Czechs and the Russians brings back memories of the tortured history shared by the former Czechoslovakia and the former Soviet Union. One only has to look at the "68" on Jaromir Jagr's back to understand that the memory of Soviet tanks crushing the Prague spring of Alexander Dubcek was very much alive 30 years later. Jagr, who was born in 1972, told reporters he wore the number to commemorate his grandfather who had been imprisoned by the Soviets after the purge. In the stands at the Big Hut, there are many who remember those days well, and their raucous cheers as the teams take the ice are tinged with a longing for revenge.

Not everyone is motivated by the past. "What happened happened," explains Martin Straka of Pittsburgh. "I wasn't even born in 1968. We don't hate Russians. Some of the guys on that team are my friends." For Hasek, the political conflict was a story heard from parents and grandparents. "We used to hate the Russian team, because of the politics," he recalls. "Their army was in our country, they told us what to do. I didn't hate the Russians personally; I was born a little later, it wasn't as bad as it used to be. But the people hated them, I heard the stories from my grandpa. If somebody said they didn't like the regime, they could lose their jobs or worse. We couldn't beat them in politics, but maybe we can beat them on the ice."

Before the opening face-off, Robert Reichel says something to

Hasek. The Islander taps both of the goalie's leg pads, both of his gloves, both of his shoulders, and finally his mask. Tanks be damned — the Czechs will need good luck, as well as the game of their lives, to stop these Russians.

Two days earlier, the Czechs had watched Pavel Bure single-handedly destroy Finland with five goals in the other semifinal. The strategy for the Czechs will be to stop Bure and Federov and the rest of the Russian speedsters from gaining momentum in the neutral zone. And while Hasek may be the best goalie in the world on breakaways, his team won't win if it gives up as many lightning counter-attacks as the Finns surrendered.

Before the game, coach Hlinka has stressed the importance of remaining a cohesive, five-man unit when moving up the ice to prevent Russian breakaways. German head coach George Kingston had earlier explained the strategy: players should think of themselves as being under a blanket, he said, and when one pulls too far from the others on the big ice, the blanket rips. "In modern hockey, you need a first wave on the attack, but you also need a support wave following them," Kingston said. "The key is the fourth and occasionally the fifth man into the rush. More and more, these are the players scoring these days. To be successful you need four or five players — including defensemen — comfortable handling the puck, creating offense. That was one of the things lacking for Canada in the Olympics."

North American defensemen tend simply to dump the puck to a safe spot on the ice, agrees Tod Hartje, the American who played in Russia. "This is in stark contrast to the method employed in the Soviet Elite league where the puck was virtually never moved without a D to D (defenseman to defenseman) regroup. Teams even went so far as to pass the puck to their own goaltender. Although I'm not suggesting we adopt that strategy completely, I do believe a strong dose of Soviet style and mentality, and the skill their defensemen bring to the game, would benefit North American players and fans alike."

One only has to see the puck-handling skills of Boris and Dmitri Mironov, Kasparitis, and Zhitnik (as well as the absent Ozolinsh and Sergei Zubov) to understand what Hartje means about the Russian defensemen's participation on offense. On the Czech side, Svoboda, Hamrlik, and Slegr are also highly proficient at completing these five-man units. Just how proficient quickly becomes obvious: the two teams fly up and down the ice for the first five and a half minutes of the gold-medal game without a whistle. The first stoppage doesn't come until Hasek takes Pavel Bure's shot in the midsection and holds on.

Midway through the first period, Hasek lifts the puck over the glass. He's assessed a delay-of-game penalty by referee Bill McCreary. It's a borderline call, considering the low glass at Big Hat, but McCreary goes by the book. For two minutes, the Russians swarm the Czech goal. Hasek is a dervish killing the penalty, twice bolting out of his net to flip the puck up the boards, then scampering back. The Russians fail to mount a serious threat. Hasek had said before the Games that the international ice surface was too big for him to do much roaming, but he's moved into another zone this week, and neither wild horses nor Ivan Hlinka's baleful gaze will constrain him.

The Czechs set up a forest of legs and sticks in front of Hasek, and the Russian forwards who do carry any speed into the offensive zone see their passes and shots rattle around this obstacle course. Hasek gets into the act himself late in the period. Federov carries deep behind the Czech net and eludes a defender; in front of the net Andrei Kovalenko, alone, awaits his pass. All Federov needs to do is push the puck in front. But Hasek deftly lays his paddle down in the line of the pass, two or three feet in front of his crease, and the puck bounces harmlessly off the stick into his waiting glove. Kovalenko slaps the ice in frustration. The first period ends scoreless.

It's more of the same in the second. Russian attacks are thwarted mostly at the Czech defense. Hasek sees only six shots, all of which he stops. At one point, he loses his stick in a scramble, but by now everyone believes he could play goal with a kitchen broom and stop everything short of a cruise missile. "It's not only the way he plays," Russian coach Yurzinov will say after the game. "He made a major psychological impact, because at times I felt we were not quite sure if we could score at all. Period."

At the other end, Mikhail Shtalenkov faces tougher chances, but he too is up to the level of the gold-medal game. With the stinginess of the goalies, whispers are already starting about another shootout. The speculation grows more intense until, eight minutes into the third period, Pavel Patera — one of the Czech unknowns — beats Ottawa's Alexei Yashin on a face-off in the left circle of the Russian zone. Maple Leaf winger Martin Prochaska — another less-than-household name — relays the puck back to Petr Svoboda at the point. It would be hard to imagine a less likely candidate for gold-medal-winning heroics than a journeyman defenseman who'd averaged fewer than four goals a year during a 15-season NHL career in Montreal, Buffalo, and Philadelphia, but Svoboda's rising slapshot finds its way through a maze of legs and sticks, beating the screened Shtalenkov. Resounding cheers, chants, and air horns fill the Big Hat.

From there, the Czechs, confident that Hasek will yield nothing, simply grind it out. Hasek stops a dangerous Kamensky slapshot with his blocker. The Russians try to rough him up; Nemchinov backs into him, knocking him backwards with his legs trapped beneath him — anything to rattle him, tie the game. As the final seconds tick down, however, the Russians are unable even to force a face-off in the Czech zone. On the bench, the Czech players join arm in arm to celebrate the improbable. On press row, a Czech announcer shouts, "Do you believe in miracles?" When the horn signals the end of the game,

Hasek leaps deliriously in the air for a third straight game, then is buried under a wall of teammates. An enormous Czech flag is produced, and the players wrap themselves in the red, white, and blue as they take their victory skate around the ice, Hasek leading the way. He has shut out the Russians 1–0, his second shutout of the tournament. In six games plus an overtime period, he has allowed just six goals, a goals-against average of 0.97. He wins the top goaltender award at the Games, of course. More importantly, he has keyed the first gold medal for men's hockey from the Czech Republic or its predecessor, Czechoslovakia.

For the Russians, it is a bittersweet moment. Almost as maligned as the Czechs, they came within a hair of the gold. "If you had asked me two weeks ago, I would have said this is my dream," sighs coach Yurzinov. "Today I could say we did have a chance to win. I feel that I failed to properly coach the team for this final game."

After the gold medal has been draped over his neck, Hasek bites it, seemingly unsure if he's dreaming. His slightly goofy grin gets even wider as the Czech flag goes up and the anthem of his nation, so recently truncated from Slovakia, swells through Big Hat. Forget 1980 at Lake Placid, this is the story of the impossible Olympic dream. While NHL commissioner Bettman licks his wounds after the rude exit of the United States, and CBS counts its losses in the TV ratings, and Canada embarks on a soul-searching inquiry into the flaws in its system of hockey development, the men from the land of Kafka have authored a great story of their own.

Within moments of the medal ceremony, Hasek is standing at rink side, flowers in one hand, cell phone in the other. On the line is President Václav Havel and 50,000 of his screaming countrymen jammed into Old Town Square in downtown Prague. The city has gone mad for these hockey underdogs, and Hasek is addressing the revelers via this long-distance hookup. Havel says he is sending a plane tonight to gather the entire team and bring them to Prague for the celebration.

When Hasek gets through to his father in Pardubice, there is some confusion. Jan Hasek thinks he's talking to Dominik's brother, Martin, in Prague. It takes the goaltender a minute to convince his father that hey, it's me, Dom, calling from Japan, and we won! Nearby, Martin Rucinsky is trying to talk to his mother in Most. She cannot hear him over the din in the streets outside her home. The Republic has turned upside down for their heroes. In the media zone beneath the now-deserted stands of the Big Hat, Svoboda, the unlikely hero, is patiently making his way down the line of journalists. While his teammates bathe in champagne in the dressing room, Svoboda is replaying the greatest moment in his hockey life to anyone who will listen. In two languages he seeks to describe what his smile is saying so much more eloquently.

"I got lucky, man. It was a great face-off. The guys gave me time to look, and it just went through. We all feel like heroes here. We had a great team." From now until they stop writing about sport in his country, he knows, his and Hasek's names will be part of Czech history.

True to his word, Havel next day sends the presidential plane to pick up the players and fly them to a hero's welcome in Prague. Despite having had just two hours' sleep, Hasek and his teammates party with 100,000 of their countrymen. Wearing a kamikaze bandanna, he sprays his fellow citizens in Wenceslas Square with champagne. This is more than a sports triumph: it's the first great moment in the life of a new nation.

Within hours of the revelry in Prague, Hasek is on another plane — this one bound for Buffalo, half a world away from Japan. Barely 48 hours after Wenceslas Square, he takes the ice at the Marine Midland Arena against Toronto. "Ladies and gentlemen, let's greet tonight's starting goalie, Number 39 of the Buffalo Sabres and gold medalist for the Czech Republic, Dominik Hasek!" This time the cheering is heartfelt and sustained. The applause signals not only the fans' official forgiveness, but also their recognition that they are watching a goaltender who, after his Olympian feats, will go down in hockey history as one of the greatest who ever played.

THREE WEEKS LATER, at the Marine Midland Center, the Florida Panthers launch 32 shots at Hasek. Only a perfect drive to the top corner by Viktor Kozlov beats him in a 6–1 Buffalo victory. He has continued his superb play, and the middling Sabres are parlaying his brilliance into a late-season run that will take them from a last-place start to a second-place finish in the Northeast Division. Hasek's performance — he'll end the season with 13 shutouts, two fewer than Tony Esposito's NHL record — will earn him more honors, including another Hart Trophy, another Jennings Trophy, another Vezina Trophy, another Lester B. Pearson Award, and another berth on the first all-star team. The same coolness under pressure he demonstrated in Nagano will carry the Sabres to playoff victories over Philadelphia and Ottawa before they finally yield to another hot goaltender, Olaf Kolzig, and a vastly more talented and experienced Washington team in the conference finals.

The volatile character of the previous year's playoffs will be replaced by a more balanced Hasek. After whiffing on a long shot that costs the Sabres a 2–1 loss in the Washington series, he'll appear for practice the next day wearing "Kramer, The Swiss Cheese" across his shoulders. He will also donate nearly a million dollars to a charity in the inner city of Buffalo.

This March night, however, is notable for other reasons. After the victory over Florida, Hasek — the first star — acknowledges the fans' salute as he skates across the ice en route to the dressing room. The Sabres have just rewarded him with an extraordinary contract that will earn him $9 million a season starting in 1999. Friends wait outside the dressing room to celebrate while Hasek changes out of his bulky equipment. Ten, twenty, thirty minutes pass; the other Sabres have long since showered and left. His friends exchange anxious glances. Where's Dom?

Finally, 45 minutes after the game, Hasek emerges from the workout room, bathed in sweat. Without his goalie equipment he looks more like a Czech high school teacher than a superb athlete who's just won a giant windfall. Tall, wiry, his long face set in a shy smile, he explains to his friends he "doesn't feel quite right" in his shoulders. "I need to work out some more," he tells them. "Why don't you come in with me till I finish?" With that he returns to the workout room.

On the night that Dominik Hasek nails down the highest salary for a goalie in history — $23 million over three years — he ends his workday with 90 gruelling minutes on the exercise bike and the Nautilus machine. Only then, when his shoulders finally feel right, does he join his friends for a celebratory dinner.

INDEX

A

Adams, Jack, 193, 245
Alexander, Les, 218
Alfredsson, Daniel, 141
Ali, Muhammad, 133
Allaire, Francois, 10, 250, 257, 261–62, 263, 264
Allison, Jason, 44, 105
Allison, Scott, 161
American Hockey League, 182, 249
Amonte, Tony, 44, 93, 115, 147
Anderson, Glenn, 156, 159, 173, 176, 199
Anderson, John, 165
Antoski, Shawn, 64
Antropov, Nikolai, 227, 228
Apps, Syl, 58–59
Arbour, Al, 192, 193
Armstrong, George, 165, 216
Arnason, Chuck, 166
Arnott, Jason, 156, 179, 182, 183, 184, 185, 187, 219, 220
Art Ross Trophy, 215, 281
Atlanta Flames. *See* Calgary Flames
Audette, Donald, 113, 133
Awrey, Dave, 118

B

Ballard, Harold, 165, 178, 214, 280
Bancroft, Steve, 166
Bandura, Jeff, 163
Bannister, Drew, 169
Barnaby, Matthew, 267, 276, 282
Barrasso, Tom, 262
Barrie Colts, 227
Bastien, Baz, 177, 178
Bathgate, Andy, 41, 132
Bauer, Father David, 8, 126, 188
Baun, Bob, 105
Beauregard, Stephane, 237
Beck, Barry, 163

Bedard, Jim, 260, 265–66
Beddoes, Dick, 57
Belfour, Ed, 86, 87, 150, 212, 226, 236, 237, 238, 245, 261, 269
Beliveau, Jean, 10, 11, 52, 117
Bell, Mike, 281
Belleville Bulls, 159, 166
Berard, Bryan, 106, 120, 121
Berehowsky, Drake, 95, 185
Bergeron, Michel, 13, 64, 129, 202–3
Bernacci, Michael, 2
Bessel, Steve, 256–57
Bettman, Gary, 78, 79, 100, 110, 138, 146, 215, 228, 271, 297
Beukeboom, Jeff, 95, 131
Bilodeau, Brent, 166
Binkley, Les, 170
Blake, Rob, 67, 119, 150
Blake, Toe, 54, 192, 206, 248–49, 251
Boivin, Leo, 105, 216
Bondra, Peter, 80, 105, 279
Bonsignoire, Jason, 160, 219, 228
Bossy, Mike, 4, 10, 163, 165
Boston Bruins, 9, 11, 35, 38, 44, 59, 89, 96, 157, 158, 162, 164, 167, 169, 183, 192, 204, 205, 209, 244, 245, 251, 254, 269, 272
Bouchard, Emile "Butch," 102
Boughner, Bob, 95, 166
Bourne, Bob, 165
Bourque, Ray, 9, 34, 37, 67, 68, 73, 94, 96, 104, 120, 131, 150
Bower, Cindy, 41
Bower, Johnny, 41, 165, 247, 248, 252
Bowman, Scotty, 6, 16, 22, 33, 36, 52, 53–55, 58, 66, 80, 110, 127, 178, 192, 187, 199–200, 201, 202, 206, 207, 208, 209, 214, 265, 266

Boyer, Paul, 60
Bradley, Bill, 49
Bradley, Brian, 38
Brantford Steelers, 19
Brewer, Carl, 25, 105, 187–88, 192
Bridgman, Mel, 162
Brimsek, Frankie, 250
Brind'amour, Rod, 66, 71
Broadhurst, Chris, 100–1, 103, 135, 145
Broda, Turk, 250
Brodeau, Martin, 35, 42, 96, 161, 239, 250, 260, 263
Brooks, Herb, 121
Brown, Doug, 63, 260
Brown, Jeff, 60, 271
Buchberger, Kelly, 124
Buechner, Helmut, 107
Buffalo Sabres, 61, 77, 92, 113, 133, 147, 193, 203, 208, 209, 227, 228, 232, 236, 238, 239, 241, 242, 251, 253, 259, 264–65, 266, 267–76, 277, 285, 286, 296, 299
Bure, Pavel, 2, 13, 26, 28, 41, 96, 112, 280, 288, 289, 294, 295
Bure, Valeri, 114, 288, 289
Burke, Brian, 137, 139, 179
Burke, Sean, 185, 186, 262, 268, 276
Burns, Pat, 89, 204–5, 209
Burridge, Randy, 22
Butcher, Garth, 123
Butkus, Dick, 90

C

Calder Trophy, 4, 141, 255
Calgary Flames, 109, 113, 183, 207, 283
Caloun, Jan, 287
Campbell, Clarence, 29
Campbell, Colin, 209
Campbell, Joseph, 18, 47
Canada Cup: (1981)197;

(1984) 222; (1991)137, 201
See also World Cup
Canada–Russia series (1972), 189, 195, 253, 254, 255
Canadian Hockey, 30, 125
Canadian Hockey League, 22, 23, 24
Canadian National Team, 188
Carbonneau, Guy, 49, 97
Carkner, Terry, 22
Carolina Hurricanes, 104, 105, 106, 114, 180, 182, 183, 185, 186–87, 219, 220, 267, 268, 269–76, 277, 283, 285
Carney, Keith, 120, 131
Carson, Jimmy, 11, 176
Casey, Jon, 31–32
Cashman, Wayne, 59, 70, 108, 139, 208, 283
Challenge Cup (1979), 197
Chara, Zdeno, 105
Charbonneau, Jose, 166
Charron, Eric, 166
Cheevers, Gerry, 247, 254
Chelios, Chris, xix, 6, 13, 34, 59, 64, 67, 68, 75, 84–102, 104, 105–6, 112, 114–16, 120, 126–28, 130, 131, 132–33, 134, 135–37, 138, 140, 141, 142, 143, 144, 145, 147, 148, 149, 150, 151, 152–53, 178–79, 190, 196, 236–37, 283, 290
Chelios, Gus, 88, 105–6, 138
Chelios, Steve, 88
Chelios, Tracee, 84, 88, 100, 138
Cherry, Don, xvii, xviii, 3, 125, 156, 189, 192, 279–80, 281
Chiasson, Steve, 187, 271, 273
Chicago Blackhawks, 4, 15, 37, 44, 59, 84, 85, 86, 87, 100, 105, 111, 114–16, 118, 127, 133, 150, 151, 159, 179, 236, 237–38, 243, 255, 268, 274, 283, 284
Ciccone, Enrico, 105
Clapper, Dit, 107
Clark, Wendel, 134, 265
Clarke, Bobby, 66, 120, 189, 219, 222

Cleary, Daniel, 159
Coaching, 27, 187–90, 191, 192–214, 249
Coffey, Paul, 10, 24, 37, 39, 104, 119, 128, 159, 173, 174, 175, 179, 198, 201
Colorado Avalanche, 5, 34, 85, 122, 123, 134, 143, 209, 210, 212, 224–25, 239, 244, 260, 264
Columbus Blue Jackets, 205
Conacher, Charlie, 246
Conn Smythe Trophy, 80, 81, 128, 265
Constantine, Kevin, 207, 208
Corey, Ronald, 97, 264
Corson, Shayne, 66, 69, 71, 114
Courtnall, Geoff, 56, 165
Crawford, Marc, 67, 70, 73, 76, 209, 210, 222, 224, 225
Crha, Jiri, 234
Crisp, Terry, 209

D

Daigle, Alexandre, 164
Dallas Stars, 34, 38, 42, 44, 52, 58, 77, 80, 89, 111, 114, 127, 182, 209–10, 211–13, 224, 226, 227, 266, 267, 269, 279, 290
Damphousse, Vincent, 115, 165
Davidson, John, 64, 243, 250, 251
Deadmarsh, Adam, 142, 147
Dean, Barry, 162
Delvecchio, Alex, 178
Demers, Jacques, 2, 53, 58, 99, 189, 203–4, 205, 206–7, 210, 213
Demitra, Pavol, 44, 46
Desjardins, Eric, 72, 119, 201
Detroit Red Wings, 1–2, 3, 4, 11, 12, 14, 15, 16–17, 21, 32–33, 41, 44, 45–47, 49–50, 54–55, 59, 62–63, 77–80, 85, 104, 107, 110, 112, 113, 123, 133, 166, 170, 176, 178, 180, 185,

193, 207, 210, 212, 214, 227, 231, 245, 246, 251, 260, 264, 265–66, 283, 288
Devellano, Jimmy, 32, 164
Deveraux, Boyd, 158, 159
Devorski, Paul, 273
Dineen, Kevin, 272, 274
Dionne, Marcel, 3, 105
Disney Corporation, 15, 181
Dollas, Bobby, 219, 224
Domi, Tie, 22, 202–3
Dopita, Jiri, 286
Draper, Kris, 77, 80
Druce, John, 22
Dryden, Dave, 22
Dryden, Ken, 26, 54, 125, 181–82, 188, 198, 199, 203, 254–55, 256, 281–82
Duff, Dick, 165
Duguay, Ron, 163
Durnan, Bill, 246

E

Eagleson, Alan, 72, 84, 86, 87, 94, 164, 177, 194, 203, 214, 215, 216
Edmonton Oilers, 28, 36, 59, 63, 109, 111, 119, 133, 136, 150, 155, 156, 157, 158, 159–60, 161, 167, 169, 170, 171, 172, 173, 174–76, 178, 179, 181, 182–87, 191, 193, 197–98, 204, 205, 206, 207, 210, 212, 216, 218–21, 222, 224–28, 238, 257, 275, 286
Edwards, Don, 251
Emerson, Nelson, 274, 275
Equipment:
goaltending, 41–42, 109, 244, 245, 247, 250–52, 256–58, 260, 270
hockey sticks, 33, 43, 108, 132, 133–35
skates, 36–39, 108, 133, 270
Eriksson, Anders, 139
Errey, Bob, 22
Esposito, Phil, 64, 118, 178, 219, 227, 254
Esposito, Tony, 177–78, 255, 268

European players, 26–30,
40–41, 46, 55, 91, 119, 120,
123–24, 138, 139, 166, 171,
188, 196–97, 203, 260–61,
279–84, 294–95

F

Farkas, Jeff, 161
Farrish, Dave, 95
Fasel, Rene, 146
Featherstone, Glen, 42
Federov, Sergei, 4, 5, 28, 39,
41, 54, 56, 78, 80, 90, 96,
166, 180, 282, 288, 294,
295
Ferguson, John, 54, 106–7
Fetisov, Viacheslav, 6, 26, 55,
60, 79, 207, 282, 283, 287
Fischer, Jiri, 30
Fischer, Jim, 173
Flaman, Fernie, 35
Flatley, Pat, 5, 6–7, 36, 55, 63,
89, 92, 156, 193, 236, 282
Fletcher, Cliff, 170
Fleury, Theo, 2, 11, 68, 73, 74,
113, 134, 279, 291
Florida Panthers, 205, 208,
209, 299
Foote, Adam, 34, 72, 95, 120
Forsberg, Kent, 141
Forsberg, Peter, 5, 55, 123–24,
139, 140–41, 224, 280
Francis, Emile, 250
Francis, Ron, 5, 10, 45, 105
Fraser, Barry, 159, 160, 227,
228
Fraser, Kerry, 190
Fraser, Scott, 224
Free agency system, 180–81
Friday, Bill, 191
Friesen, Peter, 104
Fuhr, Grant, 46, 47, 159, 160,
172, 176, 198, 204, 238

G

Gadsby, Bill, 248
Gaetz, Link, 155
Gainey, Bob, 17, 22, 95, 111,
116, 129, 210
Gallant, Gerard, 5

Game, The (Dryden), 40, 125,
188, 254
Gardiner, Charlie, 245
Gary, Jim 37, 38
Gauthier, Gerard, 51
Gelinas, Martin, 176
Geoffrion, Danny, 166
Geoffrion, Bernie, 41, 117
Giacomin, Ed, 248, 251
Gilchrist, Brent, 50, 51, 62
Gill, Hal, 105
Gill, Todd, 95
Gillies, Clark, 165
Gillis, Mike, 157
Gilmour, Doug, 5, 37, 132,
133
Gladney, Bob, 163
Goaltending, xvii, 242–64, 278
Goddard, Ron, 21
Goodenow, Bob, 86, 180, 229
Goodman, T.R., 101, 102, 104,
127
Goring, Butch, 165
Grant, Danny, 22
Gratton, Chris, 96, 112, 167
Gratton, Gilles, 244
Graves, Adam, 176
Green, Gary, 22
Green, Rick, 94
Green, Ted, 206
Green, Travis, 24
Gregg, Randy, 173
Gregson, Terry, 190
Gretzky, Walter, 19, 48, 233
Gretzky, Wayne, 3, 4, 9, 10, 11,
12, 15, 17–18, 19, 20, 28,
39, 44, 45, 47–48, 66–67,
68, 70, 71, 72, 73, 75, 76,
77, 85, 96, 105, 108, 113,
125, 129, 130–31, 133, 134,
136, 137, 143, 146–47, 160,
170, 171, 172, 173–74, 176,
187, 191, 198, 199, 201,
202, 222, 269, 279, 291
Greer, Mike, 182, 183
Griffith, Coleman, 19
Grimson, Stu, 106, 274
Grosek, Michal, 270, 276
Guerin, Bill, 136, 219, 221,
224, 225

Guidolin, Bep, 158, 170
Gzowski, Peter, 19, 168

H

Hachborn, Len, 19
Hall, Glenn, 243, 246–47, 249,
252, 262, 263–64, 269
Hallin, Mats, 282
Hamilton, Al, 191
Hamilton Bulldogs, 223
Hamrlik, Roman, 71, 120, 219,
220, 224, 278, 286, 295
Hannan, Dave, 24
Harris, Billy, 165
Harris, Ron, 102
Hart, Gene, 215
Hart Trophy, 215, 239, 242,
277, 299
Hartford Whalers. *See* Carolina
Hurricanes
Hartje, Tod, 27, 283–84, 294,
295
Hartsburg, Craig, 86, 88, 94,
116, 127, 150
Harvey, Doug, 58, 59, 117, 192
Hasek, Alena, 231, 232, 240,
290
Hasek, Dominik, 35, 46, 68,
69, 70, 71, 72, 73, 74, 75,
76, 77, 78, 96, 139, 143,
144, 146, 147, 148, 149,
203, 222–23, 231–42, 245,
247, 248, 249, 250, 251,
253, 254, 255, 256, 257,
258–60, 264, 265, 266–78,
281, 282, 284–92, 293–94,
295
Hasek, Dominika, 231, 242
Hasek, Jan, 234, 298
Hasek, Martin, 233, 298
Hasek, Michael, 231, 242, 277
Hatcher, Derian, 38, 105, 137,
148
Hatcher, Kevin, 45, 67, 137,
140
Havel, Václav, 297–98
Hay, Don, 208
Hayward, Brian, 198
Healy, Glenn, 50, 51, 258
Hebert, Guy, 14

Hedberg, Anders, 26, 113–14, 171
Heidiger, Heini, 90–91
Henderson, Paul, 216
Henning, Lorne, 165
Henrich, Michael, 227
Henry, "Sugar" Jim, 244
Hextall, Bryan, 263
Hextall, Ron, 90, 263, 273
Hitchcock, Ken, 12, 58, 209–14, 219, 226, 269
Hlinka, Ivan, 147, 286, 294, 295
Hockey:
    cross-sport comparisons, xvi, xvii, 23, 40, 162, 216
    low-scoring, 35–36, 52, 109–10, 111, 119
    Soviet system. *See* European players
    territoriality in, 107–11
    videotape analysis of, 8, 11, 22, 33–34, 52, 184–85, 206
    xenophobia in, 279–83
    (*See also* Minor hockey; Team dynamics)
Hockey Canada. *See* Canadian Hockey
Hockey development. *See* Skills development
Hockey expansion, 25, 109, 186, 189, 252
Hockey Hall of Fame, 4, 7, 10, 93, 96, 105, 117, 159, 160, 163, 192, 198, 214, 215–18, 221, 245, 249, 268
Hockey Handbook, The (Percival), 7, 8, 40
Hockey marketing, 32, 39, 270–71
Hockey News, The, 3, 215
"Hockey Night in Canada," xviii, 13, 15, 90, 237
Hockey players:
    body types/size of, 12, 105–8, 112–13, 232, 162, 265
    health and fitness of, 100–4, 145, 196
    salaries, 15, 25, 68, 87, 96,

158, 164, 167, 179–80, 203, 204, 208–9, 229, 280, 300
    top scoring, 42, 105, 117, 118, 119, 120, 128–29, 131, 140, 160, 163, 173, 203
Hockey violence, 25, 90–91, 107, 137, 189, 196
Hodson, Kevin, 265–66
Holik, Bobby, 128, 286
Holland, Ken, 31
Hollett, Flash, 117
Holmstrom, Tomas, 46
Hood, Hugh, 52
Horton, Tim, 105, 222
Horvath, Bronco, 48
Housley, Phil, 95
Houston Rockets, 65, 218
Howe, Gordie, 1, 2, 29, 41, 68, 105, 215, 216
Howe, Mark, 123
Howell, Harry, 10, 228
Hrkac, Tony, 219
Hrudey, Kelly, 165
Huddy, Charley, 173
Hull, Bobby, 4, 36, 41–42, 68, 87, 88, 105, 132, 168, 189, 216, 247, 250
Hull, Brett, 5, 13, 32, 41, 42–44, 67, 109–10, 127, 134, 136, 137, 141, 142, 143, 147, 151, 200, 203, 269
Hunter, Dale, 80
Hunter, Douglas, 249, 251

Iafrate, Al, 56, 95
Ice size, 71–72, 110–12, 123, 138, 139, 141, 142, 149, 222, 223, 272–73
Ilitch, Mike, 32, 62
Imlach, Punch, 151, 192, 194, 205, 206, 245
Indianapolis Racers, 170, 236, 237
Inness, Gary, 244
International Hockey League, 236
International Ice Hockey Federation, 138, 146–47, 292

International Olympic Committee (IOC), 147, 292
Irons, Robbie, 243–44
Irvin, Dick, 59, 199, 247, 280
Irvin, Dick, Sr., 7

J

Jack Adams Trophy, 204
Jagr, Jaromir, 5, 28, 45, 64, 69, 70, 73, 74, 105, 112, 146, 147, 148, 161, 281, 285, 286, 289, 293
James, Graham, 25
Janney, Craig, 36
Jarvis, Doug, 52
Jennings Trophy, 238, 299
Jihlava, Dukla, 234
Johansen, Trevor, 165
Johansson, Calle, 141
Johnson, Bob "Badger," 93
Johnson, Greg, 115, 116, 120
Johnston, Eddie, 251
Joly, Greg, 162
Jonsson, Tomas, 165, 282
Jordan, Michael, 20, 60
Joseph, Curtis, 120, 181, 182, 185, 212, 223, 225, 257–58
Junior hockey. *See* Minor hockey

K

Kalinin, Dmitri, 228–29
Kamensky, Valeri, 288, 296
Kamloops Blazers, 209
Kapanen, Sami, 186–87, 269, 272
Kariya, Paul, 12–16, 41, 43, 45, 64, 65, 69, 76, 90, 120, 129, 137, 180–81
Kasparitis, Darius, 65, 288, 289, 295
Keane, Mike, 226
Keenan, Mike, 3, 4, 5, 22, 70, 87, 197, 201–2, 203, 210, 237, 238, 270
Kelley, Jim, 241, 282
Kelly, Steve, 219
Kenesky, Emil "Pops," 245, 250
Kennedy, Sheldon, 25
Keon, Dave, 3

Khabibulin, Nikolai, 14, 277, 284
Kharlamov, Valeri, 26, 189, 287, 293
Kidd, Bruce, 191
Kidd, Trevor, 262
Kilrea, Brian, 52
King, Kris, 22, 116
Kingston, George, 30, 121–22, 123, 124, 294
Kitchener Rangers, 173
Kjellberg, Patrik, 141
Klassen, Ralph, 162
Klima, Petr, 133
Knox, Seymour, 242
Kocur, Joey, 31, 79
Koivu, Saku, 51, 287
Kolis, Jiri, 237, 278
Kolzig, Olaf, 262, 277, 299
Konstantinov, Vladimir, 34, 41, 50, 55, 58, 78–79, 166, 280, 283
Kordic, Dan, 101
Korn, Mitch, 264–65
Korolev, Igor, 116
Kovalenko, Andrei, 183, 295
Kozlov, Vyacheslav, 4, 53, 54, 166, 283, 287, 299
Kralik, Jiri, 234
Krivokrasov, Sergei, 114, 283
Kron, Robert, 271, 275
Krushelnyski, Mike, 172
Krutov, Vladimir, 41, 287
Kurri, Jari, 4, 76, 159, 160, 172, 176, 198, 199

L

Lacroix, Pierre, 179
Lafleur, Guy, 13, 78, 103, 105, 129, 145, 151, 163, 171, 215
Lafontaine, Pat, 32, 147, 242, 271
Laidlaw, Tom, 121
Lambert, Yvon, 108
Lamoriello, Lou, 84, 135, 136, 229
Landsberg, Michael, 281
Langenbrunner, Jaime, 22
Langevin, Dave, 165

Langway, Rod, 96, 163, 165
Lapierre, Jacques, 248
Lapointe, Guy, 119, 152
Lapointe, Martin, 45, 46, 56
Lapointe, Rick, 162
Laprade, Edgar, 216
Larionov, Igor, 2, 4, 55, 56, 80, 113, 283, 287
Lariviere, Garry, 173
Larmer, Steve, 4, 93, 151
Laxton, Gord, 162
Layne, Bobby, 2
Leadership, art of, 56, 57–59
LeClair, John, 12, 44, 64, 105, 137, 140, 148
Leeman, Gary, 56
Leetch, Brian, 37, 67, 84, 95, 96, 104, 113, 120, 128–30, 131, 135, 136, 137, 279, 290
Lefebvre, Sylvain, 120, 134
Leger, Gilles, 220
Lemaire, Jacques, 6, 53, 190, 207–8, 209, 210
Lemieux, Claude, 225
Lemieux, Mario, 2, 3, 4, 8–11, 35, 44, 45, 64, 74, 100, 109–10, 129, 156, 168, 177, 207, 215, 237, 259, 263, 269
Leroux, Francois, 105
Leschyshyn, Curtis, 186, 272
Lester B. Pearson Award, 239, 299
Lewis, Dave, 33, 34, 165, 206
Lidstrom, Nicklas, 46, 47, 51, 55, 95, 120, 139, 150, 166
Linden, Trevor, 13, 51, 70, 72
Lindros, Brett, 65
Lindros, Eric, 5, 11, 12, 15, 31, 32, 64–66, 68, 69, 71, 73, 74–75, 77, 96, 105, 112, 125, 128, 130, 143, 222
Lindsay, Ted, 1, 178, 246
Linseman, Ken, 94, 174
Los Angeles Kings, 39, 88, 172, 176, 197, 209, 214, 238
Louis, Joe, 2
Low, Ron, 183, 185, 206, 225, 228
Lowe, Ken, 206

Lowe, Kevin, 96, 159, 173, 176, 221
Ludwig, Craig, 34, 94, 132
Lumley, Harry, 250
Luongo, Roberto, 262
Lupien, Gilles, 106, 113, 263

M

McAllister, Chris, 105
McAlpine, Chris, 107
McCammon, Bob, 206
McCarty, Darren, 5, 17, 33, 50
McCauley, Alyn, 49, 50–52
McCourt, Dale, 163
McCreary, Bill, 51, 67–68, 295
MacDonald, Blair, 172
McDonald, Lanny, 163
Macfarlane, John, 191
McGillis, Kelly, 219
MacGregor, Bruce, 184, 187
MacGregor, Roy, 28, 110, 199
MacInnes, Al, 46, 120, 131–32, 134, 150
McKenzie, Johnny, 169
McKenzie, Ken, 215
McLaren, Kyle, 105
MacLean, Doug, 205, 208, 209
McNall, Bruce, 214
MacNamara, Gerry, 178
McNeil, Gerry, 246, 251
Macoun, Jamie, 96
McPhee, John, 49
McSorley, Marty, 96, 200
Mahovlich, Frank, 247
Mahovlich, Peter, 189
Makarov, Sergei, xv, 287
Malakhov, Vladimir, 114
Malarchuk, Clint, 243
Malone, Frank, 125
Maloney, Phil, 178, 194
Maltby, Kirk, 41
Maltsev, Alexander, 41, 293
Maniago, Cesare, 252
Marchant, Todd, 182
Marchment, Bryan, 219
Marleau, Patrick, 161
Marouelli, Don, 190
Marsh, Brad, 42
Martin, Jacques, 129, 163, 258, 263

Martiniuk, Ray, 166
Matheson, Jim, 175
Maurice, Paul, 276
Mayarov, Boris, 195
Meehan, Don, 97–99, 179
Meeker, Howie, xviii
Meloche, Gilles, 255
Memorial Cup, 26
Messier, Mark, 3, 49, 51, 52, 59, 66, 69, 128, 129, 156, 173–74, 175, 176, 179, 198, 199, 201, 203, 222, 279
Middleton, Rick, 38, 162
Mighty Ducks of Anaheim, 12, 13, 14, 15, 90, 137, 180–81, 208, 221, 261, 284
Mikhailov, Boris, 288
Mikita, Stan, 3, 88, 105, 132
Milford, Jake, 178
Millen, Greg, 177, 236
Mills, Dennis, 31
Minnesota North Stars, 158
Minor hockey, 22–31, 119, 122–25
Mironev, Boris, 182, 186, 288
Mironev, Dmitri, 288, 295
Modano, Mike, 44, 105, 136, 137, 141, 147, 182, 211–12, 279, 290
Modin, Frederic, 116, 139
Mogilny, Alexander, 84, 91
Mondou, Pierre, 162
Montreal Canadiens, 7, 24, 52, 53, 54, 66, 90, 93, 94, 95, 97, 102, 106, 114–15, 117, 132, 151, 152, 158, 163, 166, 171, 172, 177, 178, 181, 188, 197, 199, 200, 202, 204, 209, 245, 248, 251, 254, 260, 264, 286
Moog, Andy, 9, 115, 172, 182, 269
Moore, Dickie, 117
Morozov, Alexei, 288
Morrison, Scotty, 217
Morrow, Ken, 165
Mrionov, Dimitri, 14
Muckler, John, 172, 173, 176, 199, 206, 207, 240, 242
Mulhern, Richard, 162

Mullen, Joey, 232, 278
Muni, Craig, 96
Murphy, Joe, 84, 86, 176
Murphy, Larry, 22, 96, 112, 150
Murphy, Mike, 221
Murray, Andy, 70
Murray, Bob, 159
Murray, Rem, 183, 186
Murray, Terry, 208
Musil, Frank, 219, 237, 240, 273
Myre, Phil, 253

N

Nagano. *See* Olympics (1998)
Naslund, Mats, 93
National Hockey League (NHL): draft, 22, 23, 28, 29, 31, 106, 122–23, 156–68, 181–82, 226–27
profit-driven nature of, 25, 28, 29, 30, 31, 111, 122, 191, 208
National Hockey League Players' Association (NHLPA), 86, 87, 137, 164, 180, 194, 214, 229
Neale, Harry, 53, 65, 129, 191, 237, 258, 269
Neilson, Roger, 22, 33, 203, 206, 207, 209
Nemchinov, Sergei, 296
Nepean Raiders, 21
Nesmeth, James, 259
New Jersey Devils, 3, 37, 42, 44, 60, 136, 161, 184, 185, 190, 208, 209, 219, 229, 238, 239, 260, 296
New York Americans, 244, 245
New York Islanders, 13, 24, 32, 33, 70, 105, 141, 156, 164, 165, 178, 192, 197, 198, 206, 215, 236, 278, 286
New York Rangers, 3, 59, 113, 121, 129, 136, 158, 161, 162, 168, 184, 185, 202, 209, 216, 242, 243, 249, 260
Nicholls, Bernie, 23, 86, 150
Nicholson, Bob, 30, 125

Niedermayer, Scott, 119, 120, 222, 279
Nieuwendyk, Joe, 51, 68, 69, 72, 73, 74, 212
Nilsson, Kent, 228
Nilsson, Ulf, 168, 171, 189
Ninimaa, Janne, 120, 219, 224, 225
Nolan, Ted, 203, 208, 234, 239, 241, 242, 267, 277, 282
Norris, Bruce, 32, 214
Norris Trophy, xix, 94, 96, 105, 118, 128, 150
Norton, Jeff, 169
Nuutinen, Sami, 161
Nystrom, Bob, 165

O

Oates, Adam, 10, 80
O'Connell, Mike, 164
O'Connor, Buddy, 216
Ogrodnick, John, 5
Olajuwon, Hakeem, 65
Olmstead, Bert, 108
Olympics: (1972) 285; (1976) 285, 293; (1980) 75, 137, 285, 297; (1984), 94, 137; (1988) 287; (1992) 288; (1994) 71, 139; (1998) 15, 16, 63–64, 66–76, 111, 112, 120, 128, 135–49, 151, 152–53, 220, 221, 222–24, 225, 284, 285–300
O'Neill, Jeff, 187
Ontario Hockey League, 22, 24, 25, 106, 159, 166, 281(*See also* Minor hockey)
Orr, Bobby, 4, 10, 28, 38, 44, 68, 105, 117, 118, 120, 121, 125, 157, 167, 192, 216, 252, 254
Osgood, Chris, 79, 80, 265
Ottawa Senators, 16–17, 24, 106, 129, 141, 163, 164, 209, 234, 239–40, 258, 263, 269, 296, 299
Ottawa 67's, 281
Ozolinsh, Sander, 120, 121, 122, 288, 295

P

Page, Pierre, 207, 208
Pang, Darren, 88–89, 104, 130, 144–45
Parent, Bernie, 238, 253–54
Park, Brad, 53, 117, 118, 119
Parise, Jean Paul, 189
Parro, Dave, 163
Patera, Pavel, 73, 74, 286, 289, 296
Patrick, Craig, 113, 178
Patrick, James, 109, 111
Patrick, Lester, 192, 201
Pearson, Rob, 166
Peca, Mike, 259, 267–68, 271, 278
Peeters, Pete, 11
Percival, Lloyd, xviii, 7–8, 11, 40, 41, 43, 109, 192, 232, 261, 263
Perreault, Gil, 171
Peterborough Petes, 22, 25, 32
Philadelphia Flyers, 4, 44, 66, 89, 90, 101, 111, 128, 162, 164, 167, 171, 181, 190, 191, 206, 207, 208, 215, 219, 238, 241, 253, 254, 273, 286, 295, 296, 299
Phillips, Chris, 106
Phillips, Rod, 186
Phoenix Coyotes, 13, 14, 79, 80, 86, 95, 133, 135, 136, 208, 277, 284
Pilote, Pierre, 105
Pittsburgh Penguins, 9, 45, 64, 65, 100, 156, 158, 170, 175, 177, 178, 207, 215, 222, 237, 244, 260, 281, 286, 288, 293
Plante, Jacques, 235, 239, 241, 248, 249, 250, 251, 252, 275
Pocklington, Peter, 158, 159, 169, 170, 176, 184, 226
Poile, Bud, 178
Polano, Nick, 53
Pollock, Sam, 178, 181
Popovic, Peter, 105, 139
Potvin, Denis, 119, 165
Potvin, Felix, 250, 260

Potvin, Jean, 165
Pratt, Babe, 107
Price, Pat, 173
Primeau, Keith, 112, 143, 187, 269, 275
Probert, Bob, 84, 116
Prochaska, Michael, 296
Proctor, Brian, 27
Pronger, Chris, 22, 72, 105, 106, 120, 150
Pronovost, Marcel, 248
Propp, Brian, 89–90
Pulford, Bob, 87, 179, 216, 238
Puppa, Darren, 262

Q

Quebec Nordiques, 184, 202
(See also Colorado Avalanche)
Quenneville, Joel, 63
Quinn, Larry, 242
Quinn, Pat, 179

R

Radomski, Harry, 99
Ranford, Bill, 201
Ranheim, Paul, 274
Recchi, Mark, 24, 71, 73, 260, 279, 291
Redmond, Mickey, 22
Redquest, Greg, 244
Reekie, Joe, 95
Reese, Jeff, 254
Refereeing, 110–11, 190–91
Regier, Darcy, 242
Reich, Steve, 215
Reich, Tom, 88, 156, 180, 215
Reichel, Robert, 70, 73, 76, 286, 289, 291, 293–94
Resch, Chico, 261, 278
Rhodes, Damian, 17
Ricci, Mike, 22
Richard, Henri, 35
Richard, Maurice "Rocket," 7, 35, 216, 244, 246
Richardson, Luke, 95, 165, 181
Richer, Stephane, 24, 93, 114
Richter, Mike, 67, 85, 96, 128, 137, 140–41, 143, 144, 148, 261

Riesen, Michel, 159–60, 161, 228
Riley, Pat, 211
Rivet, Craig, 115
Roberts, Gary, 185, 186, 269
Robertson, Oscar, 49
Robinson, Larry, 39, 88, 94, 209
Robitaille, Luc, 63
Robitaille, Mike, 193–94
Rodman, Dennis, 68
Roenick, Jeremy, 86, 93, 137, 138, 140, 142, 150
Roszival, Michal, 30
Rousseau, Bobby, 216
Roy, Patrick, 34, 35, 46, 67, 69, 70, 71, 74, 75, 77, 96, 143, 144, 223, 224, 225, 239, 244, 250, 257, 260, 261, 263, 264, 279, 291
Rucinsky, Martin, 70–71, 73, 74, 115, 286
Ruff, Lindy, 209, 242, 274, 276
Ruotsalainen, Reijo, 121
Russell, Cam, 87
Russell, Scott, 21
Russian Elite League, 283–84, 294
Ruzicka, Vladimir, 69, 73, 75, 147, 148, 286

S

Sadler, Robin, 162
Sailynoja, Keijo, 161
St. Louis Blues, 31–32, 41–42, 44, 45–47, 49, 56, 63, 80, 85, 106–7, 127, 131, 158, 203, 243
St. Michael's College (Toronto), 26, 122
Sakic, Joe, 5, 32, 69, 70, 73, 76, 96, 143, 200, 224–25, 280, 300
Salaries:
coaches, 209
and free agency, 180–81
players, 15, 25, 68, 87, 96, 158, 164, 167, 179–80, 203, 204, 208–9, 229
Salming, Borje, 165

Salo, Tommy, 66, 139, 140, 141
Samuelson, Kjell, 96
Samuelsson, Ulf, 139, 140, 146–47
Sanders, Barry, 12, 60
Sanderson, Derek, xvii
Sanderson, Geoff, 185
Sandstrom, Tomas, 41, 44, 141
San Jose Sharks, 10, 23, 106, 121–22, 150, 207, 208, 219, 265, 287
Satan, Miroslav, 275
Sather, Ann, 215, 218
Sather, Glen, 28, 29, 30, 109, 110, 111, 124, 155–60, 161, 163–64, 167, 168–77, 178, 179, 180, 181, 182, 183–87, 189–90, 191, 192, 193, 197–200, 202, 204, 205, 206, 207, 209, 210, 214, 215, 216–29, 257, 275
Sather, Justin, 215, 218
Sather, Shannon, 215, 218
Sault Ste. Marie Greyhounds, 24
Sauve, Bob, 162
Savard, Denis, 97, 103
Savard, Jean, 163
Savard, Serge, 97
Sawchuk, Terry, 1, 243, 246, 250, 251, 252, 262
Schneider, Mathieu, 84, 141
Schoenfeld, Jim, 208
Schutt, Rod, 177
Scouting, 163, 164–65, 181–82
Selanne, Teemu, 5, 12, 13, 14, 28, 42, 76, 90, 112, 168, 280, 287
Semenko, Dave, 178, 228
Shanahan, Brendan, 3, 4, 17, 33, 41, 46, 63, 64, 66, 68, 69, 72, 73, 75, 79, 292
Shantz, Jeff, 116
Shero, Fred, 190, 191, 193, 194
Shields, Al, 244
Shore, Eddie, 249–50
Shtalenkov, Mikhail, 262, 284, 288, 289, 296
Shue, Gene, xv, xvi
Sillinger, Mike, 166
Simon, Chris, 84, 183

Sinden, Harry, 96, 169, 192, 205, 217, 245
Sittler, Darryl, 171
Skills development: and coaching style, 195–99, 205, 213
    disincentives to, 119–24
    and early training, 18–21, 28–29
    genetic aspects of, 17–18
    neurological aspects of, 18–20, 47–49
    "pro" style of, 121–22, 123
    skating, 39–41, 134
    Soviet system. See European players
Skinner, Jimmy, 178
Skoula, Martin, 30
Skrudland, Brian, 226
Slegr, Jiri, 71, 286, 295
Smehlik, Richard, 71, 271, 274, 276, 286, 289
Smith, Barry, 206
Smith, Bobby, 93
Smith, Dallas, 118
Smith, Dave, 18
Smith, Floyd, 165
Smith, Gary "Suitcase," 244
Smith, Jason, 115, 134
Smith, Neil, 3, 164
Smith, Ryan, 156, 182, 183
Smith, Steve, 173
Smythe, Conn, 81
Snepsts, Harold, 93
Snow, Garth, 257
Soules, Jason, 228
Spacek, Jaroslav, 71, 286
Sparta Prague, 233
Sporting News NHL Player of the Year Award, 239
Stafford, Barrie, 206
Stamberg, Grant, 120
Stanfield, Fred, 170
Stanley, Allan, 248
Stanley Cup, 2, 3, 4, 13, 14, 56, 58, 59, 76–80, 87, 89–90, 100, 105, 107, 128, 165, 166, 171, 172, 174, 175, 176, 177, 178, 182–83, 191, 193, 197, 199, 206, 208, 210, 212, 224, 225–26, 227,

231, 238, 239–40, 243, 245, 282, 252, 253, 254, 265
Stapleton, Pat, 120–21
Stastny, Peter, 10
Steen, Thomas, 61
Stefan, Greg, 19
Stein, Gil, 214–15
Stellick, Gord, 178
Stevens, Scott, 72, 95, 96, 120
Stewart, Paul, 59, 190
Straka, Martin, 293
Stumpel, Josef, 105
Sullivan, Steve, 50, 266
Summanen, Raimo, 172
Sundin, Mats, 105, 139, 140, 141, 221, 266
Suter, Gary, 15, 90, 131, 137, 138, 139, 147, 148
Sutter, Brian, 99
Sutter, Brent, 165
Sutter, Duane, 165
Svoboda, Petr, 71, 286, 290, 295, 296, 298
Sydor, Darryl, 119
Sykora, Michal, 105

T

Tarasov, Anatoli, 7, 9, 40, 41, 48, 187, 195–96, 233, 263
Taylor, Bobby, 252–53
Team Canada: (1972) 189, 195, 253, 254, 255; (1987) 3; (1991) 3, 201, 202; (1996) 4; (1998) 16, 63–64, 66–76, 111, 112, 120, 135, 139, 143, 145, 221, 222–24, 225, 290–92
Team dynamics, 55, 56–58, 107, 121, 131, 150–53, 201–2, 205, 206–7
Team North America, 126
Team USA, 84–85, 86, 94, 100, 135–49, 151, 152–53, 208, 223, 290, 291
Terreri, Chris, 114, 115, 116
Therien, Robert, 26
Thibault, Jocelyn, 262, 263
Thomas, Isiah, 2
Thornton, Joe, 106, 161, 164
Thornton, Scott, 166

Tikhonov, Viktor, 285, 287
Tikkanen, Esa, 36, 80, 172
Tinordi, Mark, 131
Titov, German, 283
Tkaczuk, Keith, 105, 135, 136, 140, 161
Tocchet, Rick, 84
Todd, Dick, 22
Tonelli, John, 163, 164
Toronto Maple Leafs, 8, 26, 37, 49, 50, 56, 58, 100, 103, 105, 113, 115–16, 133, 140, 151–52, 161, 163, 165–66, 178, 181, 203, 204, 220–21, 227, 228, 234, 243, 245, 247, 248, 254, 260, 265–66, 280, 281, 296, 298
Toronto Marlboros, 25, 165
Torrey, Bill, 164, 165, 178
Training. See Coaching; Skills development
Tremblay, Mario, 264
Tretiak, Vladislav, 73, 195, 232, 252, 255–56
Trottier, Bryan, 3, 33, 165, 198, 215
Tselios, Nikos, 105–6
Tuele, Bill, 184, 216
Turcotte, Alfie, 166
Tverdovsky, Oleg, 120

U

Ublansky, Jerry, 98
Ubriaco, Gene, xvii, 177–78
Ulmer, Michael, 10
Unified Team, 288
U.S. Olympic Committee (USOC), 152, 153

V

Vachon, Rogatien, 245
Vancouver Canucks, 15, 114, 129, 178, 179, 183, 193, 194, 206, 226, 268
Vaive, Rick, 133
Vallis, Lindsay, 166
Vanbiesbrouck, John, 137
Van Hellemond, Andy, 191, 280, 281
Van Impe, Ed, 253

Vasko, Elmer, 105
Vaydik, Greg, 162
Veitch, Darren, 173
Verbeek, Pat, 212
Vernon, Mike, 10, 41, 265
Vezina Trophy, 238, 255, 299
Vigneault, Alain, 209
Volek, David, 236

W

Waite, Jimmy, 236, 237
Walter, Ryan, 12–13, 14, 43
Wamsley, Rick, 248–49, 257, 262, 263–64
Washington Capitals, 78, 79, 80, 131, 136, 162, 173, 182, 183, 208, 227, 243, 277, 299
Watkins, Robert, 61–62
Watson, Bryan "Bugsy," 36, 175
Watson, Jimmy, 253
Watson, Phil "Fiery," 249
Watt, Tom, 188–89, 202, 205
Watters, Bill, 179
Weight, Doug, 161, 182, 185, 200, 225
Weinrich, Eric, 131
West, Jerry, 49
Western Hockey League, 209
Wharton, John, 60, 61–62, 103
Whitney, Ray, 219
Wickenheiser, Doug, 162, 166
Williams, Art, 178
Wilson, Doug, 163
Wilson, Mark, 105
Wilson, Ron, 67, 68, 135, 136, 139, 142–43, 144, 148, 182, 208
Winnipeg Jets, 61, 87, 168, 184, 189 (See also Phoenix Coyotes)
Winter, Rich, 241
Wirtz, Bill, 86, 87
Wittman, Don, 75
Woolley, Jason, 275
World Championships: (1993), 65; (1994), 222
World Cup (hockey), 4, 84–85, 86, 135, 136, 139, 143,

147–48, 149, 208, 222, 286, 288
World Cup (soccer), 72–73, 125
World Hockey Association, 82, 159, 170, 171, 173, 191, 197, 244, 252, 253
World Junior Championships, 122–23, 160
World Team vs. North American Team (1998), 277–79
Worsley, Gump, 247, 249, 251, 252
Worters, Roy "Shrimp," 245, 262
Wregget, Ken, 260

Y

Yakushev, Alexander, 26, 293
Yashin, Alexei, 17, 68, 105, 288, 296
Young, Ian, 264
Young, Scott, 93
Young, Tim, 162
Yurzinov, Vladimir, 196, 288, 296, 297
Yzerman, Isabel, 2
Yzerman, Lisa, 2, 16
Yzerman, Maria, 78
Yzerman, Mike, 18
Yzerman, Ron, 18, 20, 22, 25, 59, 61
Yzerman, Steve, 1–7, 9–10, 11, 12, 14, 16–18, 20–22, 25, 31–35, 36–39, 44, 46, 47–48, 50–51, 52–53, 54–55, 56, 57, 58–63, 66–67, 68, 70, 71, 72, 73, 76, 77–81

Z

Zamuner, Rob, 67, 69, 143
Zelepukhin, Valeri, 219
Zezel, Peter, 49
Zhamnov, Alexei, 86, 127, 288, 289
Zhitnik, Alexei, 272, 288, 295
Zholtok, Sergei, 240
Ziegler, John, 32, 203, 217
Zubov, Sergei, 120, 288, 295

h

12/07 s